Currency Trading

FOR

DUMMIES®

2ND EDITION

Currency Trading

FOR

DUMMIES®

2ND EDITION

by Brian Dolan

WILEY

Wiley Publishing, Inc.

Currency Trading For Dummies,® 2nd Edition

Published by
Wiley Publishing, Inc.
111 River St.
Hoboken, NJ 07030-5774
www.wiley.com

Copyright © 2011 by Wiley Publishing, Inc., Indianapolis, Indiana

Published by Wiley Publishing, Inc., Indianapolis, Indiana

Published simultaneously in Canada

For general information on our other products and services, please contact our Customer Care Department within the U.S. at 877-762-2974, outside the U.S. at 317-572-3993, or fax 317-572-4002.

For technical support, please visit www.wiley.com/techsupport.

Wiley also publishes its books in a variety of electronic formats. Some content that appears in print may not be available in electronic books.

Library of Congress Control Number: 2011930128

ISBN: 978-1-118-01851-4

Manufactured in the United States of America

10 9 8 7 6 5 4 3 2 1

WILEY

About the Author

Brian Dolan is the chief currency strategist at GAIN Capital Group, and a 20-plus year veteran of the interbank currency market. Brian provides research and market analysis to trading clients of GAIN Capital and FOREX.com, the retail division of GAIN Capital Group.

Brian analyzes the G10 currency markets with a blend of fundamental and technical analysis to provide actionable trading strategies.

A frequent commentator on currency-market developments and outlooks for major news media including the *Wall Street Journal,* Reuters, Bloomberg, Dow Jones, CNN Money, and MarketWatch.com, Brian has also appeared regularly as a currency analyst on financial TV networks CNBC, Bloomberg Television, Fox Business News and BNN in Canada.

In addition, he has written numerous articles on currency trading, risk management, and technical analysis for trading and investment journals such as *Currency Trader, Active Trader, SFO Magazine, Technical Analysis of Stocks & Commodities,* and *Futures.*

Prior to joining GAIN Capital, Brian was a vice president at Bank Julius Bär, where he advised hedge funds and high-net-worth individuals on currencies. He spent the first 12 years of his FX career trading major currency pairs in the interbank market in New York at some of the world's largest banks, including Credit Suisse, Dai-Ichi Kangyo Bank, and American Express Bank, as well as two years in Bermuda as a proprietary trader at Butterfield Bank. Brian is a graduate of Dartmouth College.

Dedication

To Brigid, for her love and for hanging in there through the ups and downs; and to Frank and Catherine, for inspiring me to create a work for the future, just as you are. In memoriam to my mother Peg, father Chuck, and sadly missed brother Tim, who taught me that life is not a dress rehearsal.

Acknowledgments

My efforts to translate a career's worth of currency trading experience into a book would be extremely thin were it not for the many lessons I garnered from colleagues in the market over the years. Readers of this book will benefit from the experience I've gained from many of you. Thanks to Mark Galant, for founding GAIN Capital and offering me the opportunity to write this book. To the trading team at GAIN: Tim O'Sullivan, Anthony Piccolo, Paul Spirgel, Rob Voorhees, Mike Goret, Damon Gallo, and Alan Viola — it's an honor and pleasure to work with some of the best in the business. To Glenn Stevens and Samantha Roady, for setting the whole process in motion and encouraging me to go the full distance. To Christa Conte and Henry Feintuch of Feintuch Communications, for getting the word out to the media and then some. To my research team for picking up the slack while I wrote: Eric Viloria, CMT; Chris Tevere, CMT; Kathleen Brooks; and Dan Hwang. To Susan Hobbs for her fine editing assistance that made me get to the point, clearly. To McLean D. Giles for his technical review. And to the editors and staff at Wiley Publishing, especially Stacy Kennedy, for organizing the book in the first place.

Publisher's Acknowledgments

We're proud of this book; please send us your comments at http://dummies.custhelp.com. For other comments, please contact our Customer Care Department within the U.S. at 877-762-2974, outside the U.S. at 317-572-3993, or fax 317-572-4002.

Some of the people who helped bring this book to market include the following:

Acquisitions, Editorial, and Media Development

Project Editor: Susan Hobbs

Acquisitions Editor: Stacy Kennedy

Copy Editor: Susan Hobbs

Assistant Editor: Erin Calligan Mooney

Editorial Program Coordinator: Joe Niesen

Technical Editor: McLean D. Giles

Editorial Manager: Jennifer Ehrlich

Editorial Supervisor and Reprint Editor: Carmen Krikorian

Editorial Assistants: David Lutton, Jennette ElNaggar

Art Coordinator: Alicia B. South

Cartoons: Rich Tennant (www.the5thwave.com)

Composition Services

Project Coordinator: Patrick Redmond

Layout and Graphics: Corrie Socolovitch

Proofreaders: Cara L. Buitron, Melissa Cossell

Indexer: Steve Rath

Publishing and Editorial for Consumer Dummies

    Diane Graves Steele, Vice President and Publisher, Consumer Dummies

    Kristin Ferguson-Wagstaffe, Product Development Director, Consumer Dummies

    Ensley Eikenburg, Associate Publisher, Travel

    Kelly Regan, Editorial Director, Travel

Publishing for Technology Dummies

    Andy Cummings, Vice President and Publisher, Dummies Technology/General User

Composition Services

    Debbie Stailey, Director of Composition Services

Contents at a Glance

Table of Contents

Introduction

*T*he forex market was forever the private domain of hedge funds, global banks, multinational corporations, and wealthy private investors the world over. But this all changed a few years ago when the Internet-based technological revolution of online trading spread over to the forex markets. Today, tens of thousands of individual traders and investors all over the world are discovering the excitement and challenges of trading in the forex market.

No question about it, forex markets can be one of the fastest and most volatile financial markets to trade. Money can be made or lost in a matter of seconds or minutes. At the same time, currencies can display significant trends lasting several days to weeks and even years. Most importantly, forex markets are always moving, providing an accessible and target-rich trading environment.

In contrast to stock markets, which are more familiar and relatively intuitive to most investors,, the forex market somehow remains more elusive and seemingly complicated to newcomers.

I've spent my career in the forex market as a trader at some of the world's largest financial institutions. I've written *Currency Trading For Dummies* to pull back the curtain and strip away the mystique of the currency market.

In this book, I show you how the forex market really works, what moves it, and how you can actively trade it. I also provide you with the tools to develop a structured game plan you need to trade in the forex market and not lose your shirt. I cover

- ✔ Getting a handle on the forces that drive currency movements
- ✔ Understanding forex market trading conventions and strategies
- ✔ Interpreting economic data and official statements
- ✔ Finding sources of data and market intelligence
- ✔ Gauging market psychology, sentiment, and positioning
- ✔ Identifying key traits of individual currency pairs
- ✔ Utilizing technical analysis to spot trade opportunities
- ✔ Developing a regimented and disciplined approach to trading currencies
- ✔ Focusing on risk management to minimize losses and keep more of your gains

About This Book

If you're an active trader looking for alternatives to trading stocks or futures, the forex market is hard to beat. Online trading innovations over the past decade have made it accessible, both technologically and financially.

But as an individual trader, gaining access to the forex market is only the beginning. Just because you've got the keys to a Formula One race car doesn't mean you're ready to compete in a Grand Prix. First, you have to understand how the car works. Then you have to figure out some of the tactics and strategies the pros use. And *then* you have to get behind the wheel and practice, developing your skills, instincts, and tactics as you go.

To succeed in the forex market, you're going to have to do the same. This book gives you the no-nonsense information you need, with the perspective, experience, and insight of two forex market veterans.

Whether you're an experienced trader in other markets looking to expand into currencies, or a total newcomer to trading looking to start out in currencies, this book has what you need. Best of all, it's presented in the easy to use *For Dummies* format. Divided into easy-to-follow parts, this book can serve as both your reference and troubleshooting guide.

Note: Trading foreign currencies is a challenging and potentially profitable opportunity for educated and experienced investors. However, before deciding to participate in the forex market, you should carefully consider your investment objectives, level of experience, and risk appetite. Most important, don't invest money you can't afford to lose. The leveraged nature of forex trading means that any market movement will have an equally proportional effect on your deposited funds; this may work against you as well as for you. (To manage exposure, employ risk-reducing strategies such as stop-loss or limit orders.) Any off-exchange foreign exchange transaction involves considerable exposure to risk, including, but not limited to, leverage, creditworthiness, limited regulatory protection, and market volatility that may substantially affect the price or liquidity of a currency or currency pair. Using an Internet-based trading system also involves risks, including, but not limited to, the failure of hardware, software, and Internet connection.

Conventions Used in This Book

I keep the conventions to a minimum in this book. Here are the ones I use:

✔ *Italics* are used for emphasis or to highlight new words or phrases.

✔ **Boldfaced** text indicates key words in bulleted lists or the key steps of action lists.

✔ `Monotype` font is used to refer to Web addresses and e-mail addresses.

Also, when you see references to eastern time (ET), that means whatever time it is in New York City. Part of the year, that's eastern standard time (EST) and part of the year it's eastern daylight time (EDT).

What You're Not to Read

This book is designed to be an easy-access reference guide to currency trading. I cover each subject in its entirety in individual chapters, and the information doesn't depend on what comes before or after. That means you're able to jump around to the subjects you want to focus on and skip those you feel comfortable with already or just aren't interested in.

I highly recommend that complete beginners to trading in financial markets peruse the whole book to get a solid idea of all that's involved. Experienced traders from other markets will probably want to focus more on the specific conventions and traits of the forex market — but you may also find the technical and fundamental insights as applied to currencies enlightening for your forays into trading this market.

No matter your background, you can skip paragraphs marked with the Technical Stuff icon without giving up an understanding of the primary subject. Also, sidebars supplement the primary text — you can skip them without missing the main point.

Foolish Assumptions

Making assumptions is always a risky business, but knowing where I'm coming from may help put you at ease. Obviously, not all these assumptions will apply to you, but at least I'll have it all out in the open. In writing this book, I assume that:

✔ You've heard about currency trading and you're looking to find out more about what's involved before you try it.

✔ You're intrigued by the international dimensions of the forex markets and you want to find out how to profit from currency movements.

✔ You're seeking to diversify your trading activities or hedge your investments.

- ✔ You want to discover more about technical analysis and how it can be used to improve trading results.

- ✔ You understand that trading currencies carries the risk of losses.

- ✔ You're prepared to devote the time and resources necessary to understand what's involved in currency trading.

- ✔ You have the financial resources to pursue margin trading, meaning that you'll never risk more than you can afford to lose without affecting your lifestyle.

- ✔ You aren't gullible enough to believe the infomercials that promise easy money by trading currencies.

- ✔ You understand that there is a big difference between gambling and speculating.

These assumptions should serve as a healthy reality check for you before you decide to jump in to currency trading actively. A lot of it is similar to being a weekend golfer and being disappointed when your play doesn't reach pro-level scores. But when you think about it, why should it? The pros are out there practicing and playing all day, every day — it's their full-time job. Most people can only hope to get a round in on the weekend or get to the driving range for a few hours a week. Keep your perspective about what's realistic for you, and you'll be in a much better position to profit from actively trading.

How This Book is Organized

I've divided *Currency Trading For Dummies* into five parts. In this section, I lay them all out for you.

Part 1: Trading the World's Largest Financial Market

This part introduces you to the global forex market and gives you an idea of its size and scope. You find out who the players are and what their styles and motivations are. I also look at the impact of other financial markets on currencies. This part is also where I cover the nitty-gritty of currency trading conventions and tools so you know exactly how and what you're trading.

Part II: Driving Forces behind Currencies

In this part I look at the major fundamental and economic drivers that influence currency values. Also, whether it's economic data out of the United Kingdom or a political spat in the land down under (that's Australia, mate!), the forex market moves in response to developments from around the world. I show you how to interpret the data and events like a pro, factoring in market psychology and positioning. I also draw on my years of experience to offer insights that clue you in to how major currencies typically trade so you can know what to expect before you take the plunge.

Part III: Developing a Trading Plan

The military has an old saying: "Proper planning prevents piss-poor performance." The forex market is pretty much always open and constantly moving. To swim in this ocean and avoid the sharks requires an organized and disciplined approach to trading. In this part, I detail different trading styles, highlight concrete strategies, and provide a game plan for spotting trade opportunities and being prepared to act on them. I introduce you to my preferred technical analysis tools and my approach to using them. I also explore risk-management considerations and rules in depth, because what you don't know can cost you.

Part IV: Executing a Plan

In this part, I walk you through the various ways of establishing a position in the market, how to manage the trade while it's open, and how to close out the position on the most advantageous terms. I also look at the learning curve of a trader and suggest techniques to move you up your curve faster.

Part V: The Part of Tens

Here I offer a series of lists of key characteristics of successful traders, trading pitfalls to avoid, risk management rules to live by, and resources to continue your trading education.

Icons Used in This Book

Throughout this book, you see icons in the margins, highlighting certain paragraphs. Here are the icons I use and what they mean:

Theories are fine, but anything marked with a Tip icon tells you what currency traders *really* think and respond to. These are the tricks of the trade.

Paragraphs marked with the Remember icon contain the key takeaways from this book and the essence of each subject's coverage.

Achtung, baby! The Warning icon highlights potential errors and misconceptions that can cost you money, your sanity, or both.

You can skip anything marked by the Technical Stuff icon without missing out on the main message, but you may find the information useful for a deeper understanding of the subject.

Where to Go from Here

This book is set up so you can jump right in to the topics that are of greatest interest to you. If you're an absolute newcomer to trading in general and currencies in particular, I recommend reading Parts I and II to build a foundation for the other topics. If you have more experience with trading, use the table of contents and index to find the subject you have questions about right now. This book is a reference — keep it by your computer, and turn to it whenever you have a question about currency trading.

Part I
Trading the World's Largest Financial Market

The 5th Wave

By Rich Tennant

"I'm not sure Randall is a good long term investor. He uses the word 'historically' to describe the last 4 hours."

In this part . . .

*I*ntroduce you to the global currency market with an eye to demystifying it. I begin with an overview of the currency market and how it's the ultimate traders' market. Next, I run you through a global currency trading day, so you know what to expect. I also examine how currencies and other financial markets are interconnected. Then I show you who the major players are and look at their strategies and motivations for trading in the currency market.

Chapter 1

Currency Trading 101

· ·

· ·

The foreign exchange, or *forex*, market has exploded onto the scene and is the hot new financial market. It's been around for years, but advances in electronic trading have now made it available to individual traders on a scale unimaginable just a few years ago. But just because currency trading is more accessible doesn't mean it's widely understood.

I've spent my professional career in the forex market and I can't think of a better traders' market. In my opinion, nothing quite compares to the speed and exhilaration of the forex market or the intellectual and psychological challenges of trading in it. I've always looked at my work as essentially doing the same thing every day, but no two days are ever the same. Not many people can say that about their day jobs, and I wouldn't trade it for the world, no pun intended.

Defining Currency Trading

At its heart, currency trading is speculation about the value of one currency versus another. The key words in that last sentence are *speculation* and *currency*. I think that looking at currency trading from those two angles is essential.

On the one hand, currency trading is speculation, pure and simple, just like buying an individual stock or any other financial security in the hope that it will make a profitable return. On the other hand, the securities on which you're speculating are the currencies of various countries. Viewed separately, that means currency trading is both about the dynamics of market speculation, or trading, and the factors that affect the value of currencies. Put them together and you've got the largest, most dynamic and exciting financial market in the world.

Throughout this book, I approach currency trading from those two perspectives, looking at them separately and blending them together to give you the information you need to trade in the forex market.

Speculating as an enterprise

Let me first tell you what speculating isn't; speculating is not gambling, and it's not investing. Gambling is about playing with money, even when you know the odds are stacked against you. Investing is about minimizing risk and maximizing return, usually over a long time period (months or years). Speculating, or *active trading* (I use the terms interchangeably from here out), is about taking calculated financial risks to seek a profitable return, usually over a very short time horizon (minutes, hours, or days). You may be more familiar with speculating or active trading as *day trading*, but in the 24-hour-a-day forex market it can very easily turn into overnight trading, too.

Speculating as an enterprise refers to treating your trading as a serious business venture. In my experience, many newcomers to the forex market enter it too lightly and don't appreciate the patience and diligence required to be successful. I hope you'll take to heart the following attributes I think define a successful trader in any market:

- ✔ Dedication (time and energy)
- ✔ Resources (technological and financial)
- ✔ Discipline (emotional and financial)
- ✔ Decisiveness (intellectual and psychological)
- ✔ Perseverance (risk management and opportunism)
- ✔ Knowledge (economic, political, and market dynamics)

But even if you possess all those traits, there's no substitute for developing a comprehensive trading plan (see Chapters 11, 12, and 13, as well as "Developing a Trading Plan" later in this chapter). You wouldn't open a business venture without first developing a business plan (at least I hope not!). So you shouldn't expect any success in trading if you don't develop a realistic trading plan and stick to it. Think of trading as if it were your own business, and approach it as you would a business enterprise, because that's what it is.

Above all, try not to take your trading results too personally. Financial markets are prone to seemingly irrational movements on a regular basis, and the market doesn't know or care who you are or what your trade idea is.

Currencies as the trading vehicle

If you've heard anything at all about the forex market, it's probably that it's the largest financial market in the world, at least in terms of daily trading volumes. To be sure, the forex market is unique in many respects. The volumes are, indeed, huge, which means that liquidity is ever present. It also operates around the clock, from the opening of Asia/Pacific financial centers on Monday morning to the close of North American markets on Friday afternoon, giving traders access to the market any time they need it. (In Chapter 2, I give you a sense of the scale of the forex market and how it operates on a daily basis. In Chapter 3, I look at who the major forex players are.)

Few trading restrictions exist — no daily trading limits up or down, no restrictions on position sizes, and no requirements on selling a currency pair short. (I cover all the mechanics and conventions of currency trading in Chapter 4.)

Selling a currency pair short means you're expecting the price to decline. Because of the way currencies are quoted and because currency rates move up and down all the time, going short is as common as being long.

Most of the action takes place in the major currency pairs, which pit the U.S. dollar (USD) against the currencies of the *Eurozone* (the European countries that have adopted the euro as their currency), Japan, Great Britain, and Switzerland. There's also plenty of trading opportunities in the minor pairs, which see the U.S. dollar traded against the Canadian, Australian, and New Zealand dollars (frequently called the *commodity currencies*, covered in Chapter 9).

Other minor pairs include the Scandies, referring to the Scandinavian currencies outside the euro (Sweden, Norway, Denmark), and major emerging economies like Mexico, South Africa, and Singapore, to name a few. On top of that, there's cross-currency trading that directly pits two non-USD currencies against each other, such as the Swiss franc against the Japanese yen. Altogether, there are anywhere from 30 to 50 different currency pairs, depending on which forex brokerage you deal with. (See Chapters 8 and 9 for a look at the fundamental and market factors that affect the most widely traded currency pairs.)

Most individual traders trade currencies via the Internet through a brokerage firm. Online currency trading is typically done on a margin basis, which allows individual traders to trade in larger amounts by leveraging the amount of margin on deposit.

The *leverage,* or margin trading ratios, available to forex traders ranges from 50:1 to as much as 200:1, meaning a margin deposit of $1,000 could control a position size of $50,000 (at 50:1 leverage) to $200,000 (at 200:1). But trading on margin carries its own rules and requirements and is the backdrop against which all your trading will take place. Leverage is a two-edged sword, amplifying gains and losses equally, which makes risk management the key to any successful trading strategy (see Chapter 13).

Before you ever start trading in any market, make sure you're risking money that you can afford to lose, what's commonly called *risk capital*. Risk management is the key to any successful trading plan. Without a risk-aware strategy, margin trading can be an extremely short-lived endeavor. With a proper risk plan in place, you stand a much better chance of surviving losing trades and making winning ones. (I incorporate risk management throughout this book, but especially in Chapters 12, 13, and 19.)

Information Affects Currency Rates

Information is what drives every financial market, of course, but the forex market has its own unique roster of inputs. Many different cross-currents are at play in the currency market at any given moment — financial crises, central bank interest rate decisions, economic growth data, and so on. After all, the forex market is setting the value of one currency against another, so at the minimum, you're looking at the themes affecting two major international economies. Add in 20 or more other national economies, and you've got a serious amount of information flowing through the market. But that amount of news flow means that there's plenty of trading opportunities popping up regularly. (I focus on identifying trading opportunities in Chapter 12.)

Fundamentals drive the currency market

Fundamentals are the broad grouping of news and information that reflects the macroeconomic and political fortunes of the countries whose currencies are traded. (I look at those inputs in depth in Chapters 5, 6 and 7.) Most of the time, when you hear someone talking about the fundamentals of a currency, he's referring to the economic fundamentals. Economic fundamentals are based on

- Economic data reports
- Interest rate levels
- Monetary policy
- International trade flows
- International investment flows

There are also political and geopolitical fundamentals (see Chapter 5). An essential element of any currency's value is the faith or confidence that investors place in the value of that currency. If national events, such as an election or a budget crisis, are seen to be undermining the confidence in a particular economy, the value of its currency may be negatively affected. The Great Financial Crisis of 2008–2009 (GFC), which I discuss in greater detail in Chapter 5, revealed the extreme degree of global market interconnectedness and triggered significant currency market reactions.

Gathering and interpreting all this information is just part of a currency trader's daily routine, which is one reason why dedication is put at the top of the list of successful trader attributes (see "Speculating as an enterprise," earlier in this chapter; I focus on interpreting news and data in Chapter 6.)

Unless the technicals are driving the currency market

The term *technicals* refers to *technical analysis,* a form of market analysis most commonly involving chart analysis, trend-line analysis, and mathematical studies of price behavior, such as momentum or moving averages, to mention just a couple (see Chapter 11).

I don't know of too many currency traders who don't follow some form of technical analysis in their trading. Even the stereotypical seat-of-the-pants, trade-by-your-gut traders are likely to at least be aware of technical price levels identified by others. If you've been an active trader in other financial markets, chances are you've engaged in some technical analysis or at least heard of it.

If you're not aware of technical analysis, but you want to trade actively, I strongly recommend that you familiarize yourself with some of its basics (see Chapter 11). Don't be scared off by the name. Technical analysis is just a tool, like an electric saw — you don't need to know the circuitry of the saw to know how to use it, but you do need to know how to use it properly to avoid injury. (Chapter 20 offers several great reading suggestions to expand your technical trading knowledge.)

Technical analysis is especially important in the forex market because of the amount of fundamental information hitting the market at any given time. Currency traders regularly apply various forms of technical analysis to define and refine their trading strategies, with many people trading based on technical indicators alone. (See Chapters 14, 15, and 16 for how traders really use technicals.)

Or it may be something completely different

I'm not trying to be funny here. Honest. What I am trying to do is get across the idea of the many cross-currents that are at play in the forex market at any given time. Earlier in this chapter, I note that currency trading is just one form of market speculation, and that speculative trading involves an inherent market dynamic (see "Defining Currency Trading" earlier in this chapter).

Call it what you like — trader's instinct, market psychology, sentiment, position adjustment, or more buyers than sellers. The reality is that the forex market is made up of hundreds of thousands of traders, each with a different view of the market and each expressing his view by buying or selling different currencies at various times and price levels.

That means that in addition to understanding the currency-specific fundamentals and familiarizing yourself with technical analysis, you also need to have an appreciation of the market dynamic (see Chapter 8). And that's where trading with a plan comes in (see the following section).

Developing a Trading Plan

If your e-mail inbox is anything like mine, you probably get inundated with random penny stock tips or the next great Chinese stock initial public offering (IPO). (If you're not, please send me your spam filter.)

Those are about the only times you're going to get a message telling you how to trade. The rest of the time you're going to be on your own. But isn't that what trading is all about, anyway?

Don't get me wrong; I'm not trying to scare you off. I'm just trying to make it clear that you're the only one who knows your risk appetite and your own trading style. And very likely, you may not have even settled on a trading style yet. You need a style before you can develop your plan.

Finding your trading style

Before you can develop a trading plan, settling on a trading style is essential. (See Chapter 11 for more on trading styles.) Different trading styles generally call for variations on trading plans, though there are plenty of overarching trading rules that apply to all styles.

What do I mean by a *trading style?* Basically it boils down to how you approach currency trading in terms of

- ✔ **Trade timeframe:** How long will you hold a position? Are you looking at short-term trade opportunities (day trading), trying to capture more significant shifts in currency prices over days or weeks, or something in between?

- ✔ **Currency pair selection:** Are you interested in trading in all the different currency pairs, or are you inclined to specialize in only one or two?

- ✔ **Trade rationale:** Are you fundamentally or technically inclined? Are you considering creating a systematic trading model? Are you a trend follower or a breakout trader?

- ✔ **Risk appetite:** How much are you prepared to risk, and what are your return expectations?

I don't expect you to have answers to any or all of those questions, and that's exactly the point. As you read this book, I hope you'll be thinking about what trading style you'd like to pursue. Feel free to experiment with different styles and strategies — that's why *practice accounts,* or demo accounts, are useful. (See Chapter 2 for the best way to utilize practice accounts.)

At the end of the day, though, zeroing in on a trading style that you feel comfortable with and that you can pursue on a consistent basis helps. Your own individual circumstances (including work, family, finances, temperament, and discipline) will be the key variables, and you're the only one who knows what they are.

Planning the trade

Whatever trading style you ultimately choose to follow, you won't get very far if you don't establish a concrete trading plan and stick to it (see Chapter 10). Trading plans are what keep small bad trades from becoming big bad trades and what can turn small winners into bigger winners. More than anything, though, they're your road map, helping you to navigate the market after the adrenaline and emotions start pumping, no matter what the market throws your way.

I'm not telling you that trading currencies is any easier than trading any other financial market. But I can tell you that trading with a plan will greatly improve your chances of being successful in the forex market over time. Most important, I want to caution you that trading without a plan is a surefire recipe for disaster. You may survive a few close calls, but a day of reckoning comes for any trader without a plan — it's just what happens in markets.

The starting point of any trading plan is to identify a trading opportunity (see Chapter 12). No one is going to give you a call or shoot you an e-mail telling you what and when to trade. You have to devote the effort and gray cells to spotting viable trading opportunities yourself.

Throughout this book, I offer my own observations on how the forex market behaves in many different respects. I think there are plenty of kernels for spotting trade opportunities in those observations. (In Chapter 12, in particular, I show you a number of concrete ways to look at the market with a view to spotting trade opportunities.) Above all, be patient, and wait for the market to show its hand, which it always does, one way or the other.

Executing the Trading Plan from Start to Finish

The start of any trade comes when you step into the market and open up a position. How you enter your position, or how you execute the first step of your trading plan, can be as important as the trade opportunity itself. (More on getting into a position in Chapter 14.) After all, if you never enter the position, the trade opportunity will never be exploited. And probably nothing is more frustrating as a trader than having pinpointed a trade opportunity, having it go the way you expected, but having nothing to show for it because you never put the trade on.

The effort and resources you invest in researching, monitoring, and analyzing the market come to a concrete result when you open a trade. You're now exposed to price fluctuations, and your trading account will register a profit or loss as a result. But that's just the beginning of it.

Just because you have a trading plan doesn't mean the market is necessarily going to play ball. You need to be actively engaged in managing your position to make the most of it if it's a winner and to minimize the damage if the market is not going in your favor (see Chapter 15).

Active trade management is also critical to keeping more of what you make in the market. In my experience, making money in the forex market is not necessarily the hard part. More often than not, keeping what you've made is the *really* hard part.

You need to stay on your toes, and keep thinking about and monitoring the market while your trade is still active. The market will always be moving, sometimes faster than at other times, and new information will still be coming into the market. In Chapter 15, I look at several different ways you can monitor the market while your trade is open, as well as how and when you should adjust your trade strategy depending on events and time.

Exiting each trade is the culmination of the entire process, and you're either going to be pleased with a profit or disappointed with a loss. Every trade ends in either a profit or a loss (unless you get out at the entry price); it's just the way the market works. While your trade is still active, however, you're still in control and you can choose to exit the trade at any time. In Chapter 16, I look at important tactical considerations to keep in mind when it's time to close out the trade.

Even after you've exited the position, your work is not done. If you're serious about currency trading as an enterprise, you need to review your prior trades for what they tell you about your overall trading style and trade execution. Most important, reviewing your trading results is how you stay focused and avoid lapses in discipline that could hurt you on your next trade.

Only then is it time to move on to the next trading opportunity.

Chapter 2

What Is the Forex Market?

. . . .

In This Chapter

▶ Getting inside the forex market

▶ Understanding that speculating is the name of the game

▶ Trading currencies around the world

▶ Linking other financial markets to currencies

▶ Getting a feel for currency trading with a practice account

. . . .

*T*he foreign exchange market — most often called the forex market, or simply the FX market — is the largest and most liquid of all international financial markets. I like to think of it as the Big Kahuna of financial markets. (See the "Getting liquid without getting soaked" section, later in this chapter, for my discussion of liquidity.)

The forex market is the crossroads for international capital, the intersection through which global commercial and investment flows have to move. International trade flows, such as when a Swiss electronics company purchases Japanese-made components, were the original basis for the development of the forex markets.

Today, however, global financial and investment flows dominate trade as the primary nonspeculative source of forex market volume. Whether it's an Australian pension fund investing in U.S. Treasury bonds, or a British insurer allocating assets to the Japanese equity market, or a German conglomerate purchasing a Canadian manufacturing facility, each cross-border transaction passes through the forex market at some stage.

More than anything else, the forex market is a trader's market without equal. It's a market that's open around the clock from Sunday evening ET to Friday 5 p.m. ET, enabling traders to act on news and events as they happen. It's a market where half-billion-dollar trades can be executed in a matter of seconds and may not even move prices noticeably. Try buying or selling a half-billion of anything in another market, and see how prices react.

The rise of online currency trading

Online currency trading debuted in the early 1990s when two *matching systems* were developed by Reuters and EBS for the institutional "interbank" forex market. Both systems allowed banks to enter bids and offers into the system and trade on eligible prices from other banks, based on prescreened credit limits. The systems would match buyers and sellers, and the prices dealt in these systems became the benchmarks for currency price data, such as highs and lows.

By the mid to late 1990s major, international banks were developing their own online trading platforms to allow their institutional clients, like corporations and hedge funds, to trade with them electronically. Around the same time, new companies launched online trading platforms designed specifically for individual traders. Over the past decade, the increase in electronic trading has been a major driver of growth of the overall forex market.

Remember: Most online currency platforms offer trade sizes in amounts commonly known as *lots,* with a standard-size lot equal to 100,000 base currency units and a minilot equal to 10,000 base currency units. Some retail brokerages offer trading in micro lots of $1,000 and even odd amounts, like $250, providing even more flexibility based on an individual's account size. Online brokerages offer margin ranging from 25:1 to 200:1 depending on the regulations of the country you're in, allowing individual traders to make larger trades based on the amount of margin on deposit. For example, at 50:1 leverage, a $5,000 margin deposit would enable an individual trader to control a position as large as $250,000. Retail forex brokerages offer leverage to allow individual traders to trade in larger amounts relative to the small size of pips.

Getting Inside the Numbers

Average daily currency trading volumes are now estimated to $4 trillion per day, according to the 2010 BIS survey of forex volumes. That's a mind-boggling number, isn't it? $4,000,000,000,000 — that's a lot of zeros, no matter how you slice it. To give you some perspective on that size, it's about 15 to 20 times the size of daily trading volume on all the world's stock markets *combined.*

That $4-trillion-a-day number, which you may've seen in the financial press or other books on currency trading, actually overstates the size of what the forex market is all about — spot currency trading.

Trading for spot

Spot refers to the price where you can buy or sell currencies *now,* as in "on the spot." If you're familiar with stock trading, the price you can trade at is essentially a spot price. Technically, the term refers to the nearest settlement date on which a transaction can be made and is primarily meant to differentiate spot, or cash, trading from futures trading, or trading for some future delivery date. The spot currency market is normally traded for settlement in two business days.

The Bank for International Settlements (BIS), the international supervisory body for banks around the world, surveys forex market volumes every three years. The April 2010 BIS survey (the most recent available) revealed daily spot-trading volume of $1.5 trillion, which was up from $1 trillion since the 2007 survey. Spot trading volume accounted for 37 percent of total forex market volume. The rest of the volume that makes up the $4 trillion figure is comprised of *swap* and *outright forward* currency trading (trades made for settlement dates other than spot) and currency options.

Speculating in the currency market

Although commercial and financial transactions in the currency markets represent huge nominal sums, they still pale in comparison to amounts based on speculation. By far the vast majority of currency trading volume is based on speculation — traders buying and selling for short-term gains based on minute-to-minute, hour-to-hour, and day-to-day price fluctuations.

Estimates are that upwards of 90 percent of daily trading volume is derived from speculation (meaning, commercial or investment-based FX trades account for less than 10 percent of daily global volume). The depth and breadth of the speculative market means that the liquidity of the overall forex market is unparalleled among global financial markets.

The bulk of spot currency trading, more than 75 percent by volume, takes place in the so-called "major currencies," which represent the world's largest and most developed economies. Trading in the major currencies is largely free from government regulation and takes place outside the authority of any national or international body.

Additionally, activity in the forex market frequently functions on a regional "currency bloc" basis, where the bulk of trading takes place between the USD bloc, JPY bloc, and EUR bloc, representing the three largest global economic regions.

Trading in the currencies of smaller, less-developed economies, such as Thailand or Chile, is often referred to as *emerging market* or *exotic* currency trading, and may involve currencies with local restrictions on convertibility or limited liquidity, both of which limit access and inhibit the development of an active market.

Getting liquid without getting soaked

Liquidity refers to the level of *market interest* — the level of buying and selling volume — available at any given moment for a particular asset or security. The higher the liquidity, or the *deeper* the market, the faster and easier it is to buy or sell a security.

From a trading perspective, liquidity is a critical consideration because it determines how quickly prices move between trades and over time. A highly liquid market like forex can see large trading volumes transacted with relatively minor price changes. An illiquid, or *thin,* market will tend to see prices move more rapidly on relatively lower trading volumes. A market that only trades during certain hours (futures contracts, for example) also represents a less liquid, thinner market.

I refer to liquidity, liquidity considerations, and market interest throughout this book because they're among the most important factors affecting how prices move, or *price action.*

It's important to understand that, although the forex market offers exceptionally high liquidity on an overall basis, liquidity levels vary throughout the global trading day and across various currency pairs. For individual traders, though, variations in liquidity are more of a strategic consideration rather than a tactical issue. For example, if a large hedge fund needs to make a trade worth several hundred million dollars, it needs to be concerned about the tactical levels of liquidity, such as how much its trade is likely to move market prices depending on when the trade is executed. For individuals, who generally trade in smaller sizes, the amounts are not an issue, but the ebb and flow of liquidity are an important strategic factor in knowing when and how prices are likely to move.

The next section shows how liquidity and market interest changes throughout the global trading day with an eye to what it means for trading in particular currency pairs. (I explain individual currency pairs in greater detail in Chapters 8 and 9.)

Around the World in a Trading Day

The forex market is open and active 24 hours a day, from the start of business hours on Monday morning in the Asia-Pacific time zone straight through to the Friday close of business hours in New York. At any given moment, depending on the time zone, dozens of global financial centers — such as Sydney, Tokyo, or London — are open, and currency trading desks in those financial centers are active in the market.

In addition to the major global financial centers, many financial institutions operate 24-hour-a-day currency trading desks, providing an ever-present source of market interest. It may be a U.S. hedge fund in Boston that needs to monitor currencies around the clock, or it may be a major international bank with a concentrated global trading operation in Singapore.

The opening of the trading week

There is no officially designated starting time to the trading day or week, but for all intents the market action kicks off when Wellington, New Zealand, the first financial center west of the international dateline, opens on Monday morning local time. Depending on where you live, it roughly corresponds to early Sunday afternoon in North America, Sunday evening in Europe, and very early Monday morning in Asia.

The Sunday open represents the starting point where currency markets resume trading after the Friday close of trading in North America (5 p.m. eastern time [ET]). This is the first chance for the forex market to react to news and events that may have happened over the weekend. Prices may have closed New York trading at one level, but depending on the circumstances, they may start trading at different levels at the Sunday open. The risk that currency prices open at different levels on Sunday versus their close on Friday is referred to as the *weekend gap risk* or the *Sunday open gap risk*. A *gap* is a change in price levels where no prices are tradable in between.

As a strategic trading consideration, individual traders need to be aware of the weekend gap risk and know what events are scheduled over the weekend. There's no fixed set of potential events and there's never any way of ruling out what may transpire, such as a terror attack or a natural disaster. You just need to be aware that the risk exists, and factor it into your trading strategy.

Of typical scheduled weekend events, the most common are G7 or G20 meetings (see Chapter 3 for more on the G7/G20) and national elections or referenda. Just be sure you're aware of any major events that are scheduled.

On most Sunday opens, prices generally pick up where they left off on Friday afternoon. The opening price spreads in the interbank market will be much wider than normal, because only Wellington and 24-hour trading desks are active at the time. Opening price spreads of 10 to 30 points in the major currency pairs are not uncommon in the initial hours of trading. When banks in Sydney, Tokyo, Singapore, and Hong Kong enter the market over the next few hours, liquidity begins to improve and price spreads begin to narrow to more normal levels.

Because of the wider price spreads in the initial hours of the Sunday open, most online trading platforms do not begin trading until 5 p.m. ET on Sundays, when sufficient liquidity enables the platforms to offer their normal price quotes. Make sure you're aware of your broker's trading policies with regard to the Sunday open, especially in terms of order executions.

Trading in the Asia-Pacific session

Currency trading volumes in the Asia-Pacific session account for about 22 percent of total daily global volume, according to the 2010 BIS survey. The principal financial trading centers are Wellington, New Zealand; Sydney, Australia; Tokyo, Japan; Hong Kong, and Singapore.

In terms of the most actively traded currency pairs, that means news and data reports from New Zealand, Australia, and Japan are going to be hitting the market during this session. New Zealand and Australian data reports are typically released in the early morning, local time, which corresponds to late afternoon/early evening in North America. Japanese data is typically released just before 9 a.m. Tokyo time, which equates to roughly 7 or 8 p.m. ET. Some Japanese data reports and events also take place in the Tokyo afternoon, which equates to roughly midnight to 4 a.m. ET.

The overall trading direction for the NZD, AUD, and JPY can be set for the entire session depending on what news and data reports are released and what they indicate. For example, an unexpected interest rate hike in NZ can see an outsized reaction in the NZD against other major currencies.

Also during Asia/Pacific trading, late speakers from the United States, such as Federal Reserve officials speaking on the West Coast of the United States, may offer remarks on the U.S. economy or the direction of U.S. interest rates that affect the value of the U.S. dollar against other major currencies.

With the rapid growth of China over the last decade, Chinese news and data have become critical drivers of global markets. China is now the second largest national economy after the United States and overtook Germany as the world's leading exporter in 2010. Chinese data or policy changes that indicate growth there can fuel short-term rallies in everything from stock markets to commodities, with supportive implications for commodity currencies like AUD, CAD, and NZD (see Chapter 9 for more on the commodity currencies). On the other hand, Chinese data that point to slowing growth, or policy changes intended to fight inflation, for example, that may curb growth, can send global stock and commodity markets into a tail-spin. China also holds more than $2.6 trillion in currency reserves, with more than half allocated to U.S. Treasury debt, so any news of shifts in China's currency reserve management policies can trigger strong shifts in major currencies, especially the USD.

For individual traders, overall liquidity in the major currency pairs is more than sufficient, with generally orderly price movements. In some less liquid, non-regional currencies, like GBP/USD or USD/CAD, price movements may be more erratic or nonexistent, depending on the environment. With no Canadian news out for the next 12 hours, for example, there may be little reason or interest to move that pair. But if a large market participant needs to make a transaction in that pair, the price movement could be larger than normal.

Trading in the European/London session

About midway through the Asian trading day, European financial centers begin to open up and the market gets into full swing. European financial centers and London account for more than 55 percent of total daily global trading volume, with London alone accounting for more than one-third of total daily global volume, according to the 2010 BIS survey.

The European session overlaps with half of the Asian trading day and half of the North American trading session, which means that market interest and liquidity is at its absolute peak during this session.

News and data events from the Eurozone (and individual countries like Germany and France), Switzerland, and the United Kingdom are typically released in the early-morning hours of the European session. As a result, some of the biggest moves and most active trading take place in the European currencies (EUR, GBP, and CHF) and the euro cross-currency pairs (EUR/CHF and EUR/GBP).

 Because of the larger size of the European/London session volume, market moves that started earlier in Asia can become much more pronounced after Europe/London gets started. For example, an unexpected decline in a Chinese leading index earlier in the day may see global stock markets and commodities decline only slightly in response. But after the big money in Europe/London gets to work, market-price declines could become much more severe.

Asian trading centers begin to wind down in the late-morning hours of the European session, and North American financial centers come in a few hours later, around 7 a.m. ET.

Trading in the North American session

Because of the overlap of North American and European trading sessions, the trading volumes are much more significant. Some of the biggest and most meaningful directional price movements take place during this crossover period, roughly between 7 a.m. and noon ET. On its own, however, the North American trading session accounts for roughly the same share of global trading volume as the Asia-Pacific market, or just under 20 percent of global daily trading volume.

The North American morning is when key U.S. economic data is released, and the forex market makes many of its most significant decisions on the value of the U.S. dollar. Most U.S. data reports are released at 8:30 a.m. ET, with others coming out later (between 9 and 10 a.m. ET). Canadian data reports are also released in the morning, usually between 7 and 9 a.m. ET. There are also a few U.S. economic reports that variously come out at noon or 2 p.m. ET, livening up the New York afternoon market. (See Chapter 7 for more details on individual economic data reports.)

London and the European financial centers begin to wind down their daily trading operations around noon eastern time (ET) each day. The London, or European close, as it's known, can frequently generate a volatile flurry of activity. A directional move that occurred earlier in European trading or the New York session may be reversed if enough traders decide to *take profit* (selling out or exiting long positions) or *cover shorts* (buying back short positions). Or the directional move may extend farther, as traders betting against the earlier directional move throw in the towel and decide to go with the primary move. There's no set recipe for how the European close plays out, but significant flurries of activity frequently occur around this time.

On most days, market liquidity and interest fall off significantly in the New York afternoon, which can make for challenging trading conditions. On quiet days, the generally lower market interest typically leads to stagnating price action. On more active days, where prices may have moved more significantly, the lower liquidity can spark additional outsized price movements, as fewer traders scramble to get similarly fewer prices and liquidity. Just as with the London close, there's never a set way in which a New York afternoon market move will play out, so traders just need to be aware that lower liquidity conditions tend to prevail, and adapt accordingly.

Lower liquidity and the potential for increased volatility are most evident in the least-liquid major-currency pairs, especially USD/CHF and GBP/USD and their crosses, like EUR/GBP or EUR/CHF.

North American trading interest and volume generally continue to wind down as the trading day moves toward the 5 p.m. New York close, which also sees the change in value dates take place. (See Chapter 4 for more on rollovers and value dates.) But during the late New York afternoon, Wellington and Sydney have reopened and a new trading day has begun.

Key daily times and events

In addition to the ebb and flow of liquidity and market interest during the global currency trading day, you need to be aware of the following daily events, which tend to occur around the same times each day.

Expiring options

Currency options are typically set to expire either at the Tokyo expiry (3 p.m. Tokyo time) or the New York expiry (10 a.m. ET). The New York option expiry is the more significant one because it tends to capture both European and North American option market interest. When an option expires, the underlying option ceases to exist. Any hedging in the spot market that was done based on the option being alive suddenly needs to be unwound, which can trigger significant price changes in the hours leading up to and just after the option expiry time.

The amount and variety of currency option interest is just too large to suggest any single way that spot prices will always react around the expiry (there may not even be any significant option interest expiring on many days), but you should be aware that option-related interest is most in evidence around the daily expiries.

Setting the rate at currency fixings

There are several daily currency fixings in various financial centers, but the two most important are the 8:55 a.m. Tokyo time and the 4 p.m. London time fixings. A *currency fixing* is a set time each day when the prices of currencies for commercial and financial transactions are set, or fixed. (See Chapter 3 for more on fixings.)

From a trading standpoint, these fixings may see a flurry of trading in a particular currency pair in the hour or two before the fixing that abruptly ends just after the fixing time. A sharp rally in a specific currency pair on fixing-related buying, for example, may suddenly come to an end at the fixing time and see the price quickly drop back to where it was before.

Month-end and quarter-end fixings usually see the biggest volumes as they include asset managers' portfolio hedging or *rebalancing* flows. Significant monthly gains/declines in national stock markets can mean a particular currency may need to be sold/bought to maintain hedging ratios. For example, if the U.S. S&P 500 gains 5 percent in a month, the USD value of foreign asset managers' U.S. stock portfolio will have increased. To maintain a steady hedge ratio, they will need to sell USD against their home currency.

Squaring up on the currency futures markets

The Chicago Mercantile Exchange (CME), one of the largest futures markets in the world, offers currency futures through its International Monetary

Market (IMM) subsidiary exchange. Daily currency-futures trading closes each day on the IMM at 2 p.m. central time (CT), which is 3 p.m. ET. Many futures traders like to square up or close any open positions at the end of each trading session to limit their overnight exposure or for margin requirements.

The 30 to 45 minutes leading up to the IMM closing occasionally generates a flurry of activity that spills over into the spot market. Because the amount of liquidity in the spot currency market is at its lowest in the New York afternoon, sharp movements in the futures markets can drive the spot market around this time. There's no reliable way to tell if or how the IMM close will trigger a move in the New York afternoon spot market, so you just need to be aware of it and know that it can distort prices in the short term.

The U.S. dollar index

The U.S. dollar index is a futures contract listed on the Intercontinental Exchange, or ICE, futures exchange in the United States. The dollar index is an average of the value of the U.S. dollar against a basket of six other major currencies, but it's heavily weighted toward European currencies: The European currency share of the basket — Eurozone, United Kingdom, Sweden, and Switzerland — totals 77.3 percent.

The U.S. dollar index is great parallel universe to the spot U.S. dollar currency pairs. As a currency trader, be sure to follow the U.S. dollar index, especially its technical developments. (See Chapter 11 for more on technical analysis.) When the market outlook for the U.S. dollar is uncertain or mixed against other major currencies, the U.S. dollar index can frequently provide a clearer picture. If the U.S. dollar index breaks key technical levels, many currency traders react in the major spot currency pairs, building on the break of the U.S. dollar index. The flows can go either way — sharp moves in spot currency pairs may spur similar moves in the U.S. dollar index, or breakouts in the dollar index may provoke sharp adjustments in the spot U.S. dollar pairs — so look to the U.S. dollar index as another key indicator of the overall direction of the U.S. dollar.

Currencies and Other Financial Markets

As much as I like to think of the forex market as the be all and end all of financial trading markets, it doesn't exist in a vacuum. You may even have heard of some these other markets: gold, oil, stocks, and bonds.

Risk on or risk off?

Generally speaking, currency markets overlap with other major asset markets based on the global investment environment, with *risk sentiment* as the key barometer. Risk sentiment refers to investors' moods and the level of risk appetites they're displaying: Are investors seeking risk, or are they seeking safety? When times are good, risk assets (such as stocks and commodities) tend to appreciate as growth and demand expectations are positive. When times are bad or uncertainty is high, risk assets tend to suffer, and more defensive assets (like government bonds, gold, or the USD) are sought after.

The currency market corollary breaks down by individual major currencies, with the USD, JPY, and CHF typically viewed as the *safe haven* currencies and most others viewed as *risk* currencies. Of course, the overlap between FX and other major assets classes will also be determined by what's happening to other key drivers of individual currencies, such as interest rates or growth expectations.

The U.S. dollar has a special place among major currencies because it's the primary currency for international trade, and the U.S. government bond market is the largest in the world. When there is a USD-driven movement, say the USD is weakening in a dramatic fashion due to Fed policy, the spillover effects to other markets can be quite strong, such as driving commodity prices far higher than what demand would suggest. The flip side is that when major uncertainty develops or really bad things happen (think Eurozone debt crisis), the USD tends to strengthen as investors seek safety in U.S. Treasuries.

Be very careful about getting caught up in the supposed correlations between the forex market and other financial markets. Even when a high degree of correlation is found (meaning, the two markets move in tandem or inversely to each other), it's probably over the long term (months or years) and offers little information about how the two markets will correlate in the short term (minutes, hours, and days).

Always keep in mind that all the various financial markets are markets in their own right and function according to their own internal dynamics based on data, news, positioning, and sentiment. Will markets occasionally overlap and display varying degrees of correlation? Of course, and it's always important to be aware of what's going on in other financial markets. But it's also essential to view each market in its own perspective and to trade each market individually.

With that rather lengthy disclaimer in mind, let's look at some of the other key financial markets and see what conclusions we can draw for currency trading. (See Chapter 9 for an idea of correlations.)

Gold

Gold (XAU) is commonly viewed as a hedge against inflation, an alternative to the U.S. dollar, and as a store of value in times of economic or political uncertainty. In recent years, gold has also been viewed as an alternative to major fiat currencies, with gold strengthening as both the USD and EUR came under pressure. Over the long term, gold's relationship is mostly inverse to the USD, with a weaker USD generally accompanying a higher gold price, and a stronger USD coming with a lower gold price. However, in the short run, each market has its own dynamics and liquidity, which makes short-term trading relationships more difficult to gauge.

Overall, the gold market is significantly smaller than the forex market, so if I were a gold trader, I'd sooner keep an eye on what's happening to the dollar, rather than the other way around. This is referred to as an *asymmetric bias*, where a weakening USD tends to trigger larger gold gains, while falling gold may not lend much support to the USD, and a sharply stronger USD may see outsized gold losses.

You can trade gold directly against other major currencies (like XAU/EUR, XAU/GBP or XAU/JPY), allowing you to more directly pinpoint a trade to exploit a potential currency's strength or weakness.

Despite the mania around gold in recent years, it does not possess any magical properties that ensure it will always rise in value. Always treat gold for what it really is: a speculative commodity that can rise and fall based on supply and demand. On gold's merits as a hedge against inflation, I would note that gold would need to be around $2,200 per ounce to match its inflation-adjusted high from 1980–81, meaning if you owned gold since then, you'd have lost money.

Oil

Crude oil is the largest of the global commodity markets and a finely balanced one at that. That means even minor supply disruptions can send oil prices jumping higher, whereas excess supply (seen in weekly inventory data) can send prices dropping quickly. Production disruptions from turmoil in the Middle East/North Africa in early 2011 led to a sharp rise in oil prices, but gains were prone to abrupt setbacks as fears periodically subsided. Oil demand is also a good indicator of the global growth outlook, where upbeat views may inspire higher oil prices and vice versa.

Oil is usually priced in USD so there is a tendency for oil prices to trade inversely to the value of the USD. This is especially apparent when the USD is in a weakening phase. But the real reason oil and the USD are inversely correlated is that Middle East oil producers receive oil revenue in USD, but their import purchases are mostly in EUR. If the USD weakens, their EUR purchasing power declines, so they raise long-term oil prices to compensate.

Currencies of oil producing countries like Canada and Norway tend to strengthen alongside oil prices, based on the improved outlook for domestic economic performance, but there's no guarantee that will always happen.

The best way to look at oil is as an inflation input and as a limiting factor on overall economic growth. The higher the price of oil, the higher inflation is likely to be and the slower an economy is likely to grow. The lower the price of oil, the lower inflationary pressures are likely (but not necessarily) to be. Because the United States is a heavily energy-dependent economy and also intensely consumer-driven, the United States typically stands to lose the most from higher oil prices and to gain the most from lower oil prices. I like to factor changes in the price of oil into my inflation and growth expectations, and then draw conclusions about the course of the USD from them. Above all, oil is just one input among many.

Stocks

Stocks are microeconomic securities, rising and falling in response to individual corporate results and prospects, whereas currencies are essentially macroeconomic securities, fluctuating in response to wider-ranging economic and political developments. As such, there is little intuitive reason that stock markets should be related to currencies.

In recent years, however, risk sentiment (see the "Risk on or risk off?" section, earlier in this section) has taken on greater significance in global markets, increasingly driving asset classes from stocks and commodities to currencies and precious metals.

The paths of stocks and currencies typically intersect in two main ways. When risk is on, stocks and risk currencies tend to rise, whereas safe haven assets like government bonds, USD, and JPY tend to weaken. A good example of this is carry trades, where higher yielding currencies are bought and lower yielding currencies are sold, for example buying AUD/JPY. As long as risk sentiment stays positive, stocks and carry trades tend to appreciate. But if bad news hits and investor sentiment turns sour, stocks and carry trades usually sell-off and the USD and JPY may see a rebound as shorts are covered (this typically sees USD/JPY decline).

The other main crossroad between stocks and FX is more closely based on the value of the USD. When the USD is weakening, U.S. stocks tend to benefit as the outlook for U.S. multinational corporations' profits will improve on more valuable foreign revenue. If the USD is weakening on the prospect of *easy* Fed monetary policy, stocks may also benefit on the lower interest rate outlook. At the same time, non-U.S. stocks may be more attractive to U.S.-based investors on rising currency values.

But if the outlook for more accommodative Fed monetary policy is due to a deteriorating economic outlook in the U.S., then risk sentiment is likely to be suffering and the USD may actually benefit as stocks and commodities are sold and USD-shorts are bought back. As you can see, circumstances do matter for how stocks and FX will interact.

Bonds

Fixed income or bond markets have a more intuitive connection to the forex market because they're both heavily influenced by interest rate expectations. However, short-term market dynamics of supply and demand interrupt most attempts to establish a viable link between the two markets on a short-term basis. Sometimes the forex market reacts first and fastest, depending on shifts in interest rate expectations. At other times, the bond market more accurately reflects changes in interest rate expectations, with the forex market later playing catch-up.

Overall, as currency traders, you definitely need to keep an eye on the yields of the benchmark government bonds of the major-currency countries to better monitor the expectations of the interest rate market. Changes in *yield spreads*, the difference between two countries' interest rates, exert a major influence on forex markets. (See Chapter 5 for more on interest rates and currencies.)

U.S. Treasury yields tend to have a strong positive relationship with the direction of USD/JPY. Japanese asset managers hold massive amounts of U.S. Treasury debt, and they actively hedge the currency exposure. When U.S. yields rise, prices fall and the USD value of U.S. debt holdings declines, meaning Japanese hedgers need to buy back USD they sold earlier. The opposite happens when U.S. yields fall and bond prices rise. The effect is that USD/JPY will frequently follow U.S. Treasury yields. (See more about trading USD/JPY in Chapter 8.)

Getting Started with a Practice Account

For newcomers to currency trading, the best way to get a handle on what currency trading is all about is to open a *practice account* at any of the online forex brokers. Most online forex brokers offer practice accounts to allow you to experience the real-life price action of the forex market. Practice accounts are funded with "virtual" money, so you're able to make trades with no real money at stake and gain experience in how margin trading works.

Interpreting your results realistically

Trading in a practice account is the 21st-century form of paper trading. *Paper trading* is writing down trades on paper based on real-time market prices, but not having any real money at risk. Practice accounts are a souped-up version of paper trading — you only have to click and deal, and the trading platform does all the recording for you.

Whether you're trading in an online forex practice account or paper trading on stock quotes from the morning newspaper, be sure to keep in mind that your results aren't real because you never had any real money at stake.

Think of it this way: If you make a handshake bet with a friend on a football game, you're probably not going to be too concerned with whether you win or lose. You may not even watch the game. But if you bet $50 or $100 on the game, you're probably going to be watching the whole game and cheering and yelling while you do. The difference: Your emotions come alive when real money is on the line.

Practice accounts are a great way to experience the forex market up close and personal. They're also an excellent way to test-drive all the features and functionality of a broker's platform. However, the one thing you can't simulate is the emotions of trading with real money. To get the most out of your practice-account experience, you have to treat your practice account as if it were real money, as much as you can.

Practice accounts give you a great chance to experience the minute-to-minute price movements of the forex market. You'll be able to see how prices change at different times of the day, as well as how various currency pairs may differ from each other. Be sure to check out the action when major news and economic data is released, so you can get a sense of how the forex market reacts to new information.

In addition to witnessing how the forex market really moves, you can

- ✔ Start trading in real market conditions without any fear of losing money.
- ✔ Experiment with different trading strategies to see how they work.
- ✔ Gain experience using different orders and managing open positions.
- ✔ Improve your understanding of how margin trading and leverage work.
- ✔ Start analyzing charts and following technical indicators.

 Using a practice account while you read this book is a great way to experience many of the ideas and concepts I introduce. If a picture is worth a thousand words, then a real-time currency trading platform with constantly changing prices, market updates, and charting tools, has to be worth a book. I like to think I'm pretty good at explaining how currency trading works, but nothing beats being able to see it for yourself.

I recommend that you open practice accounts with a few different forex brokers, because each trading platform has varying capabilities and functionalities. In addition, different brokers have different trading policies, charting packages, and research offerings. Also, try to get a feel for the level of customer support you'll receive as a client.

Chapter 3

Who Trades Currencies? Meet the Players

The forex market is regularly referred to as the largest financial market in the world based on trading volumes. But this massive market was unknown and unavailable to most individual traders and investors until the late 1990s.

That leaves a lot of people in the dark when it comes to exactly what the currency market is: how it's organized, who's trading it, and why. In this chapter, I discuss how the FX market is structured and who the major players are. Along the way, I clue you in to how they go about their business and what it means for your trading in the currency market.

If you believe that information is the lifeblood of financial market trading, which I certainly do, I think you'll appreciate this guide to the movers and shakers of the currency market. When you have a better understanding of who's active in the FX market, you'll be able to make better sense of what you see and hear in the market.

The Interbank Market Is "The Market"

When people talk about the forex market, they're usually referring to the *interbank market,* whether they realize it or not. The interbank market is where the really big money changes hands. Minimum trade sizes are one million of the base currency, such as €1 million of EUR/USD or $1 million of

USD/JPY. Much larger trades of between $10 million and $100 million are routine and can go through the market in a matter of seconds. Even larger trades and orders are a regular feature of the market.

For the individual trading FX online, the prices you see on your trading platform are based on the prices being traded in the interbank market.

The sheer size of the interbank market is what helps make it such a great trading market because investors of every size are able to act in the market, usually without significantly affecting prices. It's one market where I would say size really doesn't matter. I've seen spot traders be right with million-dollar trades, and sophisticated hedge funds be wrong with half-billion-dollar positions.

Daily trading volumes are enormous by any measure, dwarfing global stock trading volumes many times over. The most recent Bank of International Settlement (BIS) report, released in 2010, estimated daily FX trading volumes of nearly $4 trillion.

Getting inside the interbank market

So what is the interbank market, and where did it come from? The forex market originally evolved to facilitate trade and commerce between nations. The leading international commercial banks, which financed international trade through letters of credit and bankers' acceptances, were the natural financial institutions to act as the currency exchange intermediary. They also had the foreign branch network on the ground in each country to facilitate the currency transfers needed to settle FX transactions.

The result over years was the development of an informal interbank market for currency trading. As the prefix suggests, the *interbank* market is "between banks," with each trade representing an agreement between the banks to exchange the agreed amounts of currency at the specified rate on a fixed date. The interbank market is alternatively referred to as the *cash market* or the *spot market* to differentiate it from the currency futures market, which is the only other organized market for currency trading.

Currency futures markets operate alongside the interbank market, but they are definitely the tail being wagged by the dog of the spot market. As a market, currency futures are generally limited by exchange-based trading hours and lower liquidity than is available in the spot market.

The interbank market developed without any significant governmental oversight, and it remains largely unregulated to this day. In most cases, there is no regulatory authority for spot currency trading apart from local or national banking regulations. Interbank trading essentially evolved based on credit lines between international banks and trading conventions that developed over time.

The big commercial banks used to rule the roost when it came to currency trading, whereas investment banks remained focused more on stocks and bonds. But the banking industry has undergone a tremendous consolidation over the last 20 years, as bank merger after bank merger has seen famous names subsumed into massive financial conglomerates. Today it's hard to even think of the major banks as either commercial banks or investment banks, such has been the expansion of their trading operations.

While banks formed the core of the interbank market for decades, nonbank financial institutions, like hedge/pension/mutual funds, steadily increased their activity in the forex market. The proliferation of electronic trading technology in recent years has only increased the market presence of these firms. And in 2010, for the first time ever, the BIS survey of FX trading volume showed nonbank financial firms surpassed traditional banks' FX trading volume. Nonbanks FX trading volumes surged 42 percent from 2007 levels of $1.3 trillion to $1.9 trillion in 2010. Still, the interbank market continues to serve as the primary liquidity provider to the broader forex market. There are just more nonbank players adding to the overall pool of liquidity.

Bank to bank and beyond

The interbank market is a network of international banks operating in financial centers around the world. The banks maintain trading operations to facilitate trading for their own accounts, called *proprietary trading,* or just *prop trading* for short, and to provide currency trading services for their customers. Banks' customers can range from corporations and government agencies to hedge funds and wealthy private individuals.

Trading in the interbank market

The interbank market is an over-the-counter (OTC) market, which means that each trade is an agreement between the two counterparties to the trade. There are no exchanges or guarantors for the trades, just each bank's balance sheet and the promise to make payment.

The bulk of spot trading in the interbank market is transacted through electronic matching services, such as EBS and Reuters Dealing. Electronic matching services allow traders to enter their bids and offers into the market, *hit bids* (sell at the market), and *pay offers* (buy at the market). Price spreads vary by currency pair and change throughout the day depending on market interest and volatility.

The matching systems have prescreened credit limits, and a bank will only see prices available to it from approved counterparties. Pricing is anonymous before a deal, meaning you can't tell which bank is offering or bidding, but the counterparties' names are made known immediately after a deal goes through.

The major international FX trading banks have all deployed electronic trading platforms that function via the Internet, enabling their customers to bypass banks' trading desks and deal directly in the market, potentially accessing more advantageous prices. Electronic trading also facilitates algorithmic or *system trading*, which has also contributed to the recent surge in trading volumes. Concrete numbers are hard to come by, but conservative estimates put the amount of algorithmic trading at around 25 to 30 percent of total daily volume.

Stepping onto a currency trading floor

Interbank trading rooms are staffed by a variety of different market professionals and each has a different role to play. The typical currency trading room has

- **Flow traders:** Sometimes called *execution traders,* these are the market-makers, showing two-way prices at which to buy and sell, for the bank's customers. If the customer makes a trade, the execution trader then has to cover the resulting deal in the interbank market, hopefully at a profit. These traders are also responsible for watching and executing customer orders in the market. These are the traders who are generating most of the electronic prices and price action.

- **Proprietary traders:** These traders are focused on speculative trading for the bank's own account. Their strategies can run the gamut from short-term day trading to longer-term macroeconomic bets.

- **Forward traders:** Forward traders are active in the *forward* currency market, which refers to trades made beyond the normal spot value date. The forward market is essentially an interest rate differential market, where the interest rates of the various currencies are traded. These traders provide the bank's customers with pricing for non-spot deals or currency swap agreements. They also manage the bank's interest rate exposure in the various currencies.

- **Options traders:** Options traders manage the bank's portfolio, or book, of outstanding currency options. They hedge the portfolio in the spot market, speculate for the bank's own account with option strategies, and provide pricing to the bank's customers on requested option strategies.

Hedgers and Financial Investors

The forex market sits at the crossroads of global trade and international finance and investing. Whether it's a U.S. conglomerate managing its foreign affiliates' balance sheets or a German mutual fund launching an international stock fund, they all have to go through the forex market at some point.

Participants in the forex market generally fall into one of two categories: financial transactors and speculators. _Financial transactors_ are active in the forex market as part of their overall business but not necessarily for currency reasons. For instance, an electric utility operator in the United States may need EUR to buy a German-made turbine for a new generator. _Speculators_ are in it purely for the money.

The lion's share of forex market turnover comes from speculators. BIS data suggest that nearly 90 percent of daily FX trading volume is based solely on speculation. I look at the types and roles of speculators in the "Speculators" section of this chapter, but here I want to introduce the players who are active in the forex markets for nonspeculative reasons.

Financial transactors are important to the forex market for several reasons:

- ✔ Their transactions can be extremely sizeable, typically hundreds of million or billions.
- ✔ Their deals are frequently one-time events.
- ✔ They are generally not price sensitive or profit maximizing.

Add up those reasons and you're looking at potentially very large, one-off trading flows that are not really concerned with where the current market is trading or which way it's headed. They enter the market to do their deal and then they're gone, which can introduce an element of market inefficiency that can allow traders to take advantage of counter-trend movements.

Hedging your bets

Hedgers come in all shapes and sizes, but don't confuse them with _hedge funds._ (Despite the name, a hedge fund is typically 100 percent speculative in its investments.)

Hedging is about eliminating or reducing risk. In financial markets, hedging refers to a transaction designed to insure against an adverse price move in some underlying asset. In the forex market, hedgers are looking to insure themselves against an adverse price movement in a specific currency rate.

Hedging for international trade purposes

One of the more traditional reasons for hedging in the forex market is to facilitate international trade. Let's say you're a widget maker in Germany and you just won a large order from a UK-based manufacturer to supply it with a large quantity of widgets. To make your bid more attractive, you agreed to be paid in British pounds (GBP).

But because your production cost base is denominated in euros (EUR), you face the exchange rate risk that GBP will weaken against the EUR. That would make the amount of GBP in the contract worth fewer EUR back home, reducing or even eliminating your profit margin on the deal. To insure, or *hedge,* against that possibility, you would seek to sell GBP against EUR in the forex market. If the pound weakened against the euro, the value of your market hedge would rise, compensating you for the lower value of the GBP you'll receive. If the pound strengthens against the euro, your loss on the hedge is offset by gains in the currency conversions. (Each pound would be worth more euros.)

Trade hedgers follow a variety of hedging strategies and can utilize several different currency hedging instruments. Currency *options* can be used to eliminate downside currency risk and sometimes allow the hedger to participate in advantageous price movements. Currency *forward* transactions essentially lock in a currency price for a future date, based on the current spot rate and the interest rate differentials between the two currencies.

Trade-related hedging regularly comes into the spot market in two main forms:

✔ **At several of the daily currency fixings:** The largest is the London afternoon fixing, which takes place each day at 4 p.m. local time, which corresponds to 11 a.m. eastern time (ET). The Tokyo fixing takes place each day at 8:55 a.m. Tokyo time, which corresponds to 6:55 p.m. eastern time (ET). A *fixing* is a process sponsored by an exchange or central bank where commercial hedgers submit orders to buy or sell currencies in advance. The orders are then filled at the prevailing spot rate (the rate is fixed) at the time of the fixing.

The difference between the amount of buying and selling orders typically results in a net amount that needs to be bought or sold in the market prior to the fixing time. On some days, this can see large amounts (several hundred million dollars to a billion dollars, or more) being bought or sold in the hour or so leading up to the fixing time. After the fix, that market interest has been satisfied and disappears. Month-end and quarter-end fixings typically see the largest amounts.

Short-term traders need to closely follow live market commentaries to see when there is a substantial buying or selling interest for a fixing.

✔ **Mostly in USD/JPY, where Japanese exporters typically have large amounts of USD/JPY to sell:** Japanese exporters typically receive dollars for their exports, which must then be converted into JPY (sell USD/buy JPY). The Japanese export community tends to be closely knit and their orders are likely to appear together in large amounts at similar levels. Again, real-time market commentaries are the most likely source for individual traders to hear about Japanese exporter selling interest.

Hedging for currency options

The currency option market is a massive counterpart to the spot market and can heavily influence day-to-day spot trading. Currency option traders are typically trading a portfolio of option positions. To maximize their returns, options traders regularly engage in delta hedging and gamma trading. Without getting into a major options discussion here, option portfolios generate a synthetic, or hypothetical, spot position based on spot price movements.

To maximize the return on their options portfolios, they regularly trade the synthetic spot position as though it were a real spot position. Trading the synthetic positions generated by options is called *delta hedging* or *gamma trading*.

Option hedgers are frequently found selling at technical resistance levels or buying on support levels. When a currency pair stays in a range, it can do quite nicely. But when range breakouts occur, options traders frequently need to rush to cover those range bets, adding to the force of the directional breakout. Keep an eye out for reports of option-related buying and selling as technical levels are tested.

Another daily feature of the spot market is the 10 a.m. ET option expiry, also known as the *New York cut*, when options due to expire that day cease to exist. Any related hedging that was done for the option then needs to be unwound, though this is likely to have been done prior to the expiry if the option is well out of the money. Traders need to follow market commentaries to see if large option interest is set to expire on any given day and generally anticipate a flurry of option-related buying/selling that may suddenly reverse course after the 10 a.m. expiry.

Global investment flows

One of the reasons forex markets remain as lightly regulated as they are is that no developed nation wants to impose restrictions on the flow of global capital. International capital is the lifeblood of the developed economies and the principal factor behind the rapid rise of developing economies like China, Brazil, Russia, and India. The forex market is central to the smooth functioning of international debt and equity markets, allowing investors to easily obtain the currency of the nation they want to invest in.

Financial investors are the other main group of nonspeculative players in the forex market. As far as the forex market is concerned, financial investors are mostly just passing through on their way to another investment. More often than not, financial investors look at currencies as an afterthought because they're more focused on the ultimate investment target, be it Japanese equities, German government bonds, or French real estate.

Crossing borders with mergers and acquisitions

Mergers and acquisitions (M&A) activity is becoming increasingly international and shows no sign of abating. International firms are now involved in a global race to gain and expand market share, and cross-border acquisitions are frequently the easiest and fastest way to do that.

When a company seeks to buy a foreign business, there can be a substantial foreign exchange implication from the trade. When large M&A deals are announced, note the answers to the following two questions:

- ✓ **Which countries and which currencies are involved?** If a French electrical utility buys an Austrian power company, there are no currency implications because both countries use the euro (EUR). But if a Swiss pharmaceutical company announces a takeover of a Dutch chemical firm, the Swiss company may need to buy EUR and sell Swiss francs (CHF) to pay for the deal.

- ✓ **How much of the transaction will be in cash?** Again, if it's an all stock deal, then there are no forex market implications. But if the cash portion is large, forex markets will take note and begin to speculate on the currency pair involved.

Speculators

Speculators are market participants who are involved in the market for one reason only — to make money off directional price movements. In contrast to hedgers, who have some form of existing currency market risk, speculators have no currency risk until they enter the market. Hedgers enter the market to neutralize or reduce risk. Speculators embrace risk taking as a means of profiting from long-term or short-term price movements.

Speculators (*specs* for short) are what really make a market efficient. They add liquidity to the market by bringing their views and, most important, their capital into the market. That liquidity is what smoothes out price movements, keeps trading spreads narrow, and allows a market to expand.

In the forex market, speculators are running the show. The latest BIS survey indicates that nearly 90 percent of daily trading volume is speculative in nature. If you're trading currencies for your own account, welcome to the club. If you're trading currencies to hedge a financial risk, you can thank the specs for giving you a liquid market and reducing your transaction costs.

Speculators come in all types and sizes and pursue all different manner of trading strategies. In this section, I take a look at some of the main types of speculators to give you an idea of who they are and how they go about their business. Along the way, you may pick up some ideas to improve your own approach to the market. At the minimum, I hope this information will allow you to better understand market commentaries about who's buying and who's selling.

Hedge funds

Hedge funds are a type of *leveraged fund,* which refers to any number of different forms of speculative asset management funds that borrow money for speculation based on real assets under management. For instance, a hedge fund with $100 million under management can *leverage* those assets (through margin agreements with their trading counterparties) to give them trading limits of anywhere from $500 million to $2 billion. Hedge funds are subject to the same type of margin requirements as you or me, just with a whole lot more zeroes involved.

The other main type of leveraged fund is known as a Commodity Trading Advisor (CTA). A CTA is principally active in the futures markets. But because the forex market operates around the clock, CTAs frequently trade spot FX as well.

The major difference between the two types of leveraged funds comes down to regulation and oversight. CTAs are regulated by the Commodity Futures Trading Commission (CFTC), the same governmental body that regulates retail FX firms. As a result, CTAs are subject to a raft of regulatory and reporting requirements. Hedge funds, on the other hand, remain largely unregulated. What's important is that they all pursue similarly aggressive trading strategies in the forex market, treating currencies as a separate asset class, like stock or commodities.

In the forex market, leveraged funds can hold positions anywhere from a few hours to days or weeks. When you hear that leveraged names are buying or selling, it's an indication of short-term speculative interest that can provide clues as to where prices are going in the near future.

Speculating with algorithms, models, and systems

Many leveraged funds have opted for a *quantitative* approach to trading financial markets. A quantitative approach is one that uses mathematical formulas and models to come up with buy and sell decisions. *Algorithms* refer to the proprietary quantitative formulas used to generate the trading decisions. Data goes in, trading signals come out, and what's inside the system, no one knows. Such quantitative funds are interchangeably referred to as *algorithmic, model,* or *systems funds.* Concrete numbers are hard to come by, but conventional estimates are that between 25 and 30 percent of daily FX volume is generated by algorithmic trading systems.

Some models are based on statistical relationships between various currencies, commodities, and fixed income securities. Others are based on macroeconomic data, such as relative growth rates, inflation rates, and geopolitical risk models. Still others are based on technical indicators and price studies of the underlying currency pair. These are frequently referred to as *rules-based trading systems,* because the system will employ defined rules to enter and exit trades.

Retail FX traders are also increasingly utilizing algorithmic trading systems. Many trading platforms allow you to easily develop your own trading systems based on any number of inputs, such as moving average or momentum oscillator crossovers. These systems can be set up to automatically enter and exit trades, or they might require you to approve each trade signal, depending on your level of discretion (see "Trading with discretion" later in this chapter). Some traders opt for off-the-shelf trading systems that have been developed by third parties. One of the more popular platforms for system traders is the MetaTrader software, provided by Metaquotes, and many retail FX brokers offer the MetaTrader platform in addition to their proprietary trading platforms. (I look at system trading in greater detail in Chapter 10.)

I would caution that using a trading system offers no guarantees of success, no matter what back-testing or historical results would suggest.

Trading with discretion

The opposite of an algorithmic trading system is a *discretionary* trading fund. The discretion, in this case, refers to the fund manager's judgment and overall market view. The fund manager may follow a technical or rules-based approach but prefer to have a human make the final decision on whether a trade is initiated. A more refined version of this approach accepts the trade signals but leaves the execution up to the discretionary fund manager's trading staff, who try to maximize position entry/exit based on short-term market dynamics.

Still another variation of discretionary funds is those that base their trading strategies on macroeconomic and political analysis, known as *global-macro funds*. This type of discretionary fund manager is typically playing with a longer-time horizon in mind. The fund may be betting on a peak in an interest rate cycle or the prospect that an economy will slip into recession. Shorter-term variations on this theme may take positions based on a specific event risk, such as the outcome of the next central bank meeting or national election.

Day traders, big and small

This is where you and I fit into the big picture of the forex market. If the vast majority of currency trading volume is speculative in nature, then most of that speculation is short-term in nature. Short-term can be minute-to-minute or hour-to-hour, but rarely is it longer than a day or two. From the interbank traders who are scalping EUR/USD (high frequency in-and-out trading for few pips) to the online trader looking for the next move in USD/JPY, short-term day traders are the backbone of the market.

Intraday trading was always the primary source of interbank market liquidity, providing fluid prices and an outlet for any institutional flows that hit the market. Day traders tend to be focused on the next 20 to 30 pips in the market, which makes them the source of most short-term price fluctuations.

When you're looking at the market, look in the mirror and imagine several thousand similar faces looking back, all trying to capture the same currency trading gains that you're shooting for. It helps to imagine this so you know you're not alone and also so you know who you're up against.

The rise of online currency trading has thrust individual retail traders into the mainstream of the forex market. Daily retail FX trading volumes have increased from around $10 billion in 2001 to $125 billion in 2009, according to a study by Aite Group, a financial market consultancy, and are estimated to be around 10 percent of daily spot volume. By the way, that's a compound annual growth rate of 37 percent.

Governments and Central Banks

National governments are routinely active in the forex market, but typically not to realign or shift the values of the major currencies. (I discuss those currency policies in greater depth in Chapter 5.)

Instead, national governments are active in the forex market for routine funding of government operations, making transfer payments, and managing foreign currency reserves. The first two functions generally have little impact on the day-to-day forex market, so I won't bore you with the details. But the last one has taken on increased prominence in recent years, and all indications are that it will continue to play a major role in the years ahead.

Currency reserve management

Currency reserve management refers to how national governments develop and invest their foreign currency reserves. Foreign currency reserves are accumulated through international trade. Countries with large trade surpluses will accumulate reserves of foreign currency over time. Trade surpluses arise when a nation exports more than it imports. Because it is receiving more foreign currency for its exports than it is spending to buy imports, foreign currency balances accumulate.

The USD has historically been the primary currency for international reserve holdings of most countries. International Monetary Fund (IMF) data from early 2010 showed that the USD accounted for about 62 percent of global currency reserve holdings, with EUR (27 percent), GBP and JPY (both 3 to 4 percent) as the next most widely held currencies.

In recent years, however, the United States has run up massive trade and current account deficits with the rest of the world. The flip side has been the accumulation of large trade surpluses in other countries, most clearly in Asia. The U.S. deficits essentially amount to the United States borrowing money from the countries with trade surpluses, while those other countries buy IOUs in the form of U.S. Treasury debt securities.

The problem is one of perception and also of prudent portfolio management.

✔ **The perception problem stems from the continuing growth of U.S. deficits, which equates to your continually borrowing money from a bank.** At a certain point, no matter how good your credit is, the bank will stop lending you money because you've already borrowed so much in the first place. In the case of the United States, no one is sure exactly where that point is, but let's just say we don't want to find out.

✔ **The portfolio-management problem arises from the need to diversify assets in the name of prudence.** This point has taken on added importance since the U.S. dollar began to weaken more significantly against other major currencies starting in 2002. Not only had emerging market governments allowed their foreign currency reserves to reach massive levels and kept the proportion of USDs in them very high, but now the U.S. dollar was starting to weaken as well.

The result has been an effort by many national governments to begin to diversify their reserves away from the USD and into other major currencies. The euro, the Japanese yen, and, to a lesser extent, the British pound have been the principal beneficiaries of this shift. But before you think the sky is falling, the USD remains the primary reserve currency globally and most reserve diversification efforts are focused on new reserves being generated.

The sovereign debt crisis plaguing Eurozone countries in the aftermath of the Great Financial Crisis of 2008–09 (GFC) has also cast the EUR in a less-than-flattering light. As of spring 2011, European officials appear to have forestalled the worst of the crisis, but Eurozone debt concerns will likely color the EUR's outlook for years to come.

Currency reserve management has taken on a market prominence in recent years that never existed before. Market talk of reserve managers buying or selling has become almost a daily occurrence. The impact of this in the market varies, but it can frequently lead to multiday highs and lows being maintained in the face of an otherwise compelling trend. At other times, such as in the case of the Eurozone debt crisis, reserve managers may go with the market flow and add strength to the unfolding trend.

Traders need to closely follow real-time market commentaries for signs of reserve management activity. You should also be aware of developments involving long-term outlooks for major currencies, like an expansion in U.S. trade deficits or the risk of a default in the Eurozone, as key drivers of currency reserve managers' decisions.

The Bank for International Settlements

The Bank for International Settlements (BIS) is the central bank for central banks. Located in Basel, Switzerland, the BIS also acts as the quasigovernment regulator of the international banking system. It was the BIS, in consultation with major national governments, that established the capital adequacy requirements for banks (known as Basel I, II, and, coming soon in the wake of the Great Financial Crisis, Basel III), which are intended to underpin the international banking system.

As the bank to national governments and central banks, the BIS frequently acts as the market intermediary of those nations seeking to diversify their currency reserves. By going through the BIS, those countries can remain relatively anonymous and prevent speculation from driving the market against them.

Market talk of the BIS being active in the market is frequently interpreted as significant reserve management interest to buy or sell. Keep an eye out for market rumors of the BIS, but also keep in mind that the BIS performs more routine and smaller trade execution on behalf of its clients.

The G-7 and the G-20

The Group of Seven, or G7, is composed of the seven largest developed economies in the world: Canada, France, Germany, Italy, Japan, the United Kingdom, and the United States. Together they account for a little over half of global GDP, down from nearly two-thirds in 2000. The fall in their relative share of global GDP is the result of economic weakness following the GFC and the coincident outperformance of major emerging economies in the subsequent recovery.

The G7 used to be the primary venue for the major global powers to express their collective will on currency values and the need for any adjustments, and past G7 statements frequently triggered major realignments. In 2008, the G7 ostensibly ceded control over currency matters to a larger grouping of economies, the G-20, in recognition of globalization and the rise of economies like Brazil, Russia, India, and China.

However, following the devastating earthquake/tsunami in Japan in March 2011, and an unwelcome surge higher in the JPY, which would further destabilize the Japanese economy, the G7 convened an emergency meeting. In support of the Japanese government, the G7 opted for concerted intervention to prevent a further rise in the JPY (see Chapter 5 for more on intervention).

The reemergence of the G7 in the forex markets was in response to an historic crisis in Japan. But it also underscored the G7's ability to act quickly, whereas the more cumbersome G20 might not have been able to reach agreement. The G7 still remains a potent force, and traders would be well advised to pay attention to the quarterly gatherings of G7 finance ministers and central bank chiefs and indications that currencies may be on the agenda.

The G-20 consists of the G-7 plus Australia, Turkey, Russia, Saudi Arabia, Indonesia, India, South Korea, China, Brazil, Argentina, Mexico, and South Africa, as well as representation from the European Union. Together those economies represent about 85 percent of global GDP and two-thirds of global population.

The G-20 is new as a global forum and its two-year track record suggests it will be less of a pivotal force for currency markets than the G7 was. The reason is that they operate on consensus, and it's much more difficult to get 20 members to agree on the need for currency adjustments. The problem is highlighted when G-20 member China is seen to be actively intervening to prevent its currency from strengthening. Still, G-20 meetings and statements bear watching because the group would be a much more formidable force in markets should they ever seek major currency adjustments.

Chapter 4

The Mechanics of Currency Trading

*T*he forex market has its own set of trading conventions, like how prices are quoted and orders executed, just like any other financial market. Then there's the forex lingo and some FX-specific transactions. If you're new to currency trading, the mechanics and terminology may take some getting used to. But at the end of the day, you'll see that most currency trade conventions are pretty straightforward.

In this chapter, I take you through the basic mechanics of forex trading, starting with how currency prices are quoted, what it means to buy and sell, and how leverage works in margin trading. I also show how to execute trades and how your trading results translate into dollars and cents. Last but not least, I run through the various types of orders forex traders use to implement a trading strategy and how orders work in the real world.

Buying and Selling Simultaneously

The biggest mental hurdle facing newcomers to currencies, especially traders familiar with other markets, is getting their head around the idea that each currency trade consists of a simultaneous purchase and sale. In the stock market, for instance, if you buy 100 shares of Google, it's pretty clear that you now own 100 shares and hope to see the price go up. When you want to exit that position, you simply sell what you bought earlier. Easy, right?

But in currencies, the purchase of one currency involves the simultaneous sale of another currency. This is the *exchange* in *foreign exchange*. To put it another way, if you're looking for the dollar to go higher, the question is "Higher against what?" The answer has to be another currency. In relative terms, if the dollar goes up against another currency, it also means that the other currency has gone down against the dollar. To think of it in stock-market terms, when you buy a stock, you're selling cash, and when you sell a stock, you're buying cash.

Currencies come in pairs

To make matters easier, forex markets refer to trading currencies by pairs, with names that combine the two different currencies being traded against each other, or exchanged for one another. Additionally, forex markets have given most currency pairs nicknames or abbreviations, which reference the pair and not necessarily the individual currencies involved.

The U.S. dollar is the central currency against which other currencies are traded. In its most recent triennial survey of the global foreign exchange market in 2010, the Bank for International Settlements (BIS) found that the U.S. dollar was on one side of about 85 percent of all reported forex market transactions.

The U.S. dollar's central role in the forex markets stems from a few basic factors:

- ✔ The U.S. economy is the largest national economy in the world.

- ✔ The U.S. dollar is the primary international reserve currency.

- ✔ The U.S. dollar is the medium of exchange for many cross-border trans-actions. For example, oil is priced in U.S. dollars. So even if you're a Japanese oil importer buying crude from Saudi Arabia, you're going to pay in U.S. dollars.

- ✔ The United States has the largest and most liquid government debt markets in the world.

- ✔ The United States is a global military superpower, with a stable political system.

The U.S. dollar remains the primary reserve currency, but recent years have increasingly seen calls for an alternative to a single global reserve currency. The euro is frequently cited as a potential replacement for the greenback, and some are calling for a basket of currencies to serve as the global reserve standard. The U.S. dollar's role as the primary reserve currency is likely to diminish in coming years, but it will be a very long-term process, likely spanning decades. As long as the United States has the largest government bond market, which is what international reserve managers ultimately seek to invest in, the U.S. dollar should remain the primary reserve currency.

Major currency pairs

The major currency pairs all involve the U.S. dollar on one side of the deal. The designations of the major currencies are expressed using International Standardization Organization (ISO) codes for each currency. Table 4-1 lists the most frequently traded currency pairs, what they're called in conventional terms, and what nicknames the market has given them.

Table 4-1	The Major U.S. Dollar Currency Pairs		
ISO Currency Pair	*Countries*	*Long Name*	*Nickname*
EUR/USD	Eurozone*/United States	Euro-dollar	N/A
USD/JPY	United States/Japan	Dollar-yen	N/A
GBP/USD	United Kingdom/ United States	Sterling-dollar	Sterling or Cable
USD/CHF	United States/ Switzerland	Dollar-Swiss	Swissy
USD/CAD	United States/ Canada	Dollar-Canada	Loonie
AUD/USD	Australia/United States	Australian-dollar	Aussie or Oz
NZD/USD	New Zealand/United States	New Zealand-dollar	Kiwi

* The Eurozone is made up of all the countries in the European Union that have adopted the euro as their currency. As of this printing, the Eurozone countries are Austria, Belgium, Cyprus, Finland, France, Germany, Greece, Ireland, Italy, Luxembourg, Malta, the Netherlands, Portugal, Slovakia, Slovenia, and Spain.

Major cross-currency pairs

Although the vast majority of currency trading takes place in the dollar pairs, cross-currency pairs serve as an alternative to always trading the U.S. dollar. A cross-currency pair, or *cross* or *crosses* for short, is any currency pair that does not include the U.S. dollar. Cross rates are derived from the respective USD pairs but are quoted independently and usually with a narrower spread than you could get by trading in the dollar pairs directly. (The *spread* refers to the difference between the bid and offer, or the price at which you can sell and buy and spreads are applied in most financial markets.)

Crosses enable traders to more directly target trades to specific individual currencies to take advantage of news or events. For example, your analysis may suggest that the Japanese yen has the worst prospects of all the major currencies going forward, based on interest rates or the economic outlook. To take advantage of this, you'd be looking to sell JPY, but against which other currency? You consider the USD, potentially buying USD/JPY (buying USD/selling JPY), but then you conclude that the USD's prospects are not much better than the JPY's. Further research on your part may point to another currency that has a much better outlook (such as high or rising interest rates or signs of a strengthening economy), say the Australian dollar (AUD). In this example, you would then be looking to buy the AUD/JPY cross (buying AUD/selling JPY) to target your view that AUD has the best prospects among major currencies and the JPY the worst.

Cross trades can be especially effective when major cross-border mergers and acquisitions (M&A) are announced. If a U.K. conglomerate is buying a Canadian utility company, the UK company is going to need to sell GBP and buy CAD to fund the purchase. The key to trading on M&A activity is to note the cash portion of the deal. If the deal is all stock, then you don't need to exchange currencies to come up with the foreign cash.

The most actively traded crosses focus on the three major non-USD currencies (namely EUR, JPY, and GBP) and are referred to as euro crosses, yen crosses, and sterling crosses. The remaining currencies (CHF, AUD, CAD, and NZD) are also traded in cross pairs. Tables 4-2, 4-3, and 4-4 highlight the key cross pairs in the euro, yen, and sterling groupings, respectively, along with their market names. (Nicknames never quite caught on for the crosses.) Table 4-5 lists other cross-currency pairs.

Table 4-2	Euro Crosses	
ISO Currency Pair	*Countries*	*Market Name*
EUR/CHF	Eurozone/Switzerland	Euro-Swiss
EUR/GBP	Eurozone/United Kingdom	Euro-sterling
EUR/CAD	Eurozone/Canada	Euro-Canada
EUR/AUD	Eurozone/Australia	Euro-Aussie
EUR/NZD	Eurozone/New Zealand	Euro-Kiwi

Table 4-3	Yen Crosses	
ISO Currency Pair	*Countries*	*Market Name*
EUR/JPY	Eurozone/Japan	Euro-yen
GBP/JPY	United Kingdom/Japan	Sterling-yen
CHF/JPY	Switzerland/Japan	Swiss-yen
AUD/JPY	Australia/Japan	Aussie-yen
NZD/JPY	New Zealand/Japan	Kiwi-yen
CAD/JPY	Canada/Japan	Canada-yen

Table 4-4	Sterling Crosses	
ISO Currency Pair	*Countries*	*Market Name*
GBP/CHF	United Kingdom/Switzerland	Sterling-Swiss
GBP/CAD	United Kingdom/Canada	Sterling-Canadian
GBP/AUD	United Kingdom/Australia	Sterling-Aussie
GBP/NZD	United Kingdom/New Zealand	Sterling-Kiwi

Table 4-5	Other Crosses	
ISO Currency Pair	*Countries*	*Market Name*
AUD/CHF	Australia/Switzerland	Aussie-Swiss
AUD/CAD	Australia/Canada	Aussie-Canada
AUD/NZD	Australia/New Zealand	Aussie-Kiwi
CAD/CHF	Canada/Switzerland	Canada-Swiss

Base currencies and counter currencies

When you look at currency pairs, you may notice that the currencies are combined in a seemingly strange order. For instance, if sterling-yen (GBP/JPY) is a yen cross, then why isn't it referred to as "yen-sterling" and written "JPY/GBP"? The answer is that these quoting conventions evolved over the years to reflect traditionally strong currencies versus traditionally weak currencies, with the strong currency coming first.

It also reflects the market quoting convention where the first currency in the pair is known as the *base currency*. The base currency is what you're buying or selling when you buy or sell the pair. It's also the *notional*, or *face*, amount of the trade. So if you buy 100,000 EUR/

JPY, you've just bought 100,000 euros and sold the equivalent amount in Japanese yen. If you sell 100,000 GBP/CHF, you just sold 100,000 British pounds and bought the equivalent amount of Swiss francs.

The second currency in the pair is called the *counter currency*, or the *secondary currency*. Hey, who said this stuff was complicated? Most important for you as an FX trader, the counter currency is the denomination of the price fluctuations and, ultimately, what your profit and losses will be denominated in. If you buy GBP/JPY, it goes up, and you take a profit, your gains are not in pounds, but in yen. (I run through the math of calculating profit and loss later in this chapter.)

The long and the short of it

Forex markets use the same terms to express market positioning as most other financial markets do. But because currency trading involves simultaneous buying and selling, being clear on the terms helps — especially if you're totally new to financial market trading.

Going long

No, I'm not talking about running out deep for a football pass. A *long position,* or simply a *long,* refers to a market position in which you've bought a security. In FX, it refers to having bought a currency pair, meaning you've bought the base currency and sold the counter currency. When you're long, you're looking for prices to move higher, so you can sell at a higher price than where you bought. When you want to close a long position, you have to sell what you bought. If you're buying at multiple price levels, you're *adding to longs* and *getting longer.*

Getting short

A *short position,* or simply a *short,* refers to a market position in which you've sold a security that you never owned. In the stock market, selling a stock short requires borrowing the stock (and paying a fee to the lending brokerage) so you can sell it. In forex markets, it means you've sold a currency *pair,* meaning you've sold the base currency and bought the counter currency. So you're still making an exchange, just in the opposite order and according to currency-pair quoting terms. When you've sold a currency pair, it's called *going short* or *getting short,* and it means you're looking for the pair's price to move lower so you can buy it back at a profit. If you sell at various price levels, you're *adding to shorts* and *getting shorter.*

In most other markets, *short selling* either comes with restrictions or is considered too risky for most individual traders. In currency trading, going short is as common as going long. "Selling high and buying low" is a standard currency trading strategy.

Currency pair rates reflect relative values between two currencies and not an absolute price of a single stock or commodity. Because currencies can fall or rise relative to each other, both in medium- and long-term trends and minute-to-minute fluctuations, currency pair prices are as likely to be going down at any moment as they are up. To take advantage of such moves, forex traders routinely use short positions to exploit falling currency prices. Traders from other markets may at first feel uncomfortable with short selling, but it's just something you have to get your head around.

Squaring up

If you have no position in the market, it's called being *square* or *flat*. If you have an open position and you want to close it, it's called *squaring up*. If you're short, you need to buy to square up. If you're long, you need to sell to go flat. The only time you have no market exposure or financial risk is when you're square.

Profit and Loss

Profit and loss (P&L) is how traders measure success and failure. You don't want to be looking at the forex market as some academic or thrill-seeking exercise. Real money is made and lost every minute of every day. If you're going to trade currencies actively, you need to get up close and personal with P&L.

A clear understanding of how P&L works is especially critical to online margin trading, where your P&L directly affects the amount of margin you have to work with. (I introduce online margin trading in Chapter 2.) Changes in your margin balance will determine how much you can trade and how long you can trade if prices move against you.

Leverage amplifies risk and reward

Online margin trading is usually based on *leverage*, where the brokerage effectively lets you borrow more money than you have deposited as collateral. Leverage refers to the ratio of that loan to your collateral. A leverage ratio of 50:1, for example, means that your collateral can be leveraged 50 times. More concretely, if you open an account with $1,000, you could trade a position size as large as $50,000. At 100:1, that same $1,000 margin deposit could control a position size of $100,000. But those calculations miss the point.

The real point of leverage is what it does to your trading results: It amplifies any gains or losses equally. If your trade is profitable, great. You just made more than you otherwise could have. But if your trade misses, the result is a larger loss than you may be willing or able to tolerate. Above all, don't be deluded into trying to maximize position size. Stay focused on your P&L targets when devising a trade strategy and what those results mean for your margin balance. (Margin/leverage considerations for trade strategies are discussed in greater depth in Chapter 13.)

Many newcomers to the currency market seek out the highest leverage ratios available, sometimes opening accounts offshore in questionable jurisdictions. Use leverage sparingly; that 50:1 is more than ample to trade actively, yet prudently.

Margin balances and liquidations

When you open an online currency trading account, you'll need to pony up cash as collateral to support the margin requirements established by your broker. That initial margin deposit becomes your opening *margin balance* and is the basis on which all your subsequent trades are collateralized. Unlike futures markets or margin-based equity trading, online forex brokerages do not issue *margin calls* (requests for more collateral to support open positions). Instead, they establish ratios of margin balances to open positions that must be maintained at all times.

If your account's margin balance falls below the required ratio, even for just a few seconds, your broker probably has the right to close out your positions without any notice to you. In most cases, that only happens when an account has losing positions. If your broker liquidates your positions, that usually means your losses are locked in and your margin balance just got smaller.

Be sure you completely understand your broker's margin requirements and liquidation policies. Requirements may differ depending on account size and whether you're trading standard lot sizes (100,000 currency units) or minilot sizes (10,000 currency units). Some brokers' liquidation policies allow for all positions to be liquidated if you fall below margin requirements. Others close out the biggest losing positions or portions of losing positions until the required ratio is satisfied again. You can find the details in the fine print of the account opening contract that you sign. Always read the fine print to be sure you understand your broker's margin and trading policies.

Unrealized and realized profit and loss

Most online forex brokers provide real-time mark-to-market calculations showing your margin balance. *Mark-to-market* is the calculation that shows your unrealized P&L based on where you could close your open positions in the market at that instant. Depending on your broker's trading platform, if you're long, the calculation will typically be based on where you could sell at that moment. If you're short, the price used will be where you can buy at that moment. Your margin balance is the sum of your initial margin deposit, your unrealized P&L, and your realized P&L.

Realized P&L is what you get when you close out a trade position, or a portion of a trade position. If you close out the full position and go flat, whatever you made or lost leaves the unrealized P&L calculation and goes into your margin balance. If you only close a portion of your open positions, only that part of the trade's P&L is realized and goes into the margin balance. Your unrealized P&L will continue to fluctuate based on the remaining open positions and so will your total margin balance.

If you've got a winning position open, your unrealized P&L will be positive and your margin balance will increase. If the market is moving against your positions, your unrealized P&L will be negative and your margin balance will be reduced. FX prices are constantly changing, so your mark-to-market unrealized P&L and total margin balance will also be constantly changing.

Calculating profit and loss with pips

Profit-and-loss calculations are pretty straightforward in terms of math — it's all based on position size and the number of pips you make or lose. A *pip* is the smallest increment of price fluctuation in currency prices. Pips can also be referred to as *points;* I use the two terms interchangeably.

It's unclear where the term *pip* came from. Some say it's an abbreviation for *percentage in point,* but it could also be the FX answer to bond traders' *bips,* which refers to *bps,* or *basis points* (meaning 1/100 of 1 percent).

Just a couple paragraphs earlier, I mentioned that the pip is the smallest increment of currency price fluctuations. Not so fast. Even the venerable pip has been broken down into *decimals* or *fractionals.* Decimals or fractionals refer to one-tenth of a pip. The good news for traders is that typically means narrower trading spreads. Instead of trading on a whole pip spread of 3 pips, you might see a spread of 2.6 or 2.2 pips, which can lead to lower transaction costs over time.

For now, though, to get a handle on P&L calculations, you're better off sticking with whole pips. Take a look at a few currency pairs to get an idea of what a pip is. (I leave out the decimalized pip version for simplicity sake for the rest of this chapter.) Most currency pairs are quoted using five digits. The placement of the decimal point depends on whether it's a JPY currency pair — if it is, there are two digits behind the decimal point. For all other currency pairs, there are four digits behind the decimal point. In all cases, that last itty-bitty digit is the pip.

Here are some major currency pairs and crosses, with the pip underlined:

- ✓ **EUR/USD:** 1.305<u>3</u>
- ✓ **USD/CHF:** 1.056<u>7</u>
- ✓ **USD/JPY:** 84.2<u>3</u>
- ✓ **GBP/USD:** 1.508<u>5</u>
- ✓ **EUR/JPY:** 110.6<u>5</u>

Focus on the EUR/USD price first. Looking at EUR/USD, if the price moves from 1.3053 to 1.3073, it's just gone up by 20 pips. If it goes from 1.3053 down to 1.3003, it's just gone down by 50 pips. Pips provide an easy way to calculate the P&L. To turn that pip movement into a P&L calculation, all you need to know is the size of the position. For a 100,000 EUR/USD position, the 20-pip move equates to $200 (EUR 100,000 × 0.0020 = $200). For a 50,000 EUR/USD position, the 50-point move translates into $250 (EUR 50,000 × 0.0050 = $250).

Whether the amounts are positive or negative depends on whether you were long or short for each move. If you were short for the move higher, that's a - (minus sign) in front of the $200; if you were long, it's a + (plus sign). EUR/USD is easy to calculate, especially for USD-based traders, because the P&L accrues in dollars.

If you take USD/CHF, you've got another calculation to make before you can make sense of it. That's because the P&L is going to be denominated in Swiss francs (CHF), because CHF is the counter currency. If USD/CHF drops from 1.0567 to 1.0527 and you're short USD 100,000 for the move lower, you've just caught a 40-pip decline. That's a profit worth CHF 400 (USD 100,000 × 0.0040 = CHF 400). Yeah, but how much is that in real money? To convert it into USD, you need to divide the CHF 400 by the USD/CHF rate. Use the closing rate of the trade (1.0527), because that's where the market was last, and you get USD 379.98.

Factoring profit and loss into margin calculations

The good news is that online FX trading platforms calculate the P&L for you automatically, both unrealized while the trade is open and realized when the trade is closed. So why did I just drag you through the math of calculating P&L using pips? Because online brokerage platforms will start calculating your P&L for you only *after* you enter a trade.

To structure your trade and manage your risk effectively (How big a position? How much margin to risk?), you're going to need to calculate your P&L outcomes *before* you enter the trade. Understanding the P&L implications of a trade strategy you're considering is critical to maintaining your margin balance and staying in control of your trading. This simple exercise can help prevent you from costly mistakes, like putting on a trade that's too large, or putting *stop-loss orders* beyond prices where your account falls below the margin requirement. At the minimum, you need to calculate the price point at which your position will be liquidated when your margin balance falls below the required ratio. (I cover this subject more extensively in Chapter 13.) Fortunately, many online brokers provide a *pip calculator* application that makes it even easier.

Understanding Rollovers and Interest Rates

One market convention unique to currencies is *rollovers*. A rollover is a transaction where an open position from one *value date* (settlement date) is rolled over into the next value date. Rollovers represent the intersection of interest-rate markets and forex markets. In short, you will either earn or pay interest on open positions held overnight.

Currency is money, after all

Rollover rates are based on the difference in interest rates of the two currencies in the pair you're trading. That's because what you're actually trading is good old-fashioned cash. That's right: Currency is cold, hard cash with a fancy name. When you're long a currency (cash), it's like having a deposit in the bank. If you're short a currency (cash), it's like having borrowed a loan. Just as you would expect to earn interest on a bank deposit or pay interest on a loan, you should expect an interest gain/expense for holding a currency position over the change in value.

The catch in currency trading is that if you carry over an open position from one value date to the next, you have two bank accounts involved. Think of it as one account with a positive balance (the currency you're long) and one with a negative balance (the currency you're short). But because your accounts are in two different currencies, the two interest rates of the different countries will apply.

The difference between the interest rates in the two countries is called the *interest-rate differential*. The larger the interest-rate differential, the larger the impact from rollovers. The narrower the interest-rate differential, the smaller the effect from rollovers. You can find relevant interest-rate levels of the major currencies from any number of financial-market websites, but www.reuters. com and www.bloomberg.com have especially good resources. Look for the base or benchmark lending rates in each country.

So how do interest rates get turned into currency rates? After all, interest rates are in percent and currency rates are, well, *not* in percent. The answer is that deposit rates yield actual cash returns, which are netted, producing a net cash return. That net cash return is then divided by the position size, which gives you the currency pips, which is the rollover rate.

The following calculation illustrates how this works. I've simplified matters by using just one interest rate for each currency. In the real world, each currency would have a slightly different interest rate depending on whether you're borrowing or lending (depositing).

> *Position:* Long AUD/USD 100,000 at 1.0200 (long AUD/short USD 102,000)
>
> AUD interest rate: 4.75 percent per annum → 1 day = $0.0475 \times (1 \div 365)$ = 0.01301 percent
>
> AUD deposit earns: $100,000 \times 0.0001301$ = AUD +13.01
>
> USD interest rate: 0.25 percent per annum → 1 day = $0.0025 \times (1 \div 365)$ = 0.0006849 percent
>
> USD loan costs: $102,000 \times 0.000006849$ = USD - 0.70
>
> Because AUD/USD pips are denominated in USD, convert the AUD to USD: AUD 13.01×1.0200 = USD 13.27.
>
> Net the USD amounts 13.27- 0.70 = USD +12.57 ÷ 100,000 = 0.0001257
>
> On a long AUD 100,000 position, the rollover earns 0.0001257 or +1.257 pips.

Value dates and trade settlement

When I talk about currency trading, I'm implicitly referring to trading the spot forex market. A *spot market* is one that's trading for immediate delivery of whatever security is being traded. But in the real world, *immediate* means a few business days, to allow banks and financial firms time to settle a trade (make payment, deliver/receive a security).

In forex markets, *spot* refers to trade settlement in *two* business days, which is called the *value date.* That time is needed to allow for trade processing across global time zones and for currency payments to be wired around the world.

The forex market operates on a 24-hour trade date basis beginning at 5 p.m. eastern time (ET) and ending the next day at 5 p.m. ET. So if it's a Monday, spot currencies are trading for value on Wednesday (assuming no holidays).

At 5 p.m. ET on Monday, the trade date becomes Tuesday and the value date is shifted to Thursday. If you have an open position on Monday at 5 p.m. ET closing, your position will be rolled over to the next value date, in this case from Wednesday to Thursday, or a *one-day rollover.*

If you close your position the next day (Tuesday) and finish the trade date square, there are no rollovers because you have no position. The same is true if you never carry a position through the daily 5 p.m. ET close.

On Wednesday trade dates, spot currencies are normally trading for a Friday value date. At 5 p.m. ET on Wednesday, the value date changes from Friday to Monday, a *weekend rollover.* In rollover calculations, that's a *three-day rollover* (Saturday, Sunday, and Monday), which means the rollover costs/gains are going to be three times as much as any other day.

The one exception to the two-day spot convention in FX are trades in USD/CAD. And that's because the main financial centers in the United States and Canada share the same time zone, so communications and wire transfers can be made more quickly. USD/CAD trades settle in one business day. The weekend rollover for USD/CAD takes place on Thursday after the 5 p.m. ET close, when the value date shifts from Friday to Monday. This only applies to USD/CAD and not to other pairs involving CAD, such as CAD/JPY or EUR/CAD.

Market holidays and value dates

Value dates are based on individual currency pairs to account for banking holidays in respective countries. Rollover periods can be longer if there is a banking holiday in one of the countries whose currency is part of the trade. For example, if it's Wednesday and you're trading GBP/USD, the normal spot value date would be Friday. But if there's a banking holiday in the United Kingdom on Friday, U.K. banks are not open to settle the trade. So the value date is shifted to the next valid banking day common to the United Kingdom and the United States, typically the following Monday. In this case, the weekend rollover would take place at the close on Tuesday at 5 p.m. ET, when the value date would change from Thursday to Monday, because of Friday's holiday. That's a *four-day rollover* (Friday, Saturday, Sunday, and Monday).

So what happens at the change in value date at Wednesday's 5 p.m. ET close? No rollovers in GBP/USD, that's what. Because the value date for trades made on Wednesday is already Monday, no rollover is needed because trades made on Thursday are also for value on Monday. That's called a *double value date,* meaning two trade dates (Wednesday and Thursday) are settling for the same value date (Monday).

A few times each year (mostly around Christmas, New Year's, and Golden Week spring holidays in Japan) when multiple banking holidays in various countries coincide over several days, rollover periods can be as long as seven or eight days. So you may earn or pay rollovers of seven or eight times normal on one day, but then not face any rollovers for the rest of the holiday period.

Applying rollovers

Rollover transactions are usually carried out automatically by your forex broker if you hold an open position past the change in value date.

Rollovers are applied to your open position by two offsetting trades that result in the same open position. Some online forex brokers apply the rollover rates by adjusting the average rate of your open position. Other forex brokers apply rollover rates by applying the rollover credit or debit directly to your margin balance. In terms of the math, its six of one, half a dozen of the other.

Here's an example of how the rollover of an open position would work under each model:

Position: Long 100,000 AUD/JPY at a rate of 90.15 for a value date of January 10

At 5 p.m. ET, the rollover takes place and the following rollover trades hit your account. (**Remember:** This is done automatically by most online brokers.)

You sell 100,000 AUD/JPY at 90.22 for a value date of January 10. (This trade closes the open position for the same value date.)

You buy 100,000 AUD/JPY at 90.206 for a value date of January 11. (This trade reopens the same position for the new value date.)

The difference in the rates represents the rollover points. (90.22 - 90.206 = 0.014, which is expressed as 1.4 points.)

If the rollover is applied to your average rate on the open position, your new average rate on the position is 90.136. (Here's the math: 90.15 - 0.014 = 90.136.) Because you're now long from a lower average price, you earned money on the rollover.

If the rollover is applied directly to you margin balance, the rollover points are multiplied by the position size (100,000 × 0.014 = JPY 1,400 earned) and converted into USD (JPY 1,400 ÷ 116.00 [the USD/JPY rate] = $12.07) and added to your margin balance.

Here's what you need to remember about rollovers:

- ✔ Rollovers are interest earned or paid based on the direction of your position.

- ✔ Rollovers are applied to open positions after the 5 p.m. ET change in value date, or trade settlement date.

- ✔ Rollovers are not applied if you don't carry a position over the change in value date. So if you're square at the close of each trading day, you'll never have to worry about rollovers.

- ✔ Rollovers reflect the interest rate return or cost of holding an open position.

- ✔ Rollovers represent the difference in interest rates between the two currencies in your open position, but they're applied in currency-rate terms.

- ✔ Rollovers can earn you money if you're long the currency with the higher interest rate and short the currency with the lower interest rate.

- ✔ Rollovers will cost you money if you're short the currency with the higher interest rate and long the currency with the lower interest rates.

- ✔ Rollovers can have spreads applied to them by some forex brokers, which can reduce any interest earned by your position.

- ✔ Rollover costs/credits are based on position size — the larger the position, the larger the cost or gain to you.

- ✔ Rollovers should be considered a cost of doing business and rarely influence overall trading decisions.

Most forex brokers publish daily rollover rates on their websites or directly on the trading platform. If you can't find them, ask. If you're going to be trading a relatively large account with an online forex broker (say, over $25,000 in margin deposited), you'll probably be able to negotiate a tighter rollover spread with your broker. This will enable you to capture more of the gains if you're positioned the right way, or to reduce your cost of carry if you're not.

Understanding Currency Prices

Now you're getting down to the brass tacks of actually making trades in the forex market. Before you get ahead of yourself, though, it's critical to understand exactly how currency prices work and what they mean to you as a trader. Earlier in this chapter, I show you that *buying* means "buying the *currency pair*" and *selling* means "selling the *currency pair.*"

Here, you look at how online brokerages display currency prices and what they mean for trade and order execution. Keep in mind that different online forex brokers use different formats to display prices on their trading platforms. A thorough picture of what the prices mean will allow you to navigate different brokers' platforms and know what you're looking at.

Bids and offers

When you're in front of your screen and looking at an online forex broker's trading platform, you'll see two prices for each currency pair. The price on the left-hand side is called the *bid* and the price on the right-hand side is called the *offer* (some call this the *ask*). Some brokers display the prices above and below each other, with the bid on the bottom and the offer on top. The easy way to tell the difference is that the bid price will always be lower than the offer price.

The price quotation of each bid and offer you see will have two components: the big figure and the dealing price. The *big figure* refers to the first three digits of the overall currency rate and is usually shown in a smaller font size or even in shadow. The *dealing price* refers to the last three digits of the over-all currency price and is brightly displayed in a larger font size. The two big numbers are the last whole pips, and the smaller number is the tenth of a pip.

For example, in Figure 4-1 the full EUR/USD price quotation is 1.40225/1.40246. The 1.40 is called the big figure and is there to show you the full price level at which the market is currently trading. The 225/246 portion of the price is the bid/offer dealing price in pips.

Figure 4-1:
A dealing box from the FOREX. com trading platform for EUR/USD.

Spreads

The *spread* is the difference between the bid price and the offer price. In one sense, you can look at the spread as the commission that the online brokers charge for executing your trades. So even if they *say* they're commission free, they may be earning the difference when one trader sells at the bid price and another trader buys at the offer price. Spreads are standard in all financial market trading.

Spreads will vary from broker to broker and by currency pairs at each broker as well. Generally, the more liquid the currency pair, the narrower the spread; the less liquid the currency pair, the wider the spread. This is especially the case for some of the less-traded crosses.

Executing a Trade

It's trigger-pulling time, pardner. In this section, I assume you've signed up for a practice account at an online forex broker and you're ready to start executing some practice trades. Getting a feel for executing deals now, before you're ready to commit any real money to a trade, will be very helpful. (See Chapters 2 and 10 for more on using a practice account.)

There are two main ways of executing trades in the FX market: live trades and orders. If you're an adrenaline junkie, don't focus only on the "Live dealing" section — the "Orders" section gives you plenty of juice to keep you going, too.

Trading online

Live dealing is how you access the market to buy or sell at current market rates. Knowing exactly what you want to do is important, because when you click the buy or sell button, it's a *done* deal. If you make a mistake, you'll have to make another trade to correct your erroneous trade, and that is very likely going to cost you real money.

There are a few different avenues to get to the market depending on how your broker is set up. In the following sections, I cover all the bases.

Click and deal or "Instant Execution"

Most forex brokers provide live streaming prices that you can deal on with a simple click of your computer mouse. On those platforms, to execute a trade:

1. **Specify the amount of the trade you want to make.**

2. **Click on the Buy or Sell button to execute the trade you want.**

   The forex trading platform will respond back, usually within a second or two, to let you know whether the trade went through:

- If the trade went through, you'll see the trade and your new position appear in your platform's list of trades.

- If the trade failed because of a price change, you need to start again from the top.

- If the trade failed because the trade was too large based on your margin, you need to reduce the size of the trade.

When the trade goes through, you have a position in the market and you'll see your unrealized P&L begin updating according to market price fluctuations.

Online platforms usually have a number of shortcuts to enable more rapid trading. Some of these are for more advanced or active traders, so be sure you know what they are before you engage them. Following are the parameters that you can usually set up in advance.

- ✔ **Preset trade amounts:** These are so you don't have to specify the amount each time you make a deal.

- ✔ **Automatic stop-loss orders at a predetermined distance from the trade-entry price:** These automatic stop-loss functions can be turned on or off, and you define the number of pips away for the stop loss. These functions are good for providing fail-safe stop-loss protection until you can enter a more detailed order for your trade strategy. *Remember:* You never know when a headline will roil the market, and you don't want to get caught with your pants down.

Some online brokers advertise narrower trading spreads as a way to attract traders. If your click-and-deal trade attempts frequently fail, and the platform then asks if you'd like to make the trade at a worse price, you're probably being re-quoted. *Re-quoting* is when brokers offer you a worse price to make your trade, meaning you end up paying a larger spread than you bargained for.

Pay attention to the rate you receive when a trade is executed, or your *fill rate*. Getting the rate you requested is a more important indicator of a forex platform's execution ability than spreads.

Phone dealing

Placing live trades over the phone is available from most online forex brokers. You need to find out from your broker whether it offers this service and exactly what its procedures are before you can be ready to use it.

The ability to make trades over the phone is critical if you're frequently trading while away from your computer or in cases of technological disruptions. At the minimum, you need to have the dealing phone number memorized and a reliable phone connection in case something goes wrong with your computer or Internet connection. If your dog chews through your mouse cable or your kid spills a sippy cup of juice on your keyboard, you'll need a fallback plan to protect your market exposure. (I discuss more such risk considerations in Chapter 13.)

To place a trade over the phone, you'll need to:

1. **Call the telephone number at your broker for placing a trade.**

2. **When you're connected to a representative, identify yourself by name and give your trading account number.**

   Be ready to provide whatever account password is needed. (Knowing what's required *before* you call to place the trade is a good idea.)

   Know what your position is. If you're not sure, your broker will be able to give you this info, but be prepared for time delays.

3. **Ask what the current price is for the currency pair you're trading.** The broker's representative will quote you a two-way bid/offer price, such as "EUR/USD is trading at 1.3213/15.

4. **If you don't want the price, say, "No, thank you."**

5. **If you want the price, specify *exactly* what trade you would like to make.**

   Don't just say "Close my position" or "Square me up." Note the direction (buy or sell), the amount (don't use lots — use the real amounts), and the currency pair. For example, "I would like to sell 140,000 EUR/USD."

   The broker should then say, "Done" or "That's agreed."

6. **Confirm with your broker exactly what trade you just made.**

   For example, say, "To confirm, I just sold 140,000 EUR/USD at 1.3213."

   Be sure the broker confirms the trade. You can double-check that the trade was correct by asking the broker to input the trade and update your position.

7. **Get the name of the broker's representative you just made the trade with in case you have to call back.**

Orders

Currency traders use orders to catch market movements when they're not in front of their screens. *Remember:* The forex market is open from Sunday evening (ET) through Friday afternoon (ET). A market move is just as likely to happen while you're asleep or in the shower as it is while you're watching your screen. If you're not a full-time trader, then you've probably got a full-time job that requires your attention when you're at work — at least your boss *hopes* he has your attention. Orders are how you can act in the market without being there.

Experienced currency traders also routinely use orders to

- ✔ Implement a trade strategy from entry to exit
- ✔ Capture sharp, short-term price fluctuations
- ✔ Limit risk in volatile or uncertain markets
- ✔ Preserve trading capital from unwanted losses
- ✔ Maintain trading discipline
- ✔ Protect profits and minimize losses

I can't stress enough the importance of using orders in currency trading. Forex markets can be notoriously volatile and difficult to predict. Using orders will help you capitalize on short-term market movements, as well as limit the impact of any adverse price moves. A disciplined use of orders will also help you to quantify the risk you're taking and, with any luck, give you peace of mind in your trading. *Bottom line:* If you don't use orders, you probably don't have a well-thought-out trading strategy — and that's a recipe for pain.

Types of orders

In this section, I introduce you to all the types of orders available in the forex market. Bear in mind that not all order types are available at all online brokers. So add order types to your list of questions to ask your prospective forex broker. (For more in-depth information, I look at tactical considerations for placing orders in Chapter 13 and offer practical tips for entering orders in Chapter 14.)

Take-profit orders

Don't you just love that name? There's an old market saying that goes, "You can't go broke taking profit." You'll use *take-profit orders* to lock in gains when you have an open position in the market. If you're short USD/JPY at 90.20, your take-profit order will be to buy back the position and be placed somewhere below that price, say at 89.80 for instance. If you're long GBP/USD at 1.5505, your take-profit order will be to sell the position somewhere higher, maybe 1.5570.

Partial take-profit orders are take-profit orders that only close a portion of your open position. Let's say you bought 200,000 EUR/USD at 1.2950 expecting it to move higher — and it does. But to take some money off the table and lock in some gains, you decide to sell half the position (100,000 EUR/USD) at 1.3000 and to allow the market to see how high it wants to go with the rest. Or you can place two partial take-profit orders to close the whole position at two different levels.

Limit orders

Technically speaking, a take-profit order is a type of *limit order*. The key difference is that take-profit orders close or reduce open positions, and limit orders open new positions or add to existing positions in the same direction.

A limit order is any order that triggers a trade at more favorable levels than the *current* market price. Think "buy low, sell high." If the limit order is to buy, it must be entered at a price below the current market price. If the limit order is to sell, it must be placed at a price higher than the current market price.

Stop-loss orders

Boo! Sound's bad doesn't it? Actually, stop-loss orders are critical to trading survival. The traditional *stop-loss order,* or just *stop order* (I use the terms interchangeably going forward), does just that: It stops losses by closing out an open position that is losing money. You'll use stop orders to limit your losses if the market moves against your position. If you don't, you're leaving it up to the market, and that's always a dangerous proposition.

Stop orders are on the other side of the current price from take-profit orders, but in the same direction (in terms of buying or selling). If you're long, your stop order will be to sell, but at a lower price than the current market price. If you're short, your stop order will be to buy, but at a higher price than the current market.

When stops don't lose, and take profits don't profit

Sometimes the roles of take-profit orders and stop-loss orders reverse. This can happen if you *adjust* your order levels *after* you've entered a position and the market has already moved away from your entry price.

With both take-profit orders and stop orders, the important price is not your entry price, but the current market price. For example, you may be short USD/JPY at 84.00 and the market is trading higher at 84.30. You originally had your take-profit limit order below to buy back at 83.60, but now you're having second thoughts. You decide to raise your take-profit order to 84.15 to try to close the position on a dip. The order is still a take profit because it is below the current market price (84.30), even though it will result in a loss if it's filled.

The same can apply to stop losses. If you bought AUD/USD at 0.9640 and the price has since moved higher to 0.9670, you may decide to raise your stop-loss sell order from its original level (0.9610) to lock in some of the gains. So you raise your stop-loss order to 0.9655. If your stop-loss sell order is triggered, you'll actually be taking profit.

Trailing stop-loss orders

A trailing stop is a beautiful little tool, especially when you've got a winning trade going. You may have heard that one of the keys to successful trading is to cut losing positions quickly, and let winning positions run. A trailing stop-loss order allows you to do just that. The idea is that when you have a winning trade on, you wait for the market to stage a reversal and take you out, instead of trying to pick the right level to exit on your own.

A trailing stop-loss order is a stop-loss order that you set at a fixed number of pips from your entry rate. The trailing stop adjusts the order rate as the market price moves, *but only in the direction of your trade*. For example, if you're long EUR/CHF at 1.3750 and you set the trailing stop at 30 pips, the stop will initially become active at 1.3720 (1.5750 - 30 pips).

If the EUR/CHF price moves higher to 1.3760, the stop adjusts higher, pip for pip, with the price and will then be active at 1.3730. The trailing stop will continue to adjust higher as long as the market continues to move higher. When the market puts in a top, your trailing stop will be 30 pips (or whatever distance you specify) below that top, wherever it may be.

If the market ever goes down by 30 pips, as in this example, your stop will be triggered and your position closed. So in this case, if you're long at 1.3750 and you set a 30-pip trailing stop, it will initially become active at 1.3720. If the market never ticks up and goes straight down, you'll be stopped out at 1.5720. If the price first rises to 1.5775 and then declines, your trailing stop will have risen to 1.5745 (1.5775 - 30 pips), and that's where you'll be stopped out.

Pretty cool, huh? The only catch is that not every online trading platform offers trailing stops. If you find a platform you like and it doesn't offer trailing stops, you can mimic a trailing stop by frequently manually changing the rate on your regular stop-loss order. But this is an imperfect solution, unless you can monitor your position constantly.

One-cancels-the-other orders

A *one-cancels-the-other order* (more commonly referred to as an OCO order) is a stop-loss order paired with a take-profit order. It's the ultimate insurance policy for any open position. Your position will stay open until one of the order levels is reached by the market and closes your position. When one order level is reached and triggered, the other order automatically cancels.

Let's say you're short USD/JPY at 90.00. You think if it goes up beyond 91.00, it's going to keep going higher, so that's where you decide to place your stop-loss buying order. At the same time, you believe that USD/JPY has downside potential to 88.50, so that's where you set your take-profit buying order. You now have two orders bracketing the market and your risk is clearly defined.

As long as the market trades between 88.50 and 91.00, your position will remain open. If 88.50 is reached first, your take profit will trigger and you'll buy back at a profit. If 91.00 is hit first, then your position is stopped out at a loss.

OCO orders are highly recommended for every open position.

Contingent orders

A *contingent order* is a fancy term for combining several types of orders to create a complete currency trade strategy. You'll use contingent orders to put on a trade while you're asleep, or otherwise indisposed, knowing that you're contingent order has got all the bases covered and your risks are defined. Contingent orders are also referred to as *if/then orders*. If/then orders require the *If* order to be *done* first, and *then* the second part of the order becomes active, so they're sometimes called *If done/then* orders.

Let's look at a trade idea and see how a contingent order works. Say NZD/USD has been trading in a range between 0.6700 and 0.6800 and is currently sitting in the middle at 0.6750/53. You think it's going to go higher, but you don't want to jump in at the middle of the range and risk watching it go down before it goes up. So you use a contingent order to implement your strategy, even if you're not watching the market.

Because you're ultimately looking to buy on a dip toward 0.6700 to get long, you would place an if/then limit order to buy at 0.6710, the *if* part of the order. The contingent, or *then,* part of the order only becomes active if the *if* part is triggered and you enter a position.

The *then* part consists of either a stop order or a take-profit order, or preferably both in the form of an OCO order.

Continuing with this example, your contingent order may be to place a stop order below 0.6700, in case the range breaks and you're wrong. So you may place your stop-loss order at 0.6690 to sell what you bought in the *if* part. This type of contingent order is called an *if/then stop loss.* You may opt for only an *if/then stop-loss order* if you want to limit your downside risk, but let your upside gains run.

If you think the upside is limited to the range highs at 0.6800, you may want to add a contingent take-profit order at 0.6790 to sell what you bought at 0.6710, in addition to your stop-loss order. Now if your position is opened at 0.6710, you have an OCO order to stop sell at 0.6690 or take profit sell at 0.6790. Now you have a complete trade strategy with defined risk parameters.

If the market continues to trade in the range, it may drop from the level you saw (0.6750/53) before you went to bed. If it hits 0.6710, then your long position is established and your OCO orders are activated. If the range holds and the price moves back up to the range highs, your take profit at 0.6790 might be triggered. If the range fails to hold, your stop-loss order will limit your losses and close out your trade for you.

Be careful about using if/then orders with only a contingent take-profit order. Not using a stop loss to protect your downside is always very risky. At the minimum, always use an if/then stop loss to limit your risks.

If you use an if/then OCO order and the market behaves as you expect, you could awaken to find that you bought at 0.6710 and took profit (sold) at 0.6790, all while you slumbered through the night. Or you could awaken to find that your *if* order to buy was done, but the market has yet to hit your stop-loss or take-profit levels. But at least your open position is protected by the activated OCO order. Worst-case scenario in this example: You wake up and find that your *if* limit order was filled and your stop was triggered on a break through the bottom of the range, giving you a loss. The key is that you effectively managed your risk.

Spreads and orders in online currency trading

Now that I've covered the different order types, I think it's important for you to be aware of how online trading platforms typically handle traders' orders. I spent some time earlier in this chapter discussing forex market spreads. There was a good reason for that: Online forex brokers accept your orders according to their trading policies, which are spelled out in detail in the contract you'll have to sign to open up an online trading account. Make sure you read that section to be absolutely certain what your broker's order execution policies are. Ideally, brokers should publish their order execution policies on their website. Either way, it should be clear and easy to understand.

The key feature of most brokers' order policies is that your orders will be executed based on the *price spread* of the trading platform. That means that your limit order to buy will only be filled if the trading platform's offer price (where they sell) reaches your buy rate. A limit order to sell will only be triggered if the trading platform's bid price (where they buy) reaches your sell rate.

In practical terms, let's say you have an order to buy EUR/USD at 1.2855 and the broker's EUR/USD spread is around 3 pips. Your buy order will only be filled if the platform's price deals 1.2852/55. If the lowest price is 1.2853/56, no cigar, because the broker's lowest offer of 56 never reached your buying rate of 55. The same thing happens with limit orders to sell.

Stop-loss execution policies are typically different than limit order executions. To prevent filling your stop order at a worse rate than you requested, most forex brokers utilize the spread to trigger the stop.

✔ Stop orders to sell are triggered if the broker's *bid* price reaches your stop order rate. In concrete terms, if your stop-loss order to sell is at 1.2820 and the broker's lowest price quote is 1.2820/23, your stop will be filled at 1.2820.

✔ Stop-loss orders to buy are triggered if the platform's *offer* price reaches your stop-loss rate. If your stop order to buy is at 1.2875 and the broker's high quote is 1.2872/75, your stop will be filled at 1.2875.

The benefit of this practice is that some firms will guarantee against slippage on your stop-loss orders in normal trading conditions. (Rarely, if ever, will a broker guarantee stop losses around the release of economic reports or other volatile events.)

Nuances and strategies of trading with orders are explored further in Chapters 13 and 14.

Part II
Driving Forces behind Currencies

"I've always used historical data analysis to rebalance my assets, but lately it's been pretty much hysterical data analysis that I've been working with."

In this part . . .

I start out by looking at the main macroeconomic drivers that move currency markets. If you slept through Econ 101, don't worry — I take a mercifully brief (yet thorough) look at the economic and structural forces that drive currency rates. Then I shift gears a bit and explore how market psychology and sentiment filter those economics and dictate day-to-day price movements. Next, I look at the key individual economic reports — both U.S. and foreign — to give you a trader's insight into what they mean and how you can profit from them. I wrap up by providing our insights into the fundamental trading behavior of the major and minor currency pairs and crosses.

Chapter 5

Looking at the Big Picture

The forex market is inherently a big-picture market. FX traders focus on

✔ Interest rates and monetary policy developments.

✔ Economic growth and inflation data.

✔ Political elections and economic policies in major economies.

✔ Geopolitical risks, trade conflicts, and terror attacks.

✔ Major movements in other financial markets.

On a daily basis, currency traders have to sort through myriad economic reports, interpret the comments of political and financial officials from around the world, take stock of geopolitical developments, and assess movements in other financial markets. They do all this to help them determine what direction major currencies are likely to move.

Unfortunately, there is no set recipe for absorbing the daily flow of data and news to produce a clear-cut answer. Even if there were, many different market actors are pursuing their own interests, which may not be profit maximizing (see Chapter 3). Throw in market sentiment and future expectations, and you're looking at market participants interpreting the same data and reaching different conclusions, or maybe reaching the same conclusions but at different times. In this chapter, I lay the foundation for building the framework to make sense of the many policy, data, and news inputs that affect the forex markets every day.

The first step in laying the foundation is to get a handle on interest rates and monetary policy, because they're the final product of most of the other inputs. Unless you're an economist or banker, following monetary policy developments probably is not one of your favorite hobbies. But if you're going to actively trade in the forex market, you need to get a handle on monetary policy and interest rates. I'm not trying to turn you into an economist or an interest-rate analyst — I just want to give you the lowdown on how interest rates affect currencies.

In this chapter, I lay it all out so you can make sense of how it works, what goes into it, and how it's communicated to the market. Later in the chapter, I get into the key elements of official currency policies and what happens when governments intervene in forex markets. Lastly, I take a look at the Great Financial Crisis of 2008–2009 (GFC) to see what lessons it holds for currency traders.

Currencies and Interest Rates

If the guiding principle in real estate is "location, location, location," in currency trading it's "interest rates, interest rates, interest rates." The most significant overall determinant of a currency's value relative to other currencies is the nature and direction of monetary policy set by a country's central bank. This is because monetary policy is aimed at influencing domestic interest rates, which drive currency rates relative to other currencies with different interest rates. Domestic interest rates also influence overall economic activity, with lower interest rates typically stimulating borrowing, investment, and consumption, while higher interest rates tend to reduce borrowing and increase saving over consumption.

Interest rates are important to currencies because they influence the direction of global capital flows and serve as benchmarks for what investors expect to earn investing in a particular country. This situation applies most directly to fixed income investing (bonds), which comprise the lion's share of investments, but it also influences equity and other investment flows. All other things being equal, if you could invest in a government-backed bond that yields 6 percent or one that yields 2 percent, which would you choose? The one with the higher yield, of course. And that's exactly what happens with currencies. Currencies with higher yields (higher interest rates) tend to go up, and currencies with lower yields (lower interest rates) tend to weaken.

Although I've stressed interest rates as one of the primary drivers of currency rates, interest rates are not the only determinant of currency values. Plenty of other elements come into play, affecting currency rates both in short-term trading and in long-term trends. To use an analogy, think of the stage in a theater. Now think of interest rates as being the backdrop and the lighting on that stage. Various actors come and go; sets and props are changed between acts; but all the action on the stage takes place against the backdrop and under the lights. Interest rates provide the backdrop and set the lighting for most major currency movements, even if they're not always the center of attention.

The future is now: Interest rate expectations

It's not just the current level of interest rates that matter. Markets are always adjusting to changing circumstances and anticipating future developments. When it comes to currencies and interest rates, forex markets are focused more on the direction of future interest rate moves (higher or lower) than they are on the current levels because they're already priced in by the market. So even though a currency may have a low interest rate, market expectations of higher interest rates in the future frequently will cause the currency to appreciate.

And what drives interest rate expectations? The evolving economic outlook based on incoming data (I look at understanding and interpreting economic data in Chapters 6 and 7), economic assessments and guidance by monetary policymakers (see "Watching the central bankers" section later in this chapter), and a host of other economic, fiscal, and political developments (some of which I look at later in this chapter).

Keep an eye on various interest rate futures markets, such as the Fed Funds futures contract for U.S. rates, to see what expectations markets are pricing in. These can be found on financial websites like Bloomberg.com, Reuters.com, and Marketwatch.com. The commentary will usually note that markets have priced in, say, 18 bps of tightening by the next FOMC meeting, meaning the market is expecting a 72 percent chance of a 25 bp rate hike (18 bps/25 bps ?= 72 percent).

The *outlook period,* or the time frame in which markets are expecting interest rates to change, can span several months or quarters into the future. Depending on the economic circumstances and the outlook, markets may price-in interest rate changes a full year in advance, driving short term yields and currency levels in the process. Subsequent currency and yield fluctuations are based on incoming data and official guidance relative to the expectations markets have priced-in.

Relative interest rates

It's important to remember that currencies always come in pairs. Rather than focusing solely on a particular currency's interest rate level or outlook, forex markets tend to focus on the potential difference between two currencies' prospective interest rate changes. If two major currencies' central banks are both expected to be raising rates by the same amount in the future, there's little reason for one to outperform the other. But if one is expected to raise rates higher or faster, there are grounds for one currency to strengthen relative to the other.

Interest-rate differentials

The difference between the interest rates of the two currencies, known as the *interest-rate differential* or *spread,* is the key rate to watch. An increasing or widening interest-rate differential will generally favor the higher-yielding currency, whereas a falling or narrowing interest-rate differential will tend to favor the lower-yielding currency.

Some of the largest currency swings occur when two countries' interest rate cycles are moving, or are thought to be set to move, in opposite directions. And they don't necessarily have to both be moving — one currency could see expectations of higher/lower rates, whereas the other's rates are set to stay on hold. By focusing on the interest-rate differential, you can detect such changes more readily than by focusing on the rates of any individual currency.

Traders should monitor the interest-rate differentials among the major currencies by looking at the spreads between short-term government debt yields to spot shifts that may not otherwise be evident. For example, U.S. 2-year yields may decline by 5 bps (basis points, or a hundredth of 1 percent) — not an unusual daily development. Around the same time, Australian 2-year yields may move 5 bps higher — again, nothing earth shattering there viewed on its own. But add the two together, and you're looking at a 10 bps move between the two, and that's something to pay attention to. If the same thing happens again the following day, now you're looking at a 20 bps change in the differential, which is nearly equivalent to a typical 25 bps interest rate change from a central bank. You can be sure that if the Reserve Bank of Australia (RBA) unexpectedly raised interest rates by ¼ percent, or the Fed surprised everyone by cutting rates by ¼ percent, there would be some sharp swings in AUD/USD. The same holds true for changes in the interest-rate differentials, and they occur on a daily basis rather than the monthly meetings of most central banks.

Nominal and real interest rates

The interest rate to focus on is not always just the *nominal interest rate* (the base interest rates you see, such as the yield on a bond). Markets focus on *real interest rates* (inflation-adjusted rates, which is the nominal interest rate minus the rate of inflation [usually consumer price index]). So even though a bond may carry a nominal yield of, say, 8.5 percent, if the annual rate of inflation in the country is 4.5 percent, the real yield on the bond is closer to 4 percent.

This phenomenon is most evident in emerging market economies facing hyperinflation. Even though nominal interest rates may be 20 percent, if the annual rate of inflation is 25 percent, the real yield is –5 percent. Hyperinflation and negative yields lead to capital flight. The result is extreme weakness in the domestic currency, even though nominal interest rates may be extremely high.

The same can be true with very low interest rates and *deflation* (negative inflation), such as what happened in Japan over the past decade. With interest rates at very low levels, eventually zero, and facing deflation, real Japanese yields were significantly higher than the nominal zero rates on offer. (***Remember:*** If you subtract a negative number, it's the same as adding that positive number.) As a result, the JPY experienced overall appreciation in this period despite very low nominal rates and abysmal economic prospects.

In the following sections, I introduce the key objectives of monetary policy, take you through the tool kits of monetary policymakers, and show you how to stay on top of the evolving interest rate picture.

Monetary Policy 101

Monetary policy is the set of policy actions that central banks use to achieve their legal mandates. Most central banks function under legislative mandates that focus on two basic objectives:

- ✔ Promoting price stability (a.k.a. restraining inflation)
- ✔ Promoting sustainable economic growth, sometimes with an explicit goal of promoting maximum employment

Although it's a no-brainer that promoting economic growth is more important to those of us who work for a living, central bankers like to focus primarily on inflation. Low inflation fosters stable business and investment environments, so central bankers see it as the best way to promote long-run economic growth. Low inflation is also an end in itself because high inflation erodes assets and undermines capital accumulation. Some central banks, such as the European Central Bank (ECB), have only one mandate — to ensure price stability — with other policy objectives (growth and employment) explicitly relegated to secondary status. Still other central banks — the Swiss National Bank, for example — have a mandate to ensure a stable currency, though most countries have delegated that responsibility to the national finance ministry/treasury department.

Looking at benchmark interest rates

The primary lever of monetary policy is changes to benchmark interest rates, such as the federal funds rate in the United States or the refinance rate in the Eurozone. Changes in interest rates effectively amount to changes in the cost of money, where higher interest rates increase the cost of borrowing and lower interest rates reduce the cost of borrowing. The benchmark rates set by central banks apply to the nation's banking system and determine the cost of borrowing between banks. Banks in turn adjust the interest rates they charge to firms and individual borrowers based on these benchmark rates, affecting domestic retail borrowing costs. Other tools in the monetary policy toolkit used by central bankers are

- ✔ **Changes to money supply:** The overall amount of money in circulation, or the greater the money supply, the lower the cost
- ✔ **Reserve requirements:** The amount of capital required to be set aside by the banking system; money that cannot be used for lending

Easy money, tight money

The main thrust (or *bias,* as markets call it) of monetary policy generally falls into two categories: expansionary or restrictive. An expansionary monetary policy aims to expand or stimulate economic growth, while a restrictive bias aims to slow economic growth, usually to fight off inflation.

Expansionary monetary policy

Expansionary monetary policy (also known as accommodative or stimulative monetary policy) is typically achieved through lowering interest rates (that is, reducing the costs of borrowing in the hope of spurring investment and consumer spending). Cutting interest rates is also known as *easing* interest rates and is frequently summed up in the term *easy monetary policy.* Central banks can also increase the money supply — the overall quantity of money in the economy — which also works to lower borrowing costs. A reduction in the reserve requirement of banks frees up capital for lending, adding to the money supply and reducing borrowing costs as well.

An expansionary monetary policy is typically employed when economic growth is low, stagnant, or contracting, and unemployment is rising. Central banks of the major economies reacted to the fallout from the GFC and the global recession by slashing interest rates to historically low levels, near zero in the case of the United States, Switzerland, and Japan.

Restrictive monetary policy

Restrictive monetary policy (also known as contractionary or *tighter monetary policy*) is achieved by raising, or "tightening," interest rates. Higher interest rates increase the cost of borrowing, and work to reduce spending and investment with the aim of slowing economic growth and lowering inflation.

Central banks typically employ a tighter monetary policy when an economy is believed to be expanding too rapidly. The fear from the central banker's perspective is that heightened demand coupled with the low cost of borrowing may lead to inflation beyond levels considered acceptable to the long-run health of an economy. With too much money chasing the same or too few goods, prices begin to rise, and inflation rears its ugly head. Rapid wage gains, for example, may lead to increased personal consumption, driving up the cost of all manner of retail products.

Changing rates incrementally

Changes in monetary policy usually involve many small shifts in interest rates, because central bankers are generally reluctant to shock an economy by adjusting interest rates too drastically. Even the *potential* for large interest rate changes could contribute to uncertainty among investors and businesses, potentially disrupting or delaying well-laid business plans, thereby harming the overall economy in the process. Typical interest rate changes among the major central banks center on ¼ percent or 25 basis points (a basis point is 1/100th of 1 percent, or 0.01 percent), with 50 bps (or ½ percent) as the next most frequent rate adjustment.

The GFC and the accompanying global recession caused key central banks to slash rates rapidly, with cuts of 75 to 100 bps coming in rapid succession in some cases. Having cut benchmark rates to near zero, several major central banks felt compelled to undertake additional *unconventional easing* measures to support their economies.

Unconventional easing

Central banks can only directly influence the level of short term interest rates. Longer-term interest rates, the ones used by markets to set business and consumer lending rates, are determined by bond investors and are based on their views of growth, inflation, and creditworthiness. For example, the 10-year U.S. Treasury rate is the benchmark for U.S. mortgage rates.

When central banks cut their benchmark rates to near-zero levels, they were faced with the zero-lower bound of interest rates. To further support their economies, they sought to drive down longer-term lending rates through unconventional means, typically large-scale asset purchase programs where the central bank buys longer-term government bonds. (Remember, bond prices move inversely to bond yields — it's just bond math. Buying longer-maturity bonds theoretically pushes bond prices higher and yields lower, hopefully sending consumer and business lending rates down in the process.)

Such large scale asset purchase programs are frequently referred to as *quantitative easing (QE)* because the central bank is increasing the money supply, the quantity, by creating money to buy the bonds. In the United States, the Federal Reserve initiated two rounds of quantitative easing, while in the UK and Japan, the Bank of England and the Bank of Japan also undertook large-scale asset purchase programs. (Japan had also pursued QE repeatedly in the prior decade, well before the GFC.)

Currencies of countries pursuing such unconventional easing typically tend to weaken because such measures may drive down interest rates relative to other countries' rates, at least while the program is in place. Some investors also view an increasing money supply as a currency negative (the greater the supply, the lower the value). But I think that's too simplistic and relies on that extra money actually entering the economy.

A good case in point is what happened when the U.S. Federal Reserve indicated in August 2010 it was considering undertaking a second round of QE, known as QE2. Initially, the USD weakened as the Fed was seen to be trying to lower rates further. But when the actual program was announced, the USD began to strengthen and U.S. yields moved higher. It might look like a case of "sell the rumor, buy the fact," but it was more in response to U.S. data and the immediate outlook: The Fed was looking at QE2 in response to a slowdown in the summer of 2010, but by the time QE2 started in November 2010, U.S. data and the outlook had rebounded. And all that money the Fed was supposedly printing? It mostly ended up back at the Fed in the form of excess reserves held by the banking system, meaning it never entered the real economy.

Watching the central bankers

If you've read this chapter from the beginning, you've probably gotten the impression that determining monetary policy is mostly an exercise in shades of gray rather than a simple black-and-white equation — and you'd be exactly right. But given the significance of monetary policy to currencies, currency traders devote a great deal of attention trying to divine the intentions of central bankers. This has not always been an easy task, but recent trends among central banks to improve the openness of communications with markets, frequently referred to as *transparency,* have made the process less of a guessing game.

Central bankers communicate with the markets in a number of ways, and their comments can provoke market reactions similar to major economic data releases — by that, we mean sharp initial price movements followed by continued volatility or a potential change in direction.

- ✔ **Rate decisions:** Interest rate setting committees of central banks meet at regularly scheduled times. At the conclusion of a meeting, they issue a formal announcement of the policy decisions made at the meeting. They can raise, lower, or hold interest rates steady. They can also make changes to reserve requirements or liquidity operations.

- ✔ **Policy statements or guidance:** Along with the interest rate decision, central banks frequently issue an accompanying statement that explains the basis for their policy action. These statements are also used to provide guidance to markets on the future course of monetary policy. The statements are carefully parsed by markets intent on discovering what the central bank is thinking, which way it's leaning, and what the timing

> may be for future changes. Rate announcements and accompanying policy statements are included on economic data/event calendars.
>
> ✔ **Public speeches:** Central bankers frequently appear before community and business groups, and address subjects ranging from trends in the financial industry (such as the rise of hedge funds or the use of derivatives) to relatively mundane governance issues (such as financial reporting requirements). But when a central banker gives a speech that assesses the economic outlook or the future course of monetary policy, forex markets are all ears.

Appearances by central bank officials typically are included on most economic event/data calendars, and you need to be aware of them to avoid being taken by surprise. Sometimes, the topic of the speech is given in advance; other times, it's not. The most important speeches are those that focus on the economic outlook or the current monetary policy assessment.

In most cases, a prepared text is released by financial newswires at the scheduled start time of the speech. Accredited news agencies receive copies of speeches in advance to allow their reporters to prepare stories and headlines, but the release of the information is embargoed until the designated time. The remarks are then encapsulated into a series of headlines that capture the main points of the speech; this is the news that markets receive at the appointed time. When these headlines hit traders' screens, market prices start to react. If a question-and-answer session follows, the central banker's comments will be posted by the newswires as they're delivered live. This setup can make for some exciting headline-driven trading.

Currency traders need to be aware of and constantly follow the current market thinking on the direction of interest rates because of the strong relationship between interest rates and currency values. The best way to do this is to follow market commentaries in print and online news media, always keeping in mind that such outlets (especially print) are usually one step behind the current market. This makes online news commentaries that much more relevant. Some of the best sites for timely insights and market reporting are Bloomberg.com, Reuters.com, and MarketWatch.com. Best of all, these sites are free.

Look for currency brokers that offer real-time market analysis and news updates.

In the next section, I delve a bit deeper into how monetary policy is presented to financial markets by central bank officials. I also look at currency-specific policies and rhetoric. Sometimes, how a message is delivered or who delivers it is more important than the message itself. This is certainly true of monetary or currency policy comments from central bank or government finance officials.

Interpreting monetary policy communications

Earlier in this chapter, I cover the various ways in which central bankers communicate their thinking to market participants (see the preceding section). But the process is far more nuanced and evolved than relying simply on official policy statements or speeches before the Rotary Club of Indianapolis. Central bankers are keenly aware that their comments have the ability to move, and potentially disrupt, financial markets all over the world. So they choose their words very carefully, leaving traders to act as interpreters. Before you start interpreting monetary policy statements and commentary, it'll help to know the following.

Not all central bankers are created equal

The interest rate setting committees of central banks, frequently known as Monetary Policy Committees (MPCs) — the Fed's FOMC is one of these — typically operate under a one-member/one-vote rule. But when it comes to delivering a message to the markets, the chairman or president of the central bank holds far more sway than any other individual member. This is partly in deference to the central bank chief's role as first among equals, but also because that person is frequently viewed as expressing the thinking of the entire committee. Central bankers strive for consensus in reaching their decisions, and who better to represent and present this view than the chairman or president?

When the head of the central bank gives an update on the economy or the outlook for interest rates, listen up. A scheduled speech by the chair of the Fed, for instance, is likely to be preceded by market speculation similar to that of a major economic data report. And the reaction to his comments can be equally sharp.

In the case of the Fed, the FOMC is composed of 12 voting members consisting of the board of governors and a *rotating* slate of regional Federal Reserve Bank presidents each year. So when a Federal Reserve Bank president is set to speak, make sure you know whether he's a voting member in the current year before acting on his comments.

Remarks by nonvoting FOMC members are frequently discounted or ignored by traders because the speaker is not going to be casting a vote at the next meeting. But this is a bit of an oversimplification and can be risky. Before downplaying a nonvoter's comments, you need to consider her comments in the context of the FOMC consensus. Is she expressing her own views or elaborating on a shift in consensus thinking?

Birds of a feather: Hawks and doves

Central bank officials are frequently a known commodity to market analysts and traders, either from past policy statements or from their academic or policy writings prior to becoming central bankers. Markets typically refer to central bankers in terms of being hawks or doves. A *hawk* is someone who generally favors an aggressive approach to fighting inflation and is not averse to raising rates even if it will hurt economic growth. A *dove,* on the other hand, is a central banker who tends to favor pro-growth and employment monetary policy, and is generally reluctant to tighten rates if it will hurt the economy. In short, hawks tend to be fixated on fighting inflation, and doves tend to stress growth and employment.

Don't get me wrong: There are plenty of central bankers in the middle who can wear both hats (or feathers, in this instance). In those cases, the middle-of-the-roaders tend to reveal their hawkish or dovish leanings only at the extremes of the policy cycles.

So if a hawk is slated to speak on the outlook for monetary policy, and he cites the risks from inflation or the need to prevent any increase in inflationary pressures, guess what? You're not going to see much of a reaction from the markets because he's a known quantity speaking true to form. You get a much sharper reaction when a hawk downplays the threats from inflation or suggests that inflationary pressures may be starting to recede. Markets will jump all over dovish comments coming from a hawk, and vice versa with hawkish comments made by a dove.

Official Currency Policies and Rhetoric

Another major influence on currency values is government policies or official stances regarding the value of individual currencies. Some of the largest changes in currency values in recent decades have been brought on by official policies and multilateral agreements among the major industrialized economies. For instance, the Plaza Accord of 1985 stands out as a watershed in forex market history, ultimately resulting in a roughly 50 percent *devaluation* of the U.S. dollar over the course of the next two years.

National governments have a great deal at stake when it comes to the value of their currencies. After all, in a sense, a nation's currency is the front door to its economy and financial markets. If the currency is viewed as unstable or too volatile, it's tantamount to slamming the front door shut. And no major economy can afford to do that today.

In this section, I look at the major objectives of national currency policies, who sets them, and how they're implemented.

Currency policy or currency stance?

Referring to official government thinking on currencies as a *currency policy* may be a mischaracterization. Instead, you may do better to think of it as a *stance* on particular currency values at a particular point in time.

Daily trading volumes in the forex market dwarf most national central bank currency reserve holdings. (*Currency reserves* are the accumulated stocks of international currencies held by central banks for use in market interventions and overall central bank reserve management.) Japan and China together have more than $2 trillion in central bank currency reserves. That may seem like a lot to you and me, but average currency trading volume in the global forex market is over $4 trillion *per day*. This means that even if national governments *wanted* to routinely manage the value of their national currency, they would be hard-pressed to overcome market forces if they were at odds with the official policy.

To summarize why governments are generally reluctant to get involved in trying to influence currency values, it comes down to the following:

- ✔ **They can't because they're too small.** Forex markets are much bigger than any one nation's foreign currency reserves.

- ✔ **They can't because of market structure.** Forex markets operate outside national jurisdictions.

- ✔ **They can't agree on what to do.** Currencies always have another country or countries on the other side of the pair. You may want your currency to weaken, but do others want their currencies to strengthen?

- ✔ **They don't want to meddle in the free market.** Tampering with international capital flows is a recipe for economic disaster.

Generally speaking, then, governments prefer to refrain from getting involved in setting currency rates or trying to influence overall currency direction. They recognize that their power is extremely limited and that it must be used sparingly, usually only when extreme circumstances demand action from the national government or collective action from several governments. Moreover, the global economic superpowers are believers in the power of free markets to best allocate capital and maximize long-run economic potential. It simply would not do for them to openly reject free-market policies by regularly seeking to influence currency rates. You have to practice what you preach, or you start losing your following. For governments, that translates to credibility — and that's a trait most governments seek to cultivate and protect.

But — and this is a big *but* — governments *do* seek to influence currency rates from time to time. And when they do, it's usually a key long-term turning point in currency values.

In the next section, I look at the principal actors in each country or currency zone and what their recent actions on currencies suggest for their currency policy goals.

Calling the shots on currencies

In the "Currency policy or currency stance?" section, earlier in this chapter, I list a number of reasons why national governments are reluctant to get involved in trying to influence the value of their currencies. Chief among these are the size and extent of the global forex market and the need for nations to reach agreement on whether adjustments are even needed. The Group of Seven (G-7) used to be the main body where currency issues would be handled, but globalization has brought more economies to the table in the form of the Group of Twenty (G-20). (I list the membership of the G7 and G20 at the end of Chapter 3.) With an even larger collection of competing national interests in the bigger G-20, collective action on currencies seems less likely.

If governments had their way, they would probably prefer to see fixed exchange rates replace floating rates and avoid the subject entirely, but that's not a realistic option for the foreseeable future. Confronted with the realities of forex markets, most government currency officials go to great lengths to avoid discussing currency values out of fear that their comments will be misinterpreted and lead to sharp exchange rate shifts. That fear was born out of experience, and today's top currency officials are much more discreet than their predecessors just a few decades ago.

Responsibility for currency matters typically falls to the finance ministry or the central bank in the nations of the most heavily traded currencies. In the following sections, I take a look at who has responsibility for setting and implementing currency policies in the five major currencies and what their major motivations are.

The United States

The Department of the Treasury has the legal mandate for all currency matters, from printing the notes and minting the coins to ensuring the soundness of the U.S. dollar in international markets. The secretary of the Treasury is the primary spokesman for the U.S. dollar. The deputy Treasury secretary for international affairs is the hands-on Treasury official responsible for day-to-day currency matters.

When the U.S. Treasury secretary speaks on the value of the dollar, or any other currency for that matter, FX markets listen.

The Eurozone

The European Central Bank (ECB) is responsible for both monetary policy and currency matters under the agreement that created the single-currency Euro in 1999. The ECB's governing council is the primary decision-making body; it's composed of the presidents of the central banks of the participating nations, with the ECB president as the group's chief policy maker and spokesman.

When the ECB needs to intervene in the market, it can do so by itself, along with the central banks of the member states on its behalf.

However, individual European countries continue to exert influence over currency policy through their finance ministers, who had responsibility for currencies prior to the introduction of the euro and the creation of the ECB. The Eurozone finance ministers meet regularly as a group and frequently weigh in on forex market developments. There still appears to be great consideration given to the member states' governments by markets with regard to currency values, with the two largest European economies — Germany and France — wielding the greatest influence. But consensus appears to be the key element in deciding if the euro is too strong or too weak, and a clear majority of member states needs to be on board in opposing market movements before the market will pay attention.

The ECB is primarily concerned with fighting inflation and seeks to achieve currency stability as a means of fostering long-term economic growth. Europe remains heavily export oriented, so extreme euro strength is the most likely risk factor for any future forex market interventions out of Europe.

Japan

The Ministry of Finance (MOF) is responsible for currency matters in Japan. The MOF is the most powerful government ministry in Japan and can wield more influence over economic affairs than even the Bank of Japan (BOJ), the central bank. The MOF devotes a great deal of attention to the value of the JPY. The primary day-to-day currency spokesman for the MOF is the vice minister for international affairs, but during periods of volatility the finance minister will frequently issue statements. It is not at all uncommon for the MOF to issue daily comments on the forex markets, particularly when JPY volatility increases. The MOF last ordered an intervention (see the next section) in September 2010 as the JPY was strengthening and USD/JPY was threatening to drop under the key 80.00 level as the Fed geared up for a second round of quantitative easing.

Japan's economy remains highly export oriented, so the value of the JPY is important to export competitiveness and corporate profitability. Excessive JPY strength, which makes exports more expensive abroad and lowers the profit from foreign sales, is usually the trigger point for the MOF to express concern and possibly take action in the market.

Great Britain

The Chancellor of the Exchequer (treasury secretary or finance minister) is the individual responsible for the British pound's fate. The governor of the Bank of England (BOE) also shares responsibility for the pound in a bit of a holdover arrangement from when the BOE became independent from the government in the late 1990s.

The chancellor/BOE generally stays out of currency matters and appears most concerned with the pound's exchange rate versus the euro, because the bulk of UK trade is conducted with the Eurozone.

The United Kingdom is closely aligned with European economies and would be a candidate to join the Eurozone single currency, but nationalism runs deep when it comes to getting rid of the pound. The standing government line is that no decision on joining the euro would be made without conducting a national referendum.

Switzerland

The Swiss National Bank (SNB) is charged with responsibility for the Swiss franc along with setting monetary policy. The SNB is most concerned with the Swiss franc's exchange rate versus the euro, because nearly 80 percent of Swiss trade is conducted with Eurozone nations. The SNB has been known to speak up in opposition to CHF strength or weakness whenever the EUR/CHF exchange rate approaches extreme levels. During the Eurozone debt crisis in late 2009–2010, EUR weakened sharply against the CHF and prompted the SNB to intervene repeatedly to stem CHF strength, but without any success.

Currency market intervention

In every big-bank currency trading room in major financial centers, there is a direct line to the open market trading desk of the central bank. When that line lights up, the whole dealing room erupts. That line is reserved for open market intervention by the central bank, and when it rings, it usually means only one thing: The central bank is intervening in the market.

Intervention refers to central banks buying or selling currencies in the open market to drive currency rates in a desired direction. Direct intervention in the market is usually taken only as a last resort. It also may be a stop-gap measure to stabilize markets upset by extreme events, such as a stock market collapse or a natural disaster. When it's not necessitated by emergency circumstances, markets are generally aware of the increasing risks of intervention.

Open market intervention is usually preceded by several less-blunt forms of official intervention. The idea from the government's point of view is to get as much bang for the buck as possible before committing real money. *Remember:* Central banks have limited firepower in relation to the overall market, so they have to pick their spots well. Sometimes, the government's objective is simply to slow a market move to restore financial market stability, and less drastic forms of intervention are not yet necessary. Some of the more subtle forms of intervention are

- ✔ **Verbal intervention or jawboning:** These are efforts by finance ministry or central bank officials to publicly suggest that current market directions are undesirable. Basically, it amounts to trying to talk up or talk down a particular currency's value. For example, if the Japanese MOF is intent on preventing further JPY strength to protect its export sector, but the USD/JPY rate keeps moving lower, senior MOF officials may indicate that "excessive exchange rate movements are undesirable." This message is a warning for currency traders to reduce their USD selling/JPY buying or risk the potential consequences. If the market ignores the warning, the MOF may take it up a notch and indicate that it is "closely monitoring exchange rates," which is language typically used before actual open market intervention.

- ✔ **Checking rates:** This is the central bank's open market desk ringing in on the direct line to major currency banks' trading desks. The traders don't know if it's going to be a real intervention or not, but they still react instinctively based on previously indicated preferences. Even rumors of a central bank checking rates are enough to trigger a significant market reaction.

In terms of actual open market intervention, there are several different forms it can take, all depending on which and how many central banks are participating. The more the merrier; better still, there's strength in numbers.

- ✔ **Unilateral intervention:** This is intervention by a single central bank to buy or sell its own currency. Unilateral intervention is generally the least effective form of intervention, because the government is perceived (usually correctly) to be acting alone and without the support of other major governments. Markets will typically revert to the earlier direction after the intervention has run its course to test the central bank's resolve and to see if it's intent on stopping the move or simply slowing it. The MOF/BOJ intervention in fall 2010 and the SNB interventions during the 2009–2010 European debt crisis were all unilateral interventions and had little success stemming the tide of JPY and CHF strength.

✔ **Joint intervention:** This is when two central banks intervene together to shift the direction of their shared currency pair. For example, if the ECB and the SNB are concerned about Swiss-franc strength versus the euro, they may decide to intervene jointly to buy EUR/CHF. This is a clear sign to markets that the two governments are prepared to work together to alter the direction of that pair's exchange rate.

✔ **Concerted intervention:** This is when multiple central banks join together to intervene in the market simultaneously, also referred to as *coordinated intervention.* This is the most powerful and effective type of intervention, because it suggests unity of purpose by multiple governments. Concerted intervention is not done lightly by major central banks — and markets don't take it lightly either. It's the equivalent of a sledgehammer to the head. Concerted intervention frequently results in major long-term trend changes.

In terms of the impact of intervention, different governments are given different degrees of respect by the market. Due to the frequency of past interventions and constant threats of it, the Japanese tend to get the least respect. The BOE, the SNB, and the ECB are treated with considerably more respect by markets, with the ECB being the linchpin of credibility for the Eurozone. Finally, when the U.S. Treasury (via the Fed) intervenes, it's considered a major event, and the market usually respects the intervention.

There is a difference between a central bank intervening for its own account and a central bank intervening on behalf of another foreign central bank. For example, during the MOF/BOJ intervention campaign in 2003 and 2004, there were several instances where the U.S. Fed bought USD/JPY during the New York trading day. The first reaction was that the U.S. Treasury was joining in and supporting the intervention by the MOF/BOJ, and this amplified the effect of the intervention. But the U.S. Treasury later denied that it had ordered the intervention. What happened was that the BOJ asked the New York Fed to intervene on its behalf during the New York trading session. Central banks have standing agreements to act as each other's representatives in their local markets. So even though the New York Fed bought dollars, it bought them for the BOJ.

Does intervention work? That is a question that frequently comes up when central banks get involved. The simple answer is an unequivocal "Yes, but . . . ." Intervention is most effective when it's backed by monetary policy moving in the same direction, such as expected higher interest rates to support a weak currency or easier monetary policy to weaken a strong one. Even then, interest rate changes are no guarantee that the intervention will be successful.

In the short run, the intervention may seem fruitless and counterproductive. This is especially the case with unilateral intervention. The market typically rejects the unilateral intervention and reverts to pushing the market in the direction opposed by the intervention. This situation can go on for weeks and months or — in the SNB's case in 2010 — years. When it's a joint or concerted intervention, the results are usually more immediate and successful.

Financial stability

The Great Financial Crisis of 2008–2009 triggered a massive global recession, the likes of which not seen since the Great Depression of the 1930s. As a result, major governments' finances were thrown into disarray, as tax revenues plunged and spending was maintained or increased through fiscal stimulus. Suddenly the creditworthiness and financial stability of major national governments was being questioned by global markets.

A currency's perceived value is intrinsically linked to the faith investors have in the financial stability of the nation(s) standing behind it. If investors fear a *sovereign debt default,* meaning government bonds won't be paid back, they're likely to sell both those bonds and the country's currency. The result can be a market frenzy in which government bond prices crash, sending yields soaring and increasing the government's borrowing costs, effectively forcing the government out of global capital markets and leading to a default.

The Eurozone debt crisis of 2009–2010 is the most obvious recent example, where bond investors fled Greek and Irish government debt, raising borrowing costs to unaffordable levels and forcing those governments to seek a bailout from wealthier Eurozone members. From the start of the Greek debt crisis in November 2009 until a temporary bailout mechanism was established in May 2010, the euro weakened against the USD by more than 20 percent, and fell even more against other currencies.

And the fallout from the GFC is not confined to government debt. Major global banks lost gazillions in the crisis, and many remain extremely fragile and on government life support. In the case of European banks in particular, they hold around half of outstanding Eurozone government debt, meaning sovereign defaults or *restructurings* (a euphemism meaning investors don't get back the full amount or payments are delayed) have the potential to cause additional massive losses to the banking sector, imperiling the Eurozone economy even further.

Debts, deficits, and growth

In the aftermath of the GFC, highly indebted European countries are certainly not alone in having investors question their financial stability. Debt levels in the United States and Japan are routinely cited as potential negatives, weighing on sentiment for those currencies from time to time. For the USD, its standing as the global reserve currency of choice is increasingly being called into question. And then there are the outliers, like Hungary, Iceland, and

Dubai, small economies overall, but credit fears over their financial stability have a way of reverberating throughout global markets and sending risk sentiment (which I discuss later in this chapter) into a tailspin.

As part of your analysis of individual currencies, you need to be aware of the financial stability of the key currency countries. The metrics to keep in mind are

- **Debt to GDP ratio.** A measure of the total amount of government debt relative to the size of the economy. Debt/GDP ratios over 85 to 90 percent of GDP tend to put countries under the credit-risk microscope.

- **Deficits as a percent of GDP.** Current and projected deficits add to the total amount of government debt, which can increase the debt/GDP ratio, potentially destabilizing a country's credit outlook.

- **Growth rates (GDP).** Low or negative growth can undermine a nation's GDP relative to its debt service obligations, increasing the burdens of debt service and raising the risk of default. The imposition of *austerity measures* (budget cuts and tax increases) in the most beleaguered Eurozone countries threatens to lock them in a cycle of underperformance, and may actually increase the potential for default.

Gauging credit risk

Just as with monetary policy and interest rate developments, financial stability evolves over a long time period. But there are day-to-day developments that impact the markets' view of individual countries' financial stability.

How can you monitor the current state of the markets' views of a nation's creditworthiness? Keep an eye on the following credit risk measures through markets' news reports and economic commentaries:

- **Credit ratings.** Although often late to the game in the GFC, the sovereign debt ratings issued by Moody's, Standard & Poor's (S&P), and Fitch still carry a lot of weight. A ratings downgrade can make government debt issues ineligible for certain institutional investors, forcing them to sell those government bonds. Prior to a ratings change (they can be upgrades as well as downgrades), the credit rating agencies will typically issue an announcement that a country's debt ratings are under review and offer a bias to that review, such as "Portugal sovereign debt placed on review; outlook negative." Such announcements can have a significant impact on the currency involved.

- **Yield spreads.** These are the difference between the yields (interest rates) of one government's bonds relative to an ostensibly safer country's bonds. In the Eurozone debt crisis of 2009[nd]2010, for example, markets fixated on the spread between yields of peripheral countries like Greece and Portugal and those of stalwart Germany. A widening spread indicates increasing credit concerns, as the bonds of the weak country are sold, sending yields higher, and bonds of the safe country are bought, sending those yields lower, widening the spread. Yield spreads fluctuate on a daily and intra-day basis, with widening spreads indicating deteriorating credit risk and narrowing spreads indicating greater relief.

✓ **Credit default swaps (CDS).** These derivatives are basically an insurance policy in the event of a default, where the buyer pays a premium and the seller is obligated to make good on the bond in the event of a default. CDS are an active speculative counterpart to the underlying bonds themselves, and may often lead bond market moves. Rising CDS indicate increasing credit risk and falling CDS rates, expressed in basis points (bps), signal lesser concern.

✓ **Debt auction results.** Governments borrow money through regularly scheduled auctions or *issuances,* where the government offers its debt for sale to global investors. The extent of demand and the price investors are willing pay (the yield) are the key measures here. Demand is gauged according to the *bid/cover ratio,* meaning how much is bid, or sought, relative to the amount being offered. The higher the bid/cover ratio, the greater the demand and supposed security. A *failed auction,* one where the government is not able to sell, or borrow, the full amount it seeks is "not a good thing," as Martha Stewart might say. But some investors are usually willing to buy anything if the price is right, and that's where the yield comes in. If investors demand a higher yield (bid a lower price) relative to current rates, it's an indication of concern. For U.S. Treasury debt, there's yet another indicator, supposedly attesting to the international appetite for U.S. debt, with implications for the value of the USD. The amount bought by *indirect bidders* is viewed as a proxy for foreign central bank and reserve managers' demand. A low turnout by indirect bidders could be interpreted as a vote of no confidence for U.S. debt and/or the USD by other major governments. The bid/cover ratio, yield results, and amount of indirect bids measures are all interpreted relative to prior auction results for similar issuances.

Geopolitical Risks and Events

Geopolitics is nothing more than a fancy word used to describe what's going on in the world at large. As it's applied to the currency markets, geopolitics tends to focus on political, military/security, or natural disruptions to the global economy or individual regions or nations. Because currency markets are the conduits for international capital flows, they're usually the first to react to international events, as global investors shift assets in response to geopolitical developments.

Currency markets have no national or patriotic allegiances when it comes to favoring one currency over another. The forex market simply calculates the likely economic fallout from an international event and its ultimate currency impact. A recent example is the popular uprisings in the Middle East and North Africa in early 2011. Egypt is a relatively small economy, meaning that the turmoil there did not threaten the global economic outlook, and forex and other financial markets were not seriously affected. But as the unrest spread to Libya, a major oil producer, oil prices spiked on supply disruptions, and concerns grew that other oil producers could be affected. Stock markets started to wobble, and the USD weakened as oil and gold soared. You have to interpret each international event dispassionately, with an eye on the short- and long-term economic impact to determine its significance for individual currencies.

The United States tends to wield more influence on the world's stage because it's the largest national economy and the primary military superpower. In addition, the U.S. dollar is the largest global reserve currency and the de facto currency in many developing economies. Finally, with increasing global-ization of trade and markets, the U.S. dollar frequently functions as a global risk barometer (see the next section for more on risk). For these reasons, the U.S. dollar tends to experience the greatest reaction in times of global turmoil or uncertainty, and the market tends to think in USD-positive and USD-negative terms, viewing all other currencies in contrast to the U.S. dollar. When geopolitical events are looking problematic, the USD tends to suffer. If the risks or tensions come down, the dollar may go up.

Elections in individual countries, including by-elections and legislative refer-enda, also fall under the geopolitical risk umbrella, especially when the out-come may lead to a change in government or economic policies. *By-elections* (ad hoc elections to fill individual legislative seats made vacant by death or resignation, for example) are typically seen as interim votes of confidence on the governing party. Depending on how near the next general election is, and on other economic factors, by-elections may have a greater effect on political sentiment.

As important as geopolitical issues are to the market's overall assessment of a currency's value, they tend to have relatively short-run implications and must be interpreted in light of other prevailing economic fundamentals. For instance, if the USD is weakening based on a weak economic outlook, for example, and there's a disruption to oil supplies from political unrest or a natural disaster, sending oil prices higher, it's just another reason to sell USD. In contrast, if the USD is strengthening based on a more positive economic trajectory and higher rate expectations, a spike in oil prices may see the usual inverse relationship break down, and both oil and the USD move higher.

Gauging risk sentiment

In recent years, the concept of *risk sentiment* has taken hold as a way of expressing overall conditions across financial markets, including forex. Risk sentiment refers to investor behavior and whether investors are actively seeking returns by embracing riskier assets (*risk seeking* or *risk appetite*), or whether they're seeking the safety of supposed more secure assets (*risk averse* or *risk aversion*). These two behavioral modes are frequently referred to as *risk-on* and *risk-off*, or *risk-positive* and *risk-negative*.

For currency traders, the risk environment can be a critical factor in driving currency rate movements. Part of the reason has to do with the interest rates of various major currencies. Hedge funds, commodity trading advisors (CTAs), and other leveraged speculators (see Chapter 3 for more on these guys) borrow funds (the leverage) on a short-term basis at the lowest cost available, meaning currencies with the lowest interest rates are used as *funding currencies*. In a risk-on environment, they then sell those currencies and use the proceeds to buy risk assets with greater price appreciation potential. In a risk-off environment, they're compelled to sell their risk assets and buy back those funding currencies that they previously sold.

Risk on or risk off?

So what determines whether risk is on or off? In a word, volatility. *Volatility* refers to the size and speed of price movements over a short timeframe, meaning hours or days. But volatility is the symptom and not the cause of those price changes. News and events are what dictate market reactions. In the simplest sense, when news and economic data are positive and everyone's feeling good about the outlook, risk is on and risk assets tend to appreciate (see the following section for what constitutes risk assets). When the news or data turns negative or outright catastrophic in the case of the GFC, investors turn more cautious and may exit risk trades, potentially triggering widespread selling that may force prices lower and force other investors to bail out as well, amplifying the sell-off.

I have little doubt that much of the increase in the risk-on/risk-off trading dynamic in recent years is the result of algorithmic, or model-based, trading, which has taken on increased prominence in all markets. If the computer is told that an X percent change in one asset or indicator means it should exit an existing position, it will literally not "think" twice about selling out.

Gauges of risk sentiment

To follow the evolution of risk sentiment, it helps to have a good handle on the current state of market affairs and expectations (see Chapter 10 for how to get up to speed on these). For more empirical indications of risk sentiment, pay attention to the following:

- ✔ **VIX index.** This is the options volatility on the S&P 500 U.S. stock index, frequently referred to as *the fear index*. A rising VIX indicates increased risk aversion (stocks are being sold), and a falling VIX signals the outlook is calming.

- ✔ **Government bond yields.** Major government bonds, such as U.S. Treasuries, German bunds, UK Gilts, or Japanese JGBs, are considered safe assets (for now at least). Rising yields typically mean those bonds are being sold and investors are embracing risk. But sometimes those bonds are being sold on credit concerns, which is risk-negative. Falling yields suggest risk aversion, as investors are fleeing risk assets and buying the safety of government bonds.

- ✔ **Emerging-market stock performance.** Investors have become increasingly international in their perspective and buying shares in Shanghai or Rio is no longer considered exotic. Such emerging market economies have led the way out of the GFC, and their stock markets can be the canary in the coal mine—prices down, risk-off; prices up, risk-on.

Risky versus safe assets

The low interest rate environment of recent years has forced investors and speculators alike to chase returns by investing in so-called *risk assets* that offer higher potential returns. The clearest example of risk assets are stocks and commodities: A more positive outlook (risk-on) may see stocks gain as corporate profits increase, and commodities may benefit on stronger demand for raw materials and natural resources, like oil. In forex, the risk-on currencies are those linked to commodities (AUD, CAD, and NZD, in particular) and major alternatives to the USD, like EUR and GBP. A risk-on environment may also see carry trades bought, where higher yielding currencies such as those just mentioned are bought and lower yielding currencies like the JPY, USD and CHF are sold (funding currencies). For example, a positive risk environment may see AUD/JPY move higher.

On the other side of the risk equation (risk-off) are the supposedly safe assets, such as U.S. Treasury bonds, the USD, CHF, and JPY. When bad news and events hit markets (think the Great Financial Crisis or Eurozone debt bailouts), investors typically flee risk assets, selling stocks and commodities and buying the safety of government bonds and safer currencies like CHF, JPY, and the USD. Price moves in a risk-off environment can be extremely volatile because it's a one-two punch where traders exit (sell) risk-on positions and also buy safer, risk-off assets.

Pay attention to the news when potentially disruptive events threaten the economic outlook, and be aware of the risk-on/risk-off dynamic. Depending on the nature of events, especially whether they're short-term like a natural disaster, or more enduring like a debt crisis in Europe, they can offer potential opportunities to re-enter a longer-term trend from lower price levels.

Chapter 6

Understanding and Applying Market News and Information

As Roseanne Roseannadanna used to say, "It just goes to show you. It's always something. If it's not one thing, it's another." Okay, maybe I'm dating myself with a reference to the classic *Saturday Night Live* "Weekend Update" commentator, played by Gilda Radner way back in the 1970s, but her tagline fits the forex market nicely.

Any number of real-world forces are at work in the forex market at a given moment — economic data, interest rate decisions, and geopolitical events, to name just a few. And they all get filtered through the market's collective consciousness and translated into price movements.

As currency traders, we're focused on trying to make money based on those price movements, but we're not alone. A whole raft of participants is active in the currency market, and they're all analyzing the same news and data, and drawing differing conclusions. To add yet another dimension, they're making trades based on those conclusions, which is what ultimately moves currency prices.

Which brings me back to the observation: If it's not one thing, it's another. The "other" in this case boils down to how markets process information — and there's a lot of it. I've spent over 20 years in the Forex market as a trader, analyst, and strategist, and just when I think I've seen it all, something new and unexpected comes along. So you're not alone when it comes to having to sift through the mountain of information and make trading decisions.

Your aim is to avoid paralysis by analysis and to absorb and understand as much as you can about what's driving the market, all with the goal of making successful currency trades. *My* aim is to give you a better understanding of the types of information that move the market and a solid foundation to interpret and apply that information.

Sourcing Market Information

The jumping-off point for the discussion of market information has to be getting the market information in the first place. Institutional traders have teams of economists, analysts, and strategists providing them with up-to-the-minute observations and interpretations. Does this give them an advantage? Not necessarily. In the big picture, most of the information they're getting is available to individual traders, but you have to make the effort to find it, read it, and understand it.

The art of boarding a moving train

Anyone who's ever tried to jump on a moving train knows you have to start running alongside it before you reach out and try to grab hold. If you're standing flat-footed and you try to grab on, you're likely to get your arm ripped off. The forex market is no different, and any trader who tries to jump in without first getting up to speed is asking for trouble.

Getting up to speed in the forex market means learning what current themes are driving the market. To do that, you're going to need to know where to find market information and how to interpret it.

But getting up to speed takes time, so don't be in a rush to start trading based on a few days or hours of research. I recommend spending a month following the various currency pairs and familiarizing yourself with what's going on before you consider yourself up to speed. Using a practice account at an online forex broker is a great way to get up to speed. Over the course of a month, you'll be exposed to a full cycle of economic data indicators and most market events, like central bank meetings, which will give you a firsthand sense of how the market behaves and adjusts to new information.

Part of the excitement of currency trading is that there's always something going on — a train is leaving the station every few minutes. So don't worry about missing the next train, because there's always another one right behind it.

Taking the pulse of the market

As online currency trading has grown in popularity in recent years, there's been a proliferation of currency-specific websites targeted at individual traders. We can't possibly begin to review them all here, but you'd do well to start out with FXstreet.com (`www.fxstreet.com`), a comprehensive site featuring diverse sources of market analysis, many from big-name institutional contributors, all for free.

When you're looking at forex research from various information sources, be mindful of who is providing the analysis. If you don't know the identities or backgrounds of the analysts, you may be reading the work of someone with just a few months or a year of market experience — not exactly the most sophisticated insight. When in doubt, focus on the reports made available by major financial institutions.

Most online currency trading platforms also offer various types of market research and analysis, so when you're deciding which broker you should open your account with, look at the quality (not to be confused with quantity) of its research offerings.

News sources

I tend to focus on the mainstream financial press, which provides continuous coverage of the major financial markets. Their websites provide frequent intraday updates that cover data releases and announcements, usually with some institutional commentary as well, so you can better understand how and why the market is reacting. In alphabetical order, my favorites are

- ✔ Bloomberg (`www.bloomberg.com`)
- ✔ MarketWatch.com (`www.marketwatch.com`)
- ✔ Reuters (`www.reuters.com`)

When you're reading a market news report, always use a critical eye. Keep in mind that what's being reported has already happened, and the market has digested the information and adjusted prices accordingly.

When interpreting news and information always ask yourself:

- ✔ **What is the source of the information?** You need to differentiate fact from opinion or rumor.
- ✔ **How old is the information?** You need to gauge the timeliness of the information and the extent to which the market has already acted on it.

Real-time market news sources

The forex market moves on news quickly, and the institutional players generally have multiple live feeds from the major accredited newswires, such as

Dow Jones, Bloomberg, and Reuters. Individuals can get real-time news, especially data releases, from the financial TV networks, such as Bloomberg TV, CNBC, and Fox Business News.

At FOREX.com, we provide a real-time market commentary (known as Forex Insider) directly on our trading platform. The updates are provided by our research team and senior traders based on our years of experience trading in the interbank forex market. Forex Insider offers instant analysis of data releases and other news events, as well as short-term tactical trading considerations such as institutional buying and selling flows, currency option interest, and technical support and resistance levels. I think it's a great resource for individual traders and about as close as you can get to the institutional market.

Social networks like Facebook and Twitter are also being used by online forex brokerages to distribute news and research. Also, check to see which brokerages offer access to their trading platforms from mobile devices and messaging services or apps for iPhone/iPad and Android. They're a great way to keep up on the market when you're not in front of your computer.

Economic data and event calendars

The forex market revolves around economic data and events, and you're going to need to find a reliable market calendar to see what's coming down the road next. The best market calendars contain all the major upcoming economic releases, showing the time of the report, what the market is forecasting, and the prior report indicated.

Perhaps even more important than data reports are economic events like central bank rate-setting meetings, the release of the minutes of those meetings, speeches by central bankers, and important meetings such as monthly gatherings of Eurozone finance ministers. Comments from these events frequently move the market in the short term, and if you're not aware of them, you risk getting blindsided.

Later in this chapter, I look at how markets anticipate data and events, and how this anticipation can affect currency prices. But you can't anticipate if you don't know what's scheduled.

Currency forecasts

Most of the financial media are keen on institutional forecasts of where currency rates are headed, and you'll likely encounter a lot of one-month, quarterly, and year-ahead currency-rate forecasts in your market research. However, treat these as an indication of overall market sentiment and outlook instead of as a concrete trading recommendation. Most forecasts are heavily skewed to current circumstances and are a much better guide to what the market is thinking at the moment than to where rates will actually be in a month or a year.

Rumors: Where there's smoke, there's fire

As if there weren't enough legitimate news and information to contend with in the 24-hour-a-day forex market, rumors have the nasty habit of popping up at unpredictable times. All financial markets love rumors. Here is a pair of the forex market's favorites:

- ✔ **Whisper numbers:** These are rumors of economic data anywhere from a few minutes to a few hours before the scheduled release time. They tend to roil short-term positions opened in anticipation of a report, and they also influence the market's subsequent reaction to the report. For example, a whisper number suggesting a much-worse-than-expected U.S. data report, which was originally forecast to be weak anyway, may see the USD come under more intense pressure prior to the release time. When the real number comes out, and it's weak but in line with forecasts, and not as weak as the whisper number, the USD may actually rebound because the worst fears were not realized.

- ✔ **Large market orders:** These are rumors that frequently do hold water, but like everything else, not always. They're typically associated with central banks or large institutional players buying or selling, and they usually mention a price level. Pay attention to the price level as a potential source of support or resistance. If the price level is broken, the order either wasn't real or has been filled. Either way, the price level has given way, potentially triggering a further directional move.

The trouble with rumors is that you have no easy way to determine whether they're true, and even if you can, you have no way of being certain of the price reaction, which is ultimately the key to dealing with rumors. Rumors have the uncanny habit of coming out after relatively extensive directional moves or attempts to break through important technical levels, attempts that subsequently fail and see prices reverse direction.

The key is to be aware that an intraday move or test of a technical level is under way and to have a relatively tight exit strategy if the market turns tail. If there is a rumor behind a sudden reversal, you'll usually find out only after the fact anyway, but a tight exit plan will save you from getting left behind in the reversal.

Putting Market Information into Perspective: Focusing on Themes

At any given moment in the forex market, several *themes* dominate the market's attention. Market themes are the essence of the real-world forces currently holding sway in the market. Themes are what market commentators and analysts are talking about when they explain what's happening in the market. But most important, themes are the filters through which new information and data are absorbed by the market.

Market themes come in all shapes and sizes, and have differing impacts on the market over time. Some are long-term themes that can color the market's direction for months and years, such as the persistent U.S. trade deficit. Others may hold sway for only a few hours, days, or weeks, such as unexpectedly hawkish comments from a central banker.

Market themes come in two main forms that coexist in parallel universes but that also frequently overlap. The two types of themes that I like to focus on are fundamental themes and technical themes.

Driving fundamental themes

Each currency has its own set of fundamental circumstances in which it's being evaluated by the market. The basic fundamental environment is ever-present, but it's also subject to change over time, just as economic conditions will change in the course of business cycles. Fundamental themes will also shift in relative importance to one another, with certain themes being pushed to the side for a period when news or events focuses the market's attention on other, more pressing themes.

As you read the following sections, keep in mind that each theme applies to each and every currency but in varying degrees at any given moment. I include some examples of what's likely to happen to a currency based on what incoming information means for each theme; I go into more detail on how the market processes fresh data at the end of this chapter.

Rising or falling interest rates

Interest rates are usually the single most important determinant of a currency's value. (I go into greater detail on the significance of monetary policy and interest rates in Chapter 5.) But it's not just about where interest rate levels are now, though that's still important (higher interest rate currencies tend to do better against lower-yielding currencies). What matters most is their overall direction (whether they're going up or down), their future level (how high or low they're likely to go), and the timing of any changes (how fast rates are likely to change).

Markets are constantly speculating about the direction of interest rates, even though interest rate changes are relatively infrequent. Speculation over the direction and timing of interest rate changes is one of the primary drivers of a currency's value on a daily basis as well as over longer time frames.

The information inputs that drive the interest rate outlook are centered on economic growth data and inflation reports, which I cover in detail in Chapter 7. The stronger the growth picture is, or the higher inflation pressures are, the more likely interest rates are to move higher, normally improving a currency's outlook. The weaker the growth outlook or the lower the inflation readings, the more likely interest rates are to remain steady or move lower, typically hurting a currency in the process.

Bond markets also have a lot to say about the direction of interest rates and are the best real-time barometer of the market's interest rate expectations. Central banks can really only influence short-term interest rates, which are driven by the central bank's target interest rate. But longer-term bond yields, with the ten-year maturity as the benchmark, reflect the market's long-term view of an economy's outlook and the direction of likely future interest rate moves. Falling bond yields (lower interest rates) point to a weaker economic outlook and the probability of lower interest rates ahead, typically denting that currency, while higher bond yields point to economic optimism and likely higher rates, usually supporting that currency.

The effect of interest rate themes is most powerful when the interest rates of two currencies are seen to be diverging — when one currency's interest rate is expected to move higher and the other lower. Keep an eye on the three-month *yield spreads* — the difference between yields of two government bonds — for relative changes that can favor one currency over another. Rates don't necessarily have to diverge to affect currencies. One currency's yields may simply move higher faster than another, and the widening spread between the two will reveal this.

When you're looking at economic data or monetary policy rhetoric, always assess the incoming information first in terms of what it means for the interest rates of the nation's currency — the interest rate theme. A currency that is expected to see lower rates in the near future, for example, is likely to stop declining and may even rebound if an economic growth report or an inflation reading comes in higher than expected. The market will pause to consider whether its outlook for lower rates is correct. By the same token, a currency facing the prospect of lower interest rates ahead, when hit with weaker economic data or lower inflation readings, is likely to weaken further. I say "weaken further" because it was probably already under pressure and moving lower before the latest batch of data hit the market.

Looking for growth

Economic growth prospects are the linchpin to a host of currency value determinants, from the interest rate outlook to the attractiveness of a nation's investment climate (stocks and bonds). Not surprisingly, the stronger the outlook for growth, the better a particular currency is likely to perform relative to currencies of countries with weaker growth outlooks. Strong economic growth increases the likelihood of higher interest rates down the road, as central bank officials typically seek to restrain too rapid growth to head off inflationary pressures. Weaker growth data increases the prospect of potentially lower interest rates, as well as dampening the outlook for the investment environment.

Many growth data reports reflect only a particular sector of a nation's larger economy, such as the manufacturing sector or the housing market. Depending on how significant that sector is to the larger national economy, those reports will tend to be interpreted as correspondingly more or less significant. Industrial production data in Japan, for example, is more significant to the Japanese outlook than it is to the U.S. outlook because of the more prominent role manufacturing plays in Japan.

There's no set recipe for how growth data will impact a currency's value, but when the interest rate outlook is generally neutral, as in no solid conviction on the direction of two countries' rates, the growth theme becomes more important.

Fighting inflation

Inflation is the bogeyman that all central bankers have nightmares about. Even when inflation is low, they still worry about it — it's just part of the job. When inflation is running too high for their comfort, fuhgeddaboutit. As a currency trader attuned to monetary policy developments, you need to monitor inflation readings as well. (I look at the key inflation reports in greater detail in Chapter 7.)

The inflation theme is far more nuanced than the growth theme in what it implies for a currency's value. Depending on the bigger picture, it can produce starkly different outcomes for a currency. In general, if growth is good, and inflation is too high, it's a currency plus. If growth is low or weakening, and inflation is too high, it's a currency negative. Come again? Both scenarios point to steady-to-higher interest rates, which should typically be a currency plus, right? The rub is that the low-/slow-growth scenario coupled with high/higher interest rates increases the risks of an economy dropping into recession, which would ultimately result in interest rate cuts farther down the road. In this sense, currencies are a bit fickle in that they like higher interest rates some of the time, but not all of the time.

The same phenomenon can happen when a central bank holds rates too high for too long, usually based on fighting inflation, and the market begins to speculate that an economic downturn is ahead. The response is actually not that bizarre if you consider that the forex market is, first and foremost, always anticipating future interest rates.

When factoring inflation data into the interest rate theme, be aware of how the overall growth theme is holding up. If growth is good, and inflation is high because of economic strength, higher inflation readings will be currency supportive. If growth is slowing, and inflation is still too high, the currency impact will be decidedly less positive and very likely downright negative.

Seeking stability

The Great Financial Crisis of 2008–2009 (GFC) exposed financial stability as another overarching theme. In the initial phases of the crisis, the financial sector (banks and insurers) was shaken to its core and required massive government intervention to prevent a system-wide failure. The subsequent economic downturn later exposed excessive government debt levels and budget deficits as a threat to sovereign debt and economic growth. The road to recovery in the developed economies remains a tough haul, and government debt levels and the risk of a sovereign default may continue as a theme for years to come.

Whether it's high debt levels in Europe or quantitative easing in the United States, financial stability and perceptions of creditworthiness can exert a significant impact on national currencies, usually for the worse. Keep an eye on government bond yields as an indication of market fears. Higher yields may mean investors are selling a country's bonds over fears of a default and not because of positive growth expectations. If so, the currency of the at-risk country is going to suffer alongside its bonds. (See Chapter 5 for more on this topic.)

Gauging the strength of structural themes

Beyond interest rates, growth, inflation and, stability, several other prominent themes regularly assert themselves, mostly in the structural sphere (the big-picture elements of how an economy is performing).

Structural themes can be fleeting — they can be in full force one day or for several weeks or months and then drop from the radar screen altogether. These themes are also usually secondary to those I outline in the preceding sections (interest rates, growth, inflation, and stability), but structural themes can still exert significant influence on a currency on their own. Most important, they can amplify the impact of the primary themes, like throwing gas on a fire. Following are frequently recurring structural themes:

- ✔ **Employment:** Employment is the key to an economy's long-run performance and a primary driver of interest rates. As long as employment is rising, the longer-term economic outlook is supported. But if job growth begins to falter, as reflected in incoming labor market reports, economic prospects will tend to be marked down. Sharp increases in unemployment are among the fastest triggers to interest rate cuts by central bankers, going back to the primary interest rate theme.

- ✔ **Deficits:** Both fiscal and trade deficits are typically currency negatives. During times of low/slow growth, the impact of deficits can be magnified, as the very credibility of a currency can be questioned, as was recently the case with the euro. During times of steady/high growth, deficits may have less impact but are still a negative hanging over the outlook.

✔ **Geopolitical issues:** It seems like a fact of life now, but geopolitical tensions weren't always ever-present, as they seem to be today, from North Korean nuclear tests to political upheaval in the Middle East or trade disputes with China. The USD is the most vulnerable to geopolitical issues, given the size of it economy, reliance on world trade, and potential military involvement. After geopolitical tensions subside, the market is quick to revert to preexisting themes.

✔ **Political elections or uncertainty:** Changes of government and political uncertainty in the major-currency countries can certainly dent the market's sentiment toward the currency concerned. But shortly after the political situation is resolved, political issues tend to fade quickly into the background.

Analyzing technical themes

Technical themes are perhaps a little harder to grasp than fundamental themes (see the preceding section), especially if you're not familiar with technical analysis (see Chapter 11). But to make a long story short, sometimes currency prices move simply because currency prices are moving.

The fundamental economic or political themes may not have changed dramatically, but price levels have, and that is frequently enough to bring major market interest out of the woodwork.

In most cases, breaks of major technical or price levels will be in the direction suggested by the prevailing fundamental themes, but the timing is often suspect and can leave traders scratching their heads, asking what just happened. But sizeable price movements have a way of taking on a life of their own, forcing market participants to take action based on price adjustments alone.

In addition, the prevalence of technical analysis as the basis for many trading decisions can add weight to existing fundamental-driven moves, generating yet another theme to propel the move — the technical theme. It may be a trending market movement that attracts trend-following traders who don't give a hoot about the underlying fundamentals. As long as the technical trend is in place, they keep pushing the market in the direction it's going, perhaps far beyond what the fundamentals would dictate.

When a currency pair has broken through important technical levels, it's also going to attract breakout traders — speculators who focus on jumping in on breaks of key price levels, looking to get in on the move for an easy trade. (But nothing is ever quite that easy, and breakout traders can suffer when the breaks are false and the ranges survive.) The additional interest entering the market in the direction of the move again propels the price farther and faster than it may ordinarily go.

Having a sense of where a currency pair stands from a technical perspective is always important, even if you're not basing your trades on technical analysis.

The technical-theme phenomenon also stems from several real-life considerations that all relate back to the relative level of currency prices.

- ✔ **Option interest:** The currency options market is massive and is one of the reasons that the spot currency market is as large as it is. Option-related hedging is one of the biggest sources of spot market activity outside short-term spot speculation. When spot prices have been trading in well-worn territory (a relatively narrow price range, for example), option interest tends to accumulate around the recent range. If the ranges are broken, sizeable option-related interest is frequently forced to come into the market and trade in the direction of the price breakout, either to unwind hedges or to cover new exposures created by the price break, and usually some combination of both. The amounts can be staggering, propelling the directional move in an extreme way.

- ✔ **Systematic models:** I look at so-called black box or algorithmic trading in Chapter 3. Algorithmic trading has dramatically increased in scale in recent years, with some estimates suggesting 30 to 35 percent of daily volume is from algorithmic systems. In many cases, systematic models trading decisions are generated based solely on price movements. They may be short a currency pair until a certain price level on the upside is traded, for example, which triggers a signal to exit the short and go long, no questions asked.

- ✔ **Hedgers:** Large-scale hedgers may be forced to come into the market if a rapid and unexpected price movement develops. Many firms identify an internal hedging rate for corporate and financial management purposes. As long as they're able to sell above or buy below that rate, they're looking good. If the market moves sharply on them, they may be forced to jump in on the direction of the move for fear of not ever seeing the internal hedging rate again.

Reality Check: Expectations versus Actual

When it comes to reacting to data reports and market events, the forex market typically displays two responses. The first reaction is a short-term price response to the data report or news itself, which is where most of the intraday fireworks in the forex market go off. The second reaction, usually more important in the bigger picture, comes in later trading, when the underlying themes (outlined earlier in this chapter) are updated to reflect the latest piece of news or data.

In one case, the data or news may be in line with the dominant themes of the moment, and the initial directional price reaction may be extended even further in subsequent trading action. The market may be anticipating lower U.S. interest rates, for example, and a weak U.S. consumer confidence report is released, sending the USD initially lower against other currencies. Because the weaker confidence reading supports the theme that the U.S. economy may be weakening, additional selling interest may materialize and lead to further price declines in the USD.

In other cases, the data report may fly in the face of the prevailing market themes, leading to an initial reaction in the opposite direction of the recent theme. The market may be trading on the theme that Eurozone interest rates are going higher and that the Eurozone economic outlook is improving. A subsequent Eurozone retail sales report may come in on the weak side, potentially leading to an initial market reaction that sees the euro weaken. Whether the euro's move lower will be sustained depends largely on what the market decides the latest retail sales report means in terms of the larger theme of stronger European growth and higher Eurozone interest rates.

The data report may have been influenced by bad weather keeping shoppers at home, for example, and may be interpreted as just a bump in the road on the way to higher Eurozone interest rates. In such a case, initial euro weakness may be short lived and eventually reverse course higher. On the other hand, the weak retail sales report may cause the market to reconsider that higher European Central Bank (ECB) rates are a sure thing and keep on selling euro.

Of course, there's never a set recipe for how data and news are ultimately going to be acted on by the market. The potential data and event outcomes and subsequent market reactions are myriad, to say the least. That's one reason the market reaction to the data is always more important than the data itself.

But as currency traders, we still have to understand what the data means to make sense of what the subsequent market response suggests for the bigger picture. The starting point is to understand the initial market response to the data/news in terms of what the market was expecting and what it actually got. We need a baseline from which to interpret subsequent price movements.

The role of consensus expectations

Data reports and news events don't happen in a vacuum. Forex markets evaluate incoming data reports relative to market forecasts, commonly referred to as *consensus expectations* or simply the *consensus*. Consensus expectations are the average of economic forecasts made by economists from the leading financial institutions, and private firms or academia. News agencies like

Bloomberg and Reuters survey economists for their estimates of upcoming data and collate the results. The resulting average forecast is what appears on market calendars, indicating what is expected for any given data report.

The consensus becomes the baseline against which incoming data will be evaluated by the market. In the case of economic data, the market will compare the *actual* result — the economic figure that's actually reported — with what was expected (the consensus). The actual data is typically interpreted by the market in the following terms:

- ✔ **As expected or in line with expectations:** The actual data report was at or very close to the consensus forecast.

- ✔ **Better than expected:** The report was generally stronger than the consensus forecast. For inflation reports, a better-than-expected reading means inflation was lower than expected, or more *benign.*

- ✔ **Worse than expected:** The data is weaker than the consensus forecast. For inflation reports, a worse-than-expected reading means inflation was higher than forecast, or more inflationary.

Additionally, the degree to which a data report is better or worse than expected is important. The farther off the mark the data report is, the greater the likelihood and degree of a subsequent price shift following the data release.

When evaluating central bank statements and comments from monetary policymakers, the market evaluates the language used in terms of *hawkish* (leaning toward raising interest rates) and *dovish* (leaning toward steady to lower interest rates). (I look at interpreting central bank rhetoric in greater detail in Chapter 5.)

Pricing in and pricing out forecasts

But financial markets don't typically wait for news to actually be released before they start trading on it, and the currency market is no different. Currency traders begin to price consensus expectations into the market anywhere from several days to several hours before a report is scheduled. *Pricing in* is the practice of trading as though the data were already released and, usually, as though it has come out as expected. The more significant the report, the sooner markets are likely to start pricing in expectations.

Unfortunately, there's no clear way to always tell whether or how much the market has priced in consensus expectations, so you need to follow market commentaries and price action in the hours and days before a scheduled report to get a sense of how much the market has priced in any forecast. And it's not always a case of the market pricing in an as-expected result. Market sentiment may have soured (or improved) in the run-up to the release, leading the market to price in a worse-than-expected (or better-than-expected) report. Stay on top of the market reports to get a handle on the mood.

Consensus estimates can also sometimes change in the days leading up to the report, based on other interim reports. For example, Institute for Supply Management (ISM) manufacturing forecasts may be downgraded (or upgraded) if the regional Chicago purchasing managers' index, which comes out a few days before the ISM index, is weaker (or stronger) than expected. This can lead to *pricing out* of consensus expectations, depending to what degree the consensus was priced in.

When good expectations go bad

Data miss is the market euphemism for when a data report comes in outside expectations. If the consensus was for an improvement in a particular indicator, and the actual report is worse than expected or disappointing, the result may be a sharp reversal in price direction. If core U.S. durable goods orders are expected to rise, for example, but they end up falling, we may be looking at a sharp drop in the USD. If the USD has gained prior to the release on the basis of pricing in the positive consensus, those who went long are going to be dumping their positions alongside traders selling the USD on the weak result. The same thing can happen in reverse if negative expectations are met by a surprisingly positive data report.

With as-expected data reports, it's frequently a case of "buy the rumor, sell the fact" (meaning, traders have already priced in a strong report, and if it meets expectations and sometimes even exceeds them, traders who bought in advance will be looking to take profit and sell on any subsequent gains). This market phenomenon can also happen in the other direction — as in "sell the rumor, buy the fact" — depending on the currency pair involved and the nature of the consensus forecast.

Anticipating alternative outcome scenarios

I've found that it frequently helps to think through the likely reactions to major data releases to prepare for how the market may react in the very likely case that the data surprises one way or the other. It's a thoroughly academic exercise, and it won't cost you anything, but it may just give you a significant leg up on the rest of the market, if you're inclined to trade around data reports. Considering various "what if" scenarios helps me focus my attention and my trading strategies on the major themes currently operative.

Anticipating and trading on market reactions

For major U.S. releases like the nonfarm payrolls (NFP) report, retail sales, or Federal Open Market Committee (FOMC) minutes, for example, I like to construct various concrete outcome scenarios in terms of pips. Using the NFP report as an example, let's say the consensus forecast is for an increase of 100,000 jobs. In the days prior to the release, the market will likely have gravitated to a level that reflects that consensus. Using that level as a pivot, I will establish my own expectations. For example, if the NFP number comes in at +125,000 jobs, I may expect EUR/USD to drop 30 pips. If the NFP registers +150,000 jobs, I may look for EUR/USD to drop 60 pips. Then I do the same for weaker-than-expected reports. If the number comes in at only +50,000 jobs, EUR/USD may rally 50 pips, and so on.

When the number actually comes out, and prices start to react, I've got a firm sense of where prices should move based on various data readings. The real trading information comes when prices don't react as I expected them to. For example, if the NFP number comes out at +180,000, (say I expected a 90-pip drop or so), and EUR/USD drops only 40 pips and begins to stabilize, I'm thinking there's something wrong with the market's reaction to the data and something else is going on. In many cases, I'm not alone — the rest of the market is likely drawing the same conclusion. The message is clear: Cover EUR/USD shorts, and start thinking about maybe even getting long. If EUR/USD trades back up through the pre-NFP price level within the next few hours (possibly minutes), it's a clear sign the market has other ideas about where EUR/USD should be, and it's a stronger signal to get long EUR/USD.

Getting a sense of how markets should react to data comes with experience, which you gain over time and by using a practice account. But you can also get a sense of how markets should react to data by studying past data outcomes and subsequent market reactions.

For example, if the market is expecting an increase in the upcoming U.S. ISM manufacturing index, I like to ask myself what's the likely reaction if the ISM disappoints those expectations, and also what happens if it surprises to the upside and is even stronger. This makes me focus on the most recent price action, and perhaps I note that the USD has declined slightly in advance of the report based on better Eurozone data overnight.

If the ISM comes in below expectations, I'm now thinking about how many pips lower the USD is likely to fall. I pinpoint key support levels and use those as my benchmarks to gauge the subsequent market reaction. If the report should surprise to the upside, I've also identified key resistance levels above that may come into play and where the next resistance levels are after them.

When the data does come out, I have a fairly rational baseline to judge the subsequent market reaction. If ISM rises as expected, I've identified which USD resistance levels may be tested. If they're not being tested, I'm starting to think that maybe the market is more intent on buying EUR than buying the greenback, and it may not be wise to fight the near-term trend. If the ISM surprises on the weak side, I've also identified downside USD support levels (EUR/USD resistance levels), breaks of which may see further USD weakness/ EUR strength.

Think ahead about what the market is expecting based on consensus expectations and how much has been priced in. Be prepared to factor various data outcomes in the larger themes you've already identified. Think through how the market is likely to react based on those scenarios, and you're likely to be several steps ahead of the crowd. (See the "Anticipating and trading on market reactions" sidebar for a real-world look at how I prepare for market reactions to data and events.)

Chapter 7

Getting Down and Dirty with Fundamental Data

*F*undamental economic data reports are among the most significant information inputs because policy makers and market participants alike use them to gauge the state of the economy, set monetary policy, and make investment decisions. From a trader's perspective, data reports are the routine catalysts that stir up markets and get things moving.

I run through a lot of economic information in this chapter, but you don't need to understand it like an economist — you're mainly interested in what it means for the market reaction. (If you are interested in understanding data like an economist, I recommend reading *The Secrets of Economic Indicators: Hidden Clues to Future Economic Trends and Investment Opportunities,* 2nd Edition, by Bernard Baumohl.)

As I noted in Chapter 6, the significance of individual reports varies depending on the economic environment, the market's current focus, and a host of other factors. Always keep in mind that markets interpret incoming data based on what it means for the big picture outlook. If a country's economic outlook is generally viewed as promising, data pointing to stronger growth will reinforce that view, while data that disappoints may suggest a more negative reaction. Most important, the market's reaction to data is more important than the data itself.

In the first half of this chapter, I look at how to absorb the various data reports and factor them into a broader view of the economic outlook for each particular country, with its attendant implications for interest rates and currency values. In the second half of this chapter, I run through the major data reports to give you an idea of what they cover and how the market interprets them.

Finding the Data

Before you can start processing all the economic data, you need to know where to find it. In Chapter 6, I look in greater detail at where to find data info, but here's a quick overview.

The starting point is the economic calendars typically provided by online forex brokerages. Be aware that not all calendars are as comprehensive as others, so be sure to look for calendars that show events and speakers and not just data. Also, look for a broker that provides data and event previews, and real-time data and market analysis; this type of commentary will help you get a sense of what the market is expecting, how it may be positioned for the news, and how it's likely to react.

Cable TV business channels such as Bloomberg TV, CNBC, and Fox Business News typically carry U.S. data releases live on air, and they're probably your best bet for seeing U.S. data immediately. In my opinion, Bloomberg TV does the best job of covering non-U.S. data releases, and CNBC World is another option.

In addition, www.bloomberg.com, www.marketwatch.com, and www.reuters.com provide excellent data coverage, both before and after it's released, along with event calendars. Read the economic data news stories on these sites to get the inside story of the data reports, such as any subcomponent readings or significant revisions.

Also, many calendars may include some designations of market significance for each data series, like some are *high impact* or *low impact*. Remember it's the big picture that counts and even a so-called low impact report could have a big impact if it's big enough of a surprise.

In the next section I sketch out a model for understanding where the types of data fit into the big picture. It should help you determine which categories of data are most significant, depending on the particular economic environment at any given time.

Economics 101 for Currency Traders: Making Sense of Economic Data

If you're like most people, you probably have a decent idea of what certain economic reports mean, like the unemployment rate or the consumer price index (CPI). But like lots of people, you probably don't have a strong idea of how to put the data together to make sense of it all. Having a fundamental model to put the data in perspective is critical to understanding what the data means and how the market is likely to react to the data. The sooner you're able to make sense of what a specific report means and factor it into the bigger picture, the sooner you'll be able to react in the market.

In the next few sections, I suggest a basic model to interpret the deluge of economic indicators you'll encounter in the forex market. By no means is this model the be-all and end-all of economic theory, but I do think it's a solid framework on which to hang the economic indicators and see how they fit together.

The labor market

I place the employment picture first for the simple reason that jobs and job creation are the keys to the medium- and long-term economic outlook for any country or economic bloc. No matter what else is going on, always have a picture of the labor market in the back of your mind.

If jobs are being created, more wages are being paid, consumers are consuming more, and economic activity expands. If job growth is stagnant or weak, long-run economic growth will typically be constrained. Signs of broader economic growth will be seen as tentative or suspect unless job growth is also present. Both scenarios have major implications for interest rates moves and investment themes, which are key currency drivers.

From the currency-market point of view, labor-market strength is typically seen as a currency positive, because it indicates positive growth prospects going forward, along with the potential for higher interest rates based on stronger growth or wage-driven inflation. Needless to say, labor-market weakness is typically viewed as a currency negative.

The employment indicator that gets the most attention is the monthly U.S. non-farm payrolls (NFP) report. The NFP report triggers loads of attention and speculation for a few days before and after it's released, but then the market seems to stop talking about jobs. Keep an eye on the job-specific reports outlined in the "Other labor-market indicators" sidebar, later in this chapter.

To illustrate the importance that markets place on jobs, Figure 7-1 shows changes in U.S. private payrolls overlaid with the S&P 500 stock index. As you can see, major turning points in the stock market (but not necessarily the economy) are closely associated with peaks and troughs in job markets.

The consumer

If it weren't for the overarching importance of jobs to long-run economic growth, the consumer would certainly rank first in any model seeking to understand economic data. The economies of the major currencies are driven overwhelmingly by *personal consumption,* accounting for 60 to 70 percent or more of overall economic activity in developed economies.

Personal consumption (also known as *private consumption, personal spending,* and similar impersonal terms) refers to how people spend their money. In a nutshell, are they spending more, or are they spending less? Also, what's the outlook for their spending — to increase, decrease, or stay the same? If you want to gauge the short-run outlook of an economy, look no further than how the individual consumer is faring.

Figure 7-1:
Job market trends coincide very closely with stock market performance, which reflects the economic outlook (but not necessarily the current state of the economy), as seen in U.S. private payroll changes and the S&P 500.

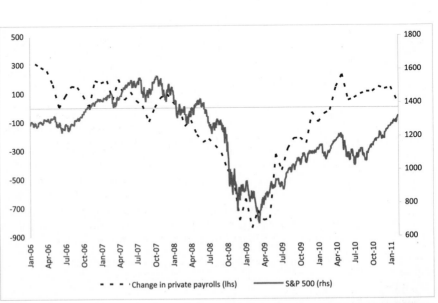

Source: Bloomberg, FOREX.com

The business sector

Businesses and firms make up the other third of overall economic activity after personal spending. (I'm leaving government out of my model to simplify matters.) Firms contribute directly to economic activity through *capital expenditures* (for example, building factories, stores, and offices; buying software and telecommunications equipment) and indirectly through growth (by hiring, meaning there's jobs again), expanding production, and producing investment opportunities.

Look at the data reports coming from the corporate sector for what they suggest about overall sentiment, capital spending, hiring, inventory management, and production going forward.

Keep in mind that the manufacturing and export sectors are more significant in many non-U.S. economies than they are in the United States. For instance, manufacturing activity in the United States accounts for only about 10 to 15 percent of overall activity versus shares of 30 to 40 percent and higher in other major-currency economies, such as Japan or Germany. So Japanese industrial production data tends to have a bigger impact on the yen than U.S. industrial production has on the dollar.

The structural

Structural indicators are data reports that cover the overall economic environment. Structural indicators frequently form the basis for currency trends and tend to be most important to medium- and long-term traders. The main structural reports focus on

- ✔ **Inflation:** Whether prices are rising or falling, and how fast. Inflation readings can be an important indicator for the direction of interest rates, which is a key determinant of currency values.

- ✔ **Growth:** Indicators of growth and overall economic activity, typically in the form of gross domestic product (GDP) reports. Structural growth reports tell you whether the economy is expanding or contracting, and how fast, which is another key input to monetary policy and the interest rate outlook. Growth forecasts from economists are important benchmarks for evaluating subsequent economic data on growth.

- ✔ **Trade balance:** Whether a country is importing more or less than it exports. The currency of a country with a *trade deficit* (the country imports more than it exports; the country loses from trade) tends to weaken because more of its currency is being sold to buy foreign goods (imports). A currency with a *trade surplus* (the country exports more than it imports; the country gains from trade) tends to appreciate because more of it is being bought to purchase that country's exports.

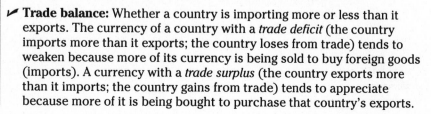

✔ **Fiscal balance:** The overall level of government borrowing and the market's perception of financial stability. Countries with high debt levels run the risks of a weakening currency if economic conditions take a turn for the worse and markets fear financial instability. Debts and deficits became a major theme for currency markets in the wake of the Great Financial Crisis of 2008–2009 (GFC), but they were always in the background.

Assessing Economic Data Reports from a Trading Perspective

The data that you find in economic textbooks is very neat and clean — but the data as it actually arrives in the market can be anything *but* neat and clean. I'm talking here not only about the imperfections of economic data gathering, but also about how markets interpret individual data reports.

In Chapter 6, I introduce the idea of consensus expectations as one of the keys to understanding how markets interpret economic news and data. In the following sections, I look at important data-reporting conventions and how they can also affect market reactions. When currencies don't react to the headlines of a data report as you would expect, odds are that one of the following elements is responsible, and you need to look more closely at the report to get the true picture.

Understanding and revising data history

Economic data reports don't originate in a vacuum — they have a history. Another popular market adage expressing this thought is "One report does not make a trend." However, that saying is mostly directed at data reports that come in far out of line with market estimates or vastly different from recent readings in the data series. To be sure, the market will react strongly when data comes in surprisingly better or worse than expected, but the sustainability of the reaction will vary greatly depending on the circumstances. If retail sales are generally increasing, for instance, does a one-month drop in retail sales indicate that the trend is over, or was it a one-off decline due to bad weather keeping shoppers at home?

When you're looking at upcoming economic data events, not only do you need to be aware of what's expected, but it also helps to know what, if any, trends are evident in the data series. The more pronounced or lengthy the trend is, the more likely the reactions to out-of-line economic reports will prove short lived. The more uneven the recent data has been, the more likely the reaction to the new data will be sustained.

The other important element to keep in mind when interpreting incoming economic data is to see whether the data from the prior period has been revised. Unfortunately, there is no rule preventing earlier economic data from being changed. It's just one of those odd facts of life in financial markets that what the market thought it knew one day (and actually traded for several weeks based on that understanding) can be substantially changed later.

When prior-period data is revised, the market will tend to net out the older, revised report with the newly released data, essentially looking at the two reports together for what they suggest about the data trend. For example, if a current report comes out worse than expected, and the prior report is revised lower as well, the two together are likely to be interpreted as more disappointing. If a current report comes out better than expected, but the prior period's revision is negative, the positive reaction to the current report will tend to be restrained by the downgrade to the earlier data.

As you can imagine, there are many different ways and degrees in which current/revised data scenarios can play out. A general rule is that the larger the revision to the prior report, the more significance it will carry into the interpretation of the current release. The key is to first be aware of prior-period revisions and to then view them relative to the incoming data. In general, current data reports tend to receive a higher weighting by the market if only because the data is the freshest available, and markets are always looking ahead.

Getting to the core

A number of important economic indicators are issued on a headline basis and a core basis. The *headline* reading is the complete result of the indicator, while the *core* reading is the headline reading minus certain categories or excluding certain items. Most inflation reports and measures of consumer spending use this convention.

In the case of inflation reports, many reporting agencies strip out or exclude highly volatile components, such as food and energy. In the United States, for instance, the consumer price index (CPI) is reported on a core basis excluding food and energy, commonly cited as *CPI ex-F&E*. (Whenever you see a data report "ex-something," it's short for "excluding" that something.) The rationale for ignoring those items is that they're prone to market, seasonal, or weather-related disruptions. For example, food prices may change rapidly due to drought, floods or unseasonably hot or cold weather. By excluding those items, the core reading is believed to paint a more accurate picture of structural, long-term price pressures, which is what concerns monetary policymakers the most.

Looking at consumer spending reports, the retail sales report in the United States is reported on a core basis excluding autos (retail sales ex-autos), which are heavily influenced by seasonal discounting and sales promotions, as well as being relatively large-ticket items in relation to other retail expenditures. The durable goods report is also issued on a core basis excluding transportation (durable goods ex-transportation), which mostly reflects aircraft sales, which are also highly variable on a month-to-month basis as well as extremely big-ticket items that can distort the overall data picture.

Markets tend to focus on the core reading over the headline reading in most cases, especially where a known preference for the core reading exists on the part of monetary-policy makers. The result can be large discrepancies between headline data and the core readings, such as headline retail sales falling 1 percent on a month-to-month basis but rising 0.5 percent on a core ex-autos basis. Needless to say, market reactions will be similarly disjointed, with an initial reaction based on the headline reading frequently followed by a different reaction to the core.

Market-Moving Economic Data Reports from the United States

Now let's get down to the nitty-gritty data. In this section, I run through the major economic data reports that come out of the United States. (I list the data reports according to the model I outlined earlier in this chapter.) My intention here is not necessarily to magnify the importance of U.S. economic data, even though the United States is the world's largest national economy and the U.S. dollar is on one side of 80 percent of currency trades.

Nope, my aim here is to kill two birds with one stone:

- ✔ Introduce you to the major economic reports issued by every major currency country, using U.S. data as the example
- ✔ Let you in on the finer points of how the market views the important data reports

At the end of this chapter, I take you through a country-by-country look at major non-U.S. data reports that don't fall into the main report categories or are too important to be ignored.

Labor-market reports

I put the job market at the top of my economic model because job creation/destruction is the single-most important driver of overall economic growth.

Every major economy issues updates on its labor market by reporting the number of jobs added/lost, the unemployment rate, or some variation of those. United States employment data holds special significance because it reflects on the world's largest economy and the primary global reserve currency. The following are the key U.S. employment reports.

U.S. monthly employment report

Typically released on the first Friday of each month and covering the prior month, the U.S. jobs report is considered among the timeliest of economic indicators. But it's also subject to large revisions to prior periods and significant statistical volatility. The main components of the report include:

- **Change in non-farm payrolls (NFP):** This is the big number everyone focuses on. The NFP change is derived from the *establishment survey* (because it's based on responses from companies), and shows the number of jobs gained or lost in the prior month. The going wisdom among economists is that the United States needs to add around 150,000 jobs each month just to offset population growth and keep the unemployment rate steady. The market's initial reaction is based on the difference between the actual and the forecast change in NFP. The prior two months' NFP changes are also revised, and those revisions will color the market's interpretation of the current report.

- **Unemployment rate:** Measures unemployed individuals seeking work as a percentage of the civilian labor force. The unemployment rate is derived from a separate survey (the *household survey* because it surveys real households), which also includes a jobs change number that may be at odds with the change in NFP. Increases in the unemployment rate are typically interpreted as a sign of weakness in the labor market and the economy overall, while declines in the rate are considered a positive sign for the job market and the overall economy.

- **Change in manufacturing payrolls:** Measures the number of jobs added or lost in manufacturing industries and is looked at as a gauge of near-term production activity.

- **Average hourly earnings:** Measures the change in employee wages and is looked as an indicator of whether incomes are rising or falling and the implications for consumer spending.

- **Average weekly hours:** Measures the average number of hours worked each week and is looked at as a rough gauge of the demand for labor, with increasing weekly hours seen as a positive for the labor market.

ADP national employment report

The ADP national employment report is put together by the payroll processing company of the same name (www.adp.com) and comes out on Wednesdays at 8:15 a.m. ET, two days before the government's NFP report (see the preceding section). ADP measures only private jobs and excludes government hiring. The ADP report is intended to serve as an alternative measurement of the labor market, but it's got a spotty track record of predicting the NFP with any accuracy. Because of that uncertainty, market reaction to the ADP is typically minor and short-lived, but economists may adjust their forecasts for the NFP depending on what the ADP indicates.

Weekly initial unemployment claims

Initial jobless claims are reported every Thursday at 8:30 a.m. ET for the week ending the prior Saturday and represent first-time filings for unemployment insurance. Initial claims are looked at as interim updates on the overall labor market between monthly NFP reports. The changes in initial claims can be volatile on a week-to-week basis — there are a fair number of hiccups caused by weather, strikes, and seasonal labor patterns — so analysts look at a four-week moving average of initial claims to factor out one-off events. Still, sharp increases or declines in initial claims data will get the market's attention, producing a market reaction on their own, as well as causing estimates of upcoming monthly NFP reports to be downgraded or upgraded.

A second part of the weekly claims report is *continuing claims,* which is a measure of the total number of people receiving unemployment benefits, excluding first-time filers. The market looks at continuing claims as another gauge of labor-market conditions. Increases in continuing claims typically suggest deterioration in the job market, because unemployed individuals are finding it difficult to get work and staying on unemployment insurance longer. Declines in continuing claims are similarly viewed as an improvement in the job market, because workers are presumably finding jobs more easily.

Other labor-market indicators

On top of the reports listed in the "Labor-market reports" section of this chapter, a number of other employment indicators come out inside other economic reports. These employment measures don't trigger market reactions in their own right, but they're used to update the overall understanding of the employment outlook. These include

✔ **Consumer confidence index (CCI):** Within the monthly consumer confidence report by the Conference Board (www.conference-board.org), respondents are asked whether "jobs are hard to get" and also whether "jobs are plentiful." The difference between the two is known as the *labor differential* and serves as another barometer of conditions in labor-markets.

✔ **Institute for Supply Management (ISM) employment indices:** The national ISM purchasing manager indices contain a subcategory asking managers to rate the employment situation at their companies, with responses over 50 indicating plans to hire and expand, and readings below 50 indicating contraction.

✔ **Regional Federal Reserve indices:** Surveys of manufacturing businesses, like the Philadelphia Fed survey, also include questions on the outlook for hiring. Readings above zero indicate plans to add employees; levels below zero suggest layoffs ahead.

Consumer-level data reports

Personal consumption accounts for two-thirds or more of most developed nations' economies, so how consumers are doing has a big impact on the economic outlook and the direction of interest rates, which are both key drivers of forex rates. Here are the main U.S. data reports focusing on personal consumption.

Consumer sentiment

Consumer psychology is at the heart of the market's attempts to interpret future consumer activity and, with it, the overall direction of the economy. The theory is that if you feel good, you'll spend more, and if you feel uncertain, you'll cut back spending. The market likes to pay attention to consumer confidence indicators even though there is little correlation between how consumers tell you they feel and how they'll actually go on to spend.

In fact, consumer sentiment is frequently the result of changes in gasoline prices, how the stock market is faring, or what recent employment indicators suggested. More reliable indicators of consumer spending are money-in-the-pocket gauges like average weekly earnings, personal income and spending, and retail sales reports. Still, the market likes to react to the main sentiment gauges, if only in the short run, with improving sentiment generally supporting the domestic currency and softer sentiment hurting it. The key confidence gauges are

- ✔ **Consumer confidence index:** A monthly report issued by the Conference Board comprised of the expectations index (looking six months ahead) and the present-situation index. The surveys ask households about their outlooks for overall economic conditions, employment, and incomes.

- ✔ **University of Michigan consumer sentiment index:** Comes out twice a month: a preliminary reading in the middle of the month and a final reading at the start of the next month.

- ✔ **ABC Consumer Confidence:** A weekly consumer-sentiment report issued each Tuesday evening. The weekly ABC confidence report can be used to update your expectations of upcoming monthly consumer confidence and University of Michigan reports.

If market forecasts envision an increase in the Michigan or Conference Board's consumer confidence index, for example, but the prior two or three weeks of the ABC survey suggest confidence is waning, you've got a pretty good indication that the monthly surveys may disappoint.

Personal income and personal spending

These two monthly reports always come out together and provide as close an indication as we can get of how much money is going into and out of consumers' pockets. The market looks at these reports to get an update on the health of the U.S. consumer and the outlook for personal consumption going forward. *Personal income* includes all wages and salaries, along with transfer payments (such as Social Security or unemployment insurance) and dividends. *Personal spending* is based on personal consumption expenditures for all types of individual outlays.

Personal income is watched as a leading indicator of personal spending on the basis that future spending is highly correlated with income. The greater the increases in personal income, the more optimistic the consumption outlook will be, and vice versa. But it's important to note that inflation-adjusted incomes are the key. If incomes are just keeping pace with inflation, the outlook for spending is less positive.

Retail sales

The monthly advance retail sales report is the primary indicator of personal spending in the United States, covering most every purchase Americans make, from gas-station fill-ups to dinner and a movie. Retail sales are reported on a headline basis as well as on a core basis (which excludes automobile purchases). The market focuses mainly on the core number to get a handle on how the consumer is behaving, but substantial strength or weakness in the auto industry doesn't go unnoticed. The advance retail sales report is a preliminary estimate based on survey samples and can be revised substantially based on later data.

Retail sales reports are subject to a variety of distorting effects, most commonly from weather. Stretches of bad weather, such as major storms or bouts of unseasonable cold or heat, can impair consumer mobility or alter shopping patterns, reducing retail sales in the affected period. Sharp swings in gasoline prices can also create illusory effects, such as price spikes leading to an apparent increase in retail sales due to the higher per-gallon price, while overall non-gas retail sales are reduced or displaced by the higher outlays at the pump.

Durable goods orders

Durable goods orders are another major monthly indicator of consumption, both by individuals and businesses. Durable goods measure the amount of orders received by manufacturers that produce items made to last at least three years. As a data series, durable goods is one of the most volatile of them all, with multiple percentage swings (as opposed to 0.1 percent or 0.3 percent changes) between months a norm rather than an exception. Durable goods are reported on a headline basis and on a core basis, excluding transportation, or ex-transportation (mostly aircraft).

Durables are generally bigger-ticket purchases, such as washing machines and furniture, so they're also looked at as a leading indicator of overall consumer spending. If consumers are feeling flush with cash and confidence, big-ticket spending is more common. If consumers are uncertain, or times are tight, high-cost purchases are the first to be postponed. Also, businesses tend to concentrate their spending in the final month of each quarter, which can distort prior months and exaggerate the last.

Housing-market indicators

The real estate or housing market is a major factor behind consumer spending since homes typically represent the largest asset on a household's balance sheet. Rising home prices are seen to support consumption through the *wealth effect* (the richer you feel, the more likely you are to spend), whereas falling house prices can be a major drag on personal spending. The U.S. real estate bubble burst in 2006–2007 and triggered the GFC and recession of 2008–2009, turning U.S. housing data into a major drag on U.S consumption, likely for many years still to come.

There's a raft of monthly housing market reports to monitor the sector, based on whether the homes are new or existing.

- ✔ **Existing-home sales** data is reported by the National Association of Realtors (NAR). Sales of preexisting homes (condos included) account for the lion's share of residential real-estate activity — about 85 percent of total home sales. Existing-home sales are reported on an annualized rate, and the market looks at the monthly change in that rate. Median home prices and the inventory of unsold homes are important clues to how the housing market is evolving. Existing-home sales are counted after a closing. Pending home sales are a separate report viewed as a leading indicator of existing-home sales. Pending home sales are counted when a contract is signed to buy an existing home.

- ✔ **New-home sales** are just that, brand-new homes and condos built for sale, reported on an annualized basis. New-home sales account for about 15 percent of residential home sales, but the sector was the fastest growing during the recent real-estate boom and has since seen activity decline steeply. New-home sales are counted when a contract is signed to purchase the new home, which means that contract cancellations (not reported) may result in lower actual sales than originally reported.

- ✔ **Housing starts** measure the number of new-home construction starts that took place in each month, reported on an annualized rate. Housing starts are considered a leading indicator of new-home sales but more recently have been looked at as an indication of home builder sentiment, as builders try to reduce inventories of unsold new homes.

- ✔ **Building permits** are the starting point of the whole new-housing cycle and are reported alongside housing starts each month. Building permits are required before construction can begin on new homes, so they're viewed as another leading indicator of housing starts and new-home sales.

Business-level data reports

Getting a handle on how businesses are faring is an important clue to the strength of the economy, which in turn drives the outlook for interest rates and the overall investment environment. The following series of data reports offer insights into how companies are responding at the enterprise level.

Institute for Supply Management and Purchasing Managers Index

The Institute for Supply Management (ISM) calculates several regional and national indices of current business conditions and future outlooks based on surveys of purchasing managers. ISM readings are based on a boom/bust scale, with 50 as the tipping point — a reading above 50 indicates expansion, whereas a reading below 50 signals contraction.

The main ISM reports to keep an eye on are

- ✔ **Chicago Purchasing Managers Index (PMI):** The Chicago PMI remains the key regional manufacturing activity index because the Chicago area and the Midwest region are still significant hubs of manufacturing activity in the United States. The Chicago PMI is also the first of the national PMIs to be reported, and the market frequently views it as a leading indicator of the larger national ISM manufacturing report, which is typically released a day after the Chicago PMI.

- ✔ **ISM manufacturing report:** The ISM manufacturing report is the monthly national survey of manufacturing activity and is one of the key indicators of the overall manufacturing sector. The ISM manufacturing report also includes a prices-paid index, which is viewed as an interim inflation reading, along with other key subsector measurements, like the employment situation. The market tends to react pretty strongly to sharp changes in the report or if the ISM is moving above or below 50, but keep in mind that the manufacturing sector accounts for a relatively small portion of overall U.S. economic activity, so the importance of the ISM manufacturing gauge tends to be exaggerated.

- ✔ **ISM nonmanufacturing report:** The ISM nonmanufacturing report is the monthly ISM report that covers the other 80 percent of the U.S. economy, namely the service sector. The ISM manufacturing report may get more attention, but the ISM non-manufacturing report is the one to focus on.

Regional Federal Reserve indices

A number of the Federal Reserve district banks issue monthly surveys of business sentiment in their regions, usually concentrated on the manufacturing sector. The regional Fed indices are looked at on their own as well as for what they suggest about subsequent national sentiment surveys, like the ISM index. The main index reading is a subjective response on general business conditions, with responses above zero indicating that conditions are improving and readings below zero indicating deterioration. The main regional Fed indices to watch are

✓ **Philadelphia Fed index:** Usually the first of the major Fed indices to be reported each month, covering the manufacturing sector in Pennsylvania, New Jersey, and Delaware. The Philly Fed index includes subindices focusing on new orders, employment, inventories and prices, among others.

✓ **New York Empire State index:** Assesses New York state manufacturers' current and six-month outlooks.

✓ **Richmond Fed manufacturing index:** A composite index based on new orders, production, and employment, covering the Middle Atlantic states.

Industrial production and capacity utilization

Industrial production measures the amount of output generated by the nation's factories, mines, and utilities on a monthly basis and is viewed as an indication of changes in the broader economy. The manufacturing sector is still viewed as a leading indicator for overall business cycles, so changes here could signal a larger swing in the economic outlook. The capacity utilization report measures actual output versus a theoretical maximum capacity and is looked at for what it suggests about inflationary pressures. High levels of capacity utilization above 80 percent may indicate price pressures are building and send a warning sign to policymakers. Lower levels of capacity utilization may signal the absence of inflationary pressures and allow monetary policymakers to keep interest rates lower.

The Fed's Beige Book

The Beige Book, named for the color of its cover, is a compilation of regional economic assessments from the Fed's 12 district banks, issued about two weeks before every Federal Open Market Committee (FOMC) policy-setting meeting. The regional Fed banks develop their summaries based on surveys and anecdotal reporting of local business leaders and economists, and the report is then summarized by one of the Fed district banks, all of which take turns issuing the report. The Beige Book is designed to serve as the basis of economic discussions at the upcoming FOMC meeting.

Markets look at the Beige Book's main findings to get a handle on how the economy is developing as well as what issues the FOMC might focus on. A typical Beige Book report may include generalized observations along the following lines: Most districts reported retail sales activity that was steady or moderately expanding; a few districts reported declines in manufacturing activity; some districts noted increased labor-market tightness and rising wage demands; all districts noted a sharp slowing in real-estate activity.

The key for the market is to assess the main themes of the report, such as:

- ✓ Is the economy expanding or contracting? How fast, and how widespread?

- ✓ Which sectors are strongest, and which sectors are weakest?

- ✓ Are there any signs of inflation?

- ✓ How does the labor market look?

The Beige Book is released in the afternoon (New York time), when liquidity is thinner, so it can generate a larger-than-normal response if its tone or conclusions are significantly different from what markets had been expecting.

Structural data reports

Structural data reports are the big picture, macroeconomic data that depict the longer-term economic outlook. What is the structure of the economy? Is it growing or contracting? If so, how fast? Is inflation under control or are prices rising too fast? Is the economy gaining or losing from trade? These reports can be some of the most significant drivers of central bank monetary policy.

Inflation gauges

Inflation reports are used to monitor overall changes in price levels of goods and services and as key inputs into setting interest rate expectations. Increases in inflation are likely to be met with higher interest rates by central-bank policy makers seeking to stamp out inflation, while moderating or declining inflation readings suggest generally lower interest-rate expectations.

There are a number of different inflation reports, with each focused on a different source of inflation or stage of the economy where the price changes are appearing. In the United States and other countries, inflation reports come out on a headline (total) basis and a core basis (which excludes food and energy to minimize distortions from these volatile inputs). Inflation indexes report changes on a month-to-month basis (abbreviated MoM, for month-over-month) to monitor short-term changes, as well as changes over the prior year's levels (YoY, for year-over-year) to gauge the longer-term rate of inflation. The main inflation reports to keep an eye on are

- ✓ **Consumer price index (CPI):** The CPI is what most people are familiar with when they think of inflation. The CPI measures the cost of a basket of goods and services at the consumer or retail level — the prices that we're paying. The CPI is looked at as the final stage of inflation.

- ✓ **Producer price index (PPI):** The PPI measures the change in prices at the producer or wholesale level, or what firms are charging one another for goods and services. The PPI looks at upstream inflation by stage of processing and may serve as a leading indicator of overall inflation.

✔ **Personal consumption expenditure (PCE):** The PCE is roughly equivalent to the CPI in that it measures the changes in price of a basket of goods and services at the consumer level. But the PCE has the distinction of being preferred by the Federal Reserve as its main inflation gauge because the composition of items in the PCE basket changes more frequently than in CPI, reflecting evolving consumer tastes and behavior. If the Fed thinks the more-dynamic basket is the one to watch, who am I to disagree? When the Fed refers to an inflation target or tolerable level of inflation, it's typically referring to core PCE readings.

✔ **Institute for Supply Management (ISM) prices paid index:** The national and regional purchasing managers indices have subcategories reporting on the level of prices paid and the level of prices received by firms. The prices-paid component usually gets the most attention as another producer-level indication of price pressures, likely to be mirrored by the PPI.

Gross domestic product

Gross domestic product (GDP) measures the total amount of economic activity in an economy over a specified period, usually quarterly and adjusted for inflation. The percentage change in GDP from one period to the next is looked at as the primary growth rate of an economy. If GDP in the first quarter of a year is reported as +0.5 percent, it means the economy expanded by 0.5 percent in the first quarter relative to the prior fourth quarter's output. GDP is frequently calculated on a quarterly basis but reported in *annualized* terms. That means a 0.5 percent quarterly GDP increase would be reported as a 2 percent annualized rate of growth for the quarter (0.5 percent × 4 quarters = 2 percent). The use of annualized rates is helpful for comparing relative growth among economies.

In most countries, GDP is reported on a quarterly basis, so it's taken as a big-picture reality check on overall economic growth. The market's economic outlook will be heavily influenced by what the GDP reports indicate. Better-than-expected growth may spur talk of the need for higher interest rates, while steady or slower GDP growth may suggest easier monetary policy ahead. At the same time, though, GDP reports cover a relatively distant economic past — a quarter's GDP report typically comes out almost midway through the next quarter and is looking back at economic activity three to four months ago. As a result, market expectations continue to evolve based on incoming data reports, so don't get too caught up in GDP for too long after its initial release.

Trade and current account balances

Two of the most important reports for the forex markets, because there are direct and potentially long-term currency implications, are trade and current account balances:

✔ **Trade balance** measures the difference between a nation's exports and its imports. If a nation imports more than it exports, it's said to have a *trade deficit;* if a nation exports more than it imports, it's said to have a *trade surplus.* Trade balances are reported on a monthly basis; prior periods are subject to revision.

✔ **Current account balance** is a broader measure of international trade, and includes financial transfers as well as trade in goods and services. Current accounts are also either in deficit or surplus, reflecting whether a country is a net borrower or lender to the rest of the world. Nations with current account deficits are net borrowers from the rest of the world, and those with current account surpluses are net lenders to the world. Current account reports are issued quarterly, and because the monthly trade balance comprises the bulk of the current account balance, markets tend to have a good handle on what to expect in current account data.

Countries with persistently large trade or current account deficits tend to see their currencies weaken relative to other currencies, whereas currencies of countries running trade surpluses tend to appreciate. The basic idea is that the currency of a deficit nation is in less demand (it's being sold to buy more foreign goods) than the currency of a surplus nation (it's being bought to pay for domestically produced goods).

For example, the U.S. dollar was under pressure for several years before the GFC, owing to its widening (increasing) trade and current account deficits. In late 2006, however, the size of the deficit stopped increasing, which removed some of the pressure on the dollar. But because the deficit remains high in absolute and historical terms, the U.S. trade deficit is still a major U.S. dollar negative.

Government debt and budget deficits

The aftermath of the GFC has exposed high debt and deficit levels in many major economies, especially in the United States, Europe, the UK, and Japan. Fears of a debt *restructuring* (where terms of a bond are altered) or default can seriously undermine confidence in a national currency, leading to an extended bout of weakness, as was seen with the euro in the 2010 European debt crisis.

There's no single data release that adequately covers the debt situations in major economies, though most national governments typically release a monthly budget statement. Instead, monitoring the debt/deficit picture of key countries depends on a series of news and data flows:

✔ **Budget and deficit forecasts:** Issued by individual governments and the IMF, these are the best way to stay on top of evolving fiscal changes.

✔ **Government bond yields, spreads, and CDS (credit default swaps):** As investors' fears increase over the creditworthiness of governments, they sell those countries' bonds, driving yields higher. *Yield spreads* are another measure of risk, noting the difference between the yields of an embattled nation and a safer alternative. Credit default swaps are a form of insurance that pays investors in the event of a default — the higher they are, the greater the perceived risk.

✔ **Government debt auctions:** When governments seek to borrow in capital markets, lack of demand or too high a price can shut them out and possibly trigger a default. Watch for indicators of demand, like the *bid/cover ratio,* which measures the amount of bids submitted relative to the issuance amount (the higher the better) and pricing (the higher the yield demanded, the greater the risk).

✔ **Sovereign credit ratings:** Major credit rating agencies, like Moody's S&P and Fitch, may announce periodic credit reviews of sovereign debt, possibly suggesting a downgrade. Actual credit rating downgrades can send investors fleeing, driving up a country's borrowing costs and increasing the risks of default.

Major International Data Reports

In the preceding sections, I cover the main economic reports using U.S. data as the basis for explaining what each report measures and how the market views them. The main data reports of other major national economies essentially mirror the U.S. data reports, but with some minor differences in calculation methods or reporting. In other words, the CPI report out of the United Kingdom is looked at the same way as the CPI report is viewed in the United States — as a measure of consumer-level inflation.

But plenty of national data reports don't have an equivalent in the United States, and others are followed more closely in local markets and require extra attention. In the next few sections, I highlight the main data reports of other national economies beyond what I cover earlier.

Eurozone

The main data reports out of the Eurozone are remarkably similar to those of the United States. The key difference is that individual European countries report national economic data, which comes out alongside Eurozone-wide reports from Eurostat or the European Central Bank (ECB).

Because the Eurozone has a common currency and central bank, the forex market focuses primarily on indicators that cover the entire region, such as Eurozone industrial production and CPI, for example. Among individual national reports, the market concentrates on data from the largest Eurozone economies, mainly Germany and France. Keep an eye on all the major reports coming out of those countries. They can generate sizeable reactions based on the idea that they're leading indicators of Eurozone-wide data. If German industrial production slumps, for instance, it may suggest that overall Eurozone industrial production is set to decline, too.

The only European reports that may escape your attention due to unusual names are the principal European confidence indicators. These reports can generate sizeable reactions depending how they compare to forecasts:

- **ZEW survey:** This survey measures growth expectations over the next six months by institutional investors and analysts. The survey is done for Germany and the whole Eurozone.

- **IFO and GfK surveys:** IFO is a corporate sentiment survey that queries businesses across Germany on current sentiment and how business is expected to develop over the next six months. The GfK survey is a monthly measure of consumer confidence

- **Purchasing Manager Indexes (PMIs):** A data firm called Markit produces monthly PMIs for the manufacturing and service sectors for Germany, France, and the whole Eurozone, similar to the Chicago PMI in the United States. The reports come out on a preliminary and final basis.

- **Eurozone Confidence:** The European Commission (EC) produces monthly confidence surveys for a variety of sectors: consumer, services, industrial, and overall economic sentiment.

Japan

When looking at Japanese data, keep in mind that the Japanese economy is still heavily export oriented. In addition to following all the usual reports, pay special attention to industrial production and manufacturing data because of their large role in the economy. Outside the standard reports to watch, keep an eye on the following:

- **Tankan index:** The Tankan survey is a quarterly survey of business outlooks produced by the Bank of Japan (BOJ). The survey produces four readings — current conditions and future outlook from both large manufacturers and large non-manufacturers. The large all-industry capital expenditures survey is an important gauge of capital spending and is often the focus of the entire Tankan survey.

✓ **Trade balance:** Japan's monthly trade balance is nearly always in surplus. The size of that surplus carries indications for the health of the export sector as well as potential political repercussions against excessive JPY weakness when the trade surplus is seen to be too large.

✓ **All-industry and tertiary industry (services) indices:** Monthly sentiment gauges of industrial and service-sector firms.

United Kingdom

In addition to the usual major government-issued data reports, be alert for the following reports that can frequently trigger sharp reactions in GBP:

✓ **Bank of England (BOE) Minutes:** Released two weeks after each Monetary Policy Committee (MPC) meeting, they show the voting results for the most recent decision. Market expectations and GBP are frequently upended when the policy discussion or vote shows a split leaning in the direction of an interest rate change.

✓ **BOE Quarterly Inflation Report:** Though it only comes out quarterly, the BOE's forecasts for growth and inflation over the next two years can have a significant impact on the interest rate outlook and GBP.

✓ **Purchasing Manager Indexes (PMIs):** A data firm called Markit produces monthly PMIs for the manufacturing, construction, and service sectors.

✓ **GfK consumer confidence and Nationwide consumer confidence:** Two separate, monthly, consumer-sentiment gauges put out by GfK, a UK/European marketing agency, and the Nationwide Building Society, a UK mortgage lender.

✓ **CBI distributive trades survey and industrial trends survey:** Two monthly reports put out by the Confederation of British Industry, a private trade group. The distributive trades survey is a measure of retail and wholesale sales, and the industrial trends survey is a survey of manufacturers' current and future outlook.

✓ **British Retail Consortium (BRC) retail sales monitor and shop price index:** Two monthly reports put out by the British Retail Consortium, a private trade organization. The retail sales monitor is another measure of retail sales, and the shop price index measures inflation at the retail level.

Canada

Canadian data mirrors U.S. data in many respects, but here are a few other important Canadian indicators to watch:

✔ **International securities transactions:** Roughly the equivalent of the U.S. Treasury's TIC report (see "Trade and current account balances," earlier in this chapter), showing net investment flows into and out of Canada on a monthly basis. High inflows typically support the CAD, and outflows tend to hurt it.

✔ **Ivey Purchasing Manager index:** A key monthly gauge of Canadian business outlooks issued by the Richard Ivey School of Business. The report covers purchases, employment, inventories, deliveries, and prices.

Australia

Australian data reports exert a strong influence on Aussie, similar in many respects to how UK data affects the pound. In particular, keep an eye on

✔ **RBA rate decisions and RBA Minutes:** The RBA's statement following a rate decision, and the subsequent release of the minutes two weeks later, can drive interest rate expectations and AUD big time.

✔ **Westpac consumer confidence and National Australia Bank (NAB) business confidence:** Two separate monthly sentiment gauges put out by two of Australia's leading banks.

New Zealand

New Zealand data is similarly provocative for the Kiwi. In addition to the main data reports and Reserve Bank of New Zealand (RBNZ) statements, keep an eye on the following Kiwi-specific data:

✔ **NZ Card Spending:** This monthly report covers purchases using credit, debit, and store cards, and gives another view of retail sales.

✔ **ANZ Consumer Confidence:** This monthly survey of consumer sentiment is conducted by ANZ Bank.

China

In early 2011, China surpassed Japan as the world's second largest national economy after the United States. Chinese growth over the last decade has been nothing short of astronomical and played a major role in supporting the global recovery after the GFC. Data out of China has taken on increased prominence as a result, with global markets frequently reeling on weaker China data or surging on stronger reports.

TIP

European Central Bank press briefings

Unlike most central banks that simply issue a statement announcing an interest rate decision and an economic outlook, the European Central Bank (ECB) conducts a press briefing after each meeting of the Governing Council. The ECB president reads a statement that surveys the economic landscape and provides a future outlook. The most important element of the ECB statement is the inflation outlook because the ECB has only a single mandate — to maintain price stability, such as fight inflation. The ECB president then takes questions from the press and frequently addresses market expectations on ECB policy. His comments in the Q&A session can significantly alter market perceptions, potentially triggering sharp moves in the euro. The ECB may have held rates steady and indicated inflation risks are contained, for example, but if the ECB president suggests that inflation risks have shifted higher, markets may take it as a signal the ECB is prepared to tighten rates soon and the euro could strengthen.

The Chinese growth outlook affects global markets through a number of different channels. Stronger Chinese growth is good for global trade and tends to positively influence stock markets around the world. Chinese demand for commodities is also influenced by its growth trajectory, with consequent implications for individual commodity markets (China also recently surpassed the U.S. as the largest oil consumer) and commodity producing countries such as Australia and South Africa. As a result, financial markets around the world are increasingly driven by Chinese growth prospects.

In terms of economic reports, Chinese data that reflects growth are the most significant, and I would highlight the trade surplus, industrial production, manufacturing PMIs, and quarterly GDP as the keys. Chinese consumers are also increasingly seen to be key to developed nations' economic outlooks and signs of rising imports and gains in retail sales are viewed as supportive of global growth.

The Chinese still manage their currency and it's not accessible to individual traders. But Chinese data can have an impact far beyond its borders due to its newfound prominence in the global economy.

Chapter 8

Getting to Know the Major Currency Pairs

A little over half of all daily trading volume takes place in just four currency pairs, known as the *majors:* EUR/USD, USD/JPY, GBP/USD, and USD/CHF. These currency pairs are the most watched barometers of the overall forex market. When you hear about the dollar rising or falling, it's usually referring to the dollar against these other currencies.

Even though these four pairs are routinely grouped together as the major currency pairs, each currency pair represents an individual economic and political relationship. In this chapter, I look at the fundamental drivers of each currency pair to see what moves them. I also look at the market's quoting conventions and what they mean for margin-based trading.

Although it's important to understand *why* a currency rate moves, I think it's also essential to have an understanding of *how* different pairs' rates move. Most currency trading is very short-term in nature, typically from a few minutes to a few days. This makes understanding a currency pair's *price action* (how a currency pair's price moves in the very short term) a key component of any trading strategy.

When you're reading this chapter, keep in mind that my observations are not hard and fast rules. As far as I know, there are no hard and fast rules in any market, anywhere, any time. Think of them as rules of thumb that apply more often than not. When it comes to applying my insights to real-life trading, you'll have to evaluate the overall circumstances each time to see if my insights make sense. The idea is that with a baseline of currency pair behavior, you'll be in a better position to anticipate, interpret, and react to market developments.

The flip side of this coin is that there is information content when my insights don't hold water. If the market usually reacts to certain events in a regular fashion, but it's not this time, it's a clue that something else is at work (usually bigger). And that can be even more valuable trading information.

The Big Dollar: EUR/USD

EUR/USD is by far the most actively traded currency pair in the global forex market. Everyone and his brother, sister, and cousin trades EUR/USD. This will come as no surprise to anyone who has traded in the forex market, because if you have, more likely than not you traded EUR/USD at some point.

The same goes for the big banks. Every major trading desk has at least one, and probably several, EUR/USD traders. This is in contrast to less liquid currency pairs such as GBP/USD or AUD/USD, for which trading desks may not have a dedicated trader. All those EUR/USD traders add up to vast amounts of market interest, which increases overall trading liquidity.

Trading fundamentals of EUR/USD

EUR/USD is the currency pair that pits the U.S. dollar against the single currency of the Eurozone, the euro. The *Eurozone* refers to a grouping of countries in the European Union (EU) that in 1999 retired their own national currencies and adopted a unified single currency. Currently, 17 of the 27 E.U. member states have the euro as their official currency. Combined, the Eurozone constitutes a regional economic bloc roughly equal to the United States in both population and GDP.

The move to a single currency was the culmination of financial unification efforts by the founding members of the European Union. In adopting the single currency, the nations agreed to abide by fiscal policy constraints that limited the ratio of national budget deficits to gross domestic product (GDP), among other requirements. The nations also delegated monetary policy (setting interest rates) to the newly founded European Central Bank (ECB). The ECB has only one policy mandate — to maintain price stability; for example, prevent inflation.

For most of the first decade of its existence, the euro functioned well and became the second largest reserve currency after the USD. The limits on deficits, however, were never really enforced, and many countries ran deficits much higher than monetary union rules permitted. Only after the Great Financial Crisis of 2008–2009 (GFC), when recessions caused tax revenues to plunge and deficits to explode, did the extent of debt levels become apparent.

Most of the highly indebted countries lie on Europe's periphery, like Ireland and Greece, which were both forced to seek bailouts from the EU/IMF in 2010. As the euro begins it second decade, Eurozone nations, led by core members Germany and France, are seeking to establish a permanent crisis resolution mechanism to prevent highly indebted nations from defaulting and give them time to get their financial houses in order. The euro weakened as the debt drama played out, but the currency union held together despite fears of a break-up. High debt and deficit levels, and the impact to growth from economic austerity measures to reduce them, are likely to color the fortunes of the euro for years to come.

Trading EUR/USD by the numbers

Standard market convention is to quote EUR/USD in terms of the number of USD per EUR. For example, a EUR/USD rate of 1.3000 means that it takes $1.30 to buy €1.

EUR/USD trades inversely to the overall value of the USD, which means when EUR/USD goes up, the euro is getting stronger and the dollar weaker. When EUR/USD goes down, the euro is getting weaker and the dollar stronger. If you believed the U.S. dollar was going to move higher, you'd be looking to sell EUR/USD. If you thought the dollar was going to weaken, you'd be looking to buy EUR/USD.

EUR/USD has the euro as the base currency and the U.S. dollar as the secondary or counter currency. That means

- ✔ **EUR/USD is traded in amounts denominated in euros.** In online currency trading platforms, standard lot sizes are €100,000, and minilot sizes are €10,000.

- ✔ The pip value, or minimum price fluctuation, is denominated in USD.

- ✔ **Profit and loss accrues in USD.** For one standard lot position size, each pip is worth $10; for one minilot position size, each pip is worth $1.

- ✔ **Margin calculations in online trading platforms are typically based in USD.** At a EUR/USD rate of 1.3000, to trade a single minilot position worth €10,000, it'll take $260 in available margin (based on 50:1 leverage). That calculation will change over time, of course, based on the level of the EUR/USD exchange rate. A higher EUR/USD rate will require more USD in available margin collateral, and a lower EUR/USD rate will need less USD in margin.

Swimming in deep liquidity

Liquidity in EUR/USD is unmatched by other major currency pairs. This is most evident in the narrower trading spreads regularly available in EUR/USD. Normal market spreads are typically around 1.5 to 2.5 pips versus 3 to 4 pips in other major currency pairs. Tight spreads make EUR/USD a great choice for high-frequency trading.

In terms of concrete numbers, EUR/USD accounted for 28 percent of global daily trading volume, according to the 2010 Bank for International Settlements (BIS) survey of the foreign exchange markets. That's more than twice the volume of the next most liquid currency pair (USD/JPY).

Liquidity in EUR/USD is based on a variety of fundamental sources, such as

- ✔ **Global trade and asset allocation:** The Eurozone constitutes the second largest economic bloc after the United States. Not only does this create tremendous commercial trade flows, but it also makes Eurozone financial markets, and the euro, the destination for massive amounts of international investment flows.

- ✔ **Central bank credibility:** The ECB has established itself in the eyes of global investors as an effective institution in fighting inflation and maintaining currency stability.

- ✔ **Enhanced status as a reserve currency:** Central banks around the world hold foreign currency reserves to support their own currencies and improve market stability. After the USD, the euro is the second largest reserve currency, accounting for about a third of global FX reserves.

The euro also serves as the primary foil to the U.S. dollar when it comes to speculating on the overall direction of the U.S. dollar in response to U.S. news or economic data. If weak U.S. economic data is reported, traders are typically going to sell the dollar, which begs the question, "Against what?" The euro is the first choice for many, simply because it's there. It also helps that it's the most liquid alternative, allowing for easy entry and exit.

This is not to say that EUR/USD only reacts to U.S. economic data or news. On the contrary, Eurozone news and data can move EUR/USD as much as U.S. data moves the pair. But the overall tendency still favors U.S. data and news as the driving force of short-term price movements.

This situation is partly a function of geography and daily trading rhythms, because European data is released about four to eight hours before U.S. economic reports are typically issued. On any given day, traders will respond to European news and data and adjust prices accordingly for several hours until U.S. data is released.

Watching the data reports

Country-specific economic reports, such as Dutch retail sales or Italian industrial production, are increasingly disregarded by the forex market in favor of Eurozone aggregate economic data. However, German and French national economic reports can still register with markets as they represent the two largest Eurozone economies. I review the major economic reports and fundamental events in greater depth in Chapter 7, but here's a list of the major European data reports and events to keep an eye on.

✔ European Central Bank (ECB) interest rate decisions and press conferences.

✔ Speeches by ECB officials and individual European finance ministers.

✔ EU-harmonized Consumer Price Index (CPI), as well as national CPI and Producer Price Index (PPI) reports.

✔ EU Commission economic sector confidence indicators.

✔ Consumer and investor sentiment surveys separately issued by three private economic research firms known by their acronyms: Ifo, ZEW and GfK.

✔ Industrial production.

Trading behavior of EUR/USD

The deep liquidity and tight trading spreads in EUR/USD make the pair ideal for both shorter-term and longer-term traders. The price action behavior in EUR/USD regularly exhibits a number of traits that traders should be aware of.

Trading tick by tick

In normal market conditions, EUR/USD tends to trade tick by tick, as opposed to other currency pairs, which routinely display sharper short-term price movements of several pips. In trading terms, if EUR/USD is trading at 1.2910/12, there are going to be traders looking to sell at 13, 14, and 15 and higher, while buyers are waiting to buy at 9, 8, 7 and lower.

In contrast, other less-liquid currency pairs, like GBP/USD and USD/CHF, typically fluctuate in a far jumpier fashion, which is reflected by the wider price spread in those pairs.

Fewer price jumps and smaller price gaps

The depth of liquidity in EUR/USD also reduces the number of *price jumps* or *price gaps* in short-term trading. A price *jump* refers to a quick movement in prices over a relatively small distance (roughly 10 to 20 pips) in the course of normal trading. A price *gap* means prices have instantaneously adjusted over a larger price distance, typically in response to a news event or data release.

Don't get me wrong, price jumps/gaps do occur in EUR/USD, as anyone who has traded around data reports or other news events can attest. But price jumps/gaps in EUR/USD tend to be generated primarily by news/data releases and breaks of significant technical levels, events which can usually be identified in advance.

This is in contrast to other major currency pairs where short-term price gaps can develop from a one-off market flow, such as a portfolio manager selling a large amount of GBP/USD or a USD/CHF stop-loss order being triggered. When price gaps do occur in EUR/USD, they tend to be smaller relative to gaps in other pairs.

Backing and filling

When prices move rapidly in one direction, they tend to reach a short-term stopping point when opposite interest enters the market. For instance, let's say EUR/USD just traded higher from 1.2910/13 to 1.2922/25 in relatively orderly fashion, tick by tick over two minutes, meaning no price gaps. When the price move higher pauses, short-term traders who were long for the quick 12-pip move higher will look to exit and sell.

As selling interest begins to enter the market and prices stop rising, other not-so-fast longs will also start *hitting bids* (selling), pushing prices lower. From the other side, traders who missed the quick run up, or who were not as long as they wanted to be, will enter their buying interest in the market. Other buyers, sensing selling interest, may wait and place their buying interest at slightly lower levels. This back-and-forth consolidation after a short-term price movement is referred to as *backing and filling*. The price *backs up* and *fills* the short-term movement, though it can happen in both up and down price movements.

When it comes to EUR/USD price action, backing and filling is quite common and tends to be more substantial than in most currency pairs, meaning a greater amount of the directional move is retraced. Look at Figure 8-1 to get a visual idea of what backing and filling looks like. When EUR/USD is not backing and filling the way you would expect, it means the directional move is stronger and with greater interest behind it.

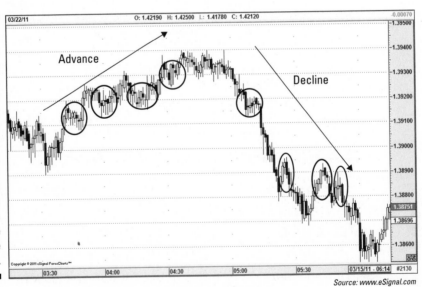

Figure 8-1:
A one-minute EUR/USD chart showing periods of backing and filling (circled areas) during a price advance and a price decline.

Advance

Decline

Source: www.eSignal.com

Prolonged tests of technical levels

When it comes to trading around technical support and resistance levels, EUR/USD can try the patience of even the most disciplined traders. I say this because EUR/USD can spend tens of minutes (an eternity in forex markets) or even several hours undergoing tests of technical levels. (See Chapter 11 for a primer on technical analysis.)

This goes back to the tremendous amount of interest and liquidity that defines the EUR/USD market. All those viewpoints come together in the form of market interest (bids and offers) when technical levels come into play. The result is a tremendous amount of market interest that has to be absorbed at technical levels, which can take time.

Looking at GBP/USD and USD/CHF as leading indicators

Given the tremendous two-way interest in EUR/USD, it can be very difficult to gauge whether a test of a technical level is going to lead to breakout or a rejection. To get an idea of whether a test of a technical level in EUR/USD is going to lead to a break, professional EUR/USD traders always keep an eye on GBP/USD and USD/CHF, as they tend to be leading indicators for the bigger EUR/USD and dollar moves in general.

If GBP/USD and USD/CHF are aggressively testing (trading at or through the technical level with very little pullback) similar technical levels to EUR/USD (for example, daily highs or equivalent trend-line resistance), then EUR/USD is likely to test that same level. If GBP/USD and USD/CHF break through their technical levels, the chances of EUR/USD following suit increases. By the same token, if GBP/USD and USD/CHF are not aggressively testing the key technical level, EUR/USD is likely to see its similar technical level hold.

GBP/USD and USD/CHF lead times can be anywhere from a few seconds or minutes to several hours and even days. Just make sure you're looking at the equivalent technical levels in each pair.

Tactical trading considerations in EUR/USD

I've looked at the major trading attributes of EUR/USD and now its time to look at how those elements translate into real-life trading tactics. After all, that's where the real money is made and lost.

Deciding whether it's a U.S. dollar move or a euro move

Earlier in this chapter, I note that EUR/USD routinely acts as the primary vehicle for forex markets to express their view on the USD. At the same time,

I also indicated that EUR/USD will also react to euro-centric news and data. So for traders approaching EUR/USD on any given day, it helps to understand whether the driving force at work is dollar-based or euro-based. Are they bearish on the USD, or are they bullish on the EUR? Or is it some combination of the two?

Having a sense of which currency is driving EUR/USD at any given moment is important so you can better adapt to incoming data and news. If it's a EUR-based move higher, for instance, and surprisingly positive USD news or data is released later in the day, guess what? You've got countertrend information hitting the market, which could spark a reversal lower in EUR/USD (in favor of the dollar). By the same token, if that U.S. data comes out weaker than expected, it's likely to spur further EUR/USD gains, because EUR-buying interest is now combined with USD-selling interest.

Being patient in EUR/USD

Earlier in this chapter I explore why EUR/USD can spend hours trading in relatively narrow ranges or testing technical levels. The key in such markets is to remain patient based on your directional view and your technical analysis. You should be able to identify short-term support that keeps an upside test alive or resistance that keeps a down-move going. If those levels fail, the move is stalling at the minimum and may even be reversing.

Taking advantage of backing and filling

Because EUR/USD tends to retrace more of its short-term movements, you can usually enter a position in your desired direction by leaving an order to buy or sell at slightly better rates than current market prices may allow. If the post–08:30 ET U.S. data price action sees EUR/USD move lower, and you think getting short is the way to go, you can leave an offer slightly (roughly 5 to 10 pips) above the current market level and use it to get short, instead of reaching out and hitting the bid on a downtick.

If your order is executed, you've got your desired position at a better rate than if you went to market, and you're probably in a better position rhythm-wise with the market (having sold on an up-tick).

Allowing for a margin of error on technical levels

When it comes to determining whether EUR/USD has broken a technical level, I like to use a 10- to 15-pip margin of error. (Shorter-term traders may want to use a smaller margin of error.) Some very short-term traders and technical purists like to pinpoint an exact price level as support or resistance. If the market trades above or below their level, they'll call it a break and that's that. But the spot forex market rarely trades with such respect for technical levels to make such a clear and pinpointed distinction. And given the amount of interest in EUR/USD, it's especially prone to hazy technical lines in the sand.

The key point to take away from this is that all sorts of interest emerges around technical levels, and it's still going through the market even though the pinpointed level might have been breached. And this is where my margin of error comes in. Again, it's not a hard and fast rule, but generally speaking, EUR/USD will have chewed through most of the market interest around a technical level within about 10 to 15 points beyond the level.

East Meets West: USD/JPY

USD/JPY is one of the more challenging currency pairs among the majors, and trading in it requires a higher degree of discipline and patience. Where other currency pairs typically display routine market fluctuations and relatively steady, active trading interest, USD/JPY seems to have an on/off switch. It can spend hours and even days in relatively narrow ranges and then rapidly adjust to a new price level.

USD/JPY can offer some of the clearest trade setups among the major pairs. When you're right in USD/JPY, the returns can be astonishingly quick. When you're wrong in USD/JPY, you'll also know it pretty quickly. The key to developing a successful trading game plan in USD/JPY is to understand what drives the pair and the how price action behaves.

Trading fundamentals of USD/JPY

The Japanese yen is the third major international currency after the U.S. dollar and the European single currency, the euro. USD/JPY accounts for 14 percent of daily global trading volume, according to the 2010 BIS survey of foreign exchange markets. Japan stands as the third largest national economy after the United States and China in terms of GDP, and the JPY represents the third major currency group after the USD and the EUR groupings.

Trading USD/JPY by the numbers

Standard market convention is to quote USD/JPY in terms of the number of JPY per USD. For example, a USD/JPY rate of 85.30 means that it takes ¥85.30 to buy $1.

USD/JPY trades in the same direction as the overall value of the USD, and inversely to the value of the JPY. If the USD is strengthening and the JPY is weakening, the USD/JPY rate will move higher. If the USD is weakening and the JPY is strengthening, the USD/JPY rate will move lower.

USD/JPY has the U.S. dollar as the base currency and the JPY as the secondary or counter currency. This means:

- ✔ **USD/JPY is traded in amounts denominated in USD.** In online currency trading platforms, standard lot sizes are $100,000, and minilot sizes are $10,000.

- ✔ The pip value, or minimum price fluctuation, is denominated in JPY.

- ✔ **Profit and loss accrues in JPY.** For one standard lot position size, each pip is worth ¥1000; for one minilot position size, each pip is worth ¥100. To convert those amounts to USD, divide the JPY amount by the USD/JPY rate. Using 85.30 as the rate, ¥1,000 = $11.72 and ¥100 = $1.17

- ✔ **Margin calculations are typically calculated in USD.** So it's a straight-forward calculation using the leverage rate to see how much margin is required to hold a position in USD/JPY. At 50:1 leverage, $200 of available margin is needed to open a minilot position of 10,000 USD/JPY.

USD/JPY is heavily influenced by U.S. interest rates

If I had to identify the main driver of USD/JPY, it would easily be the movements in U.S. interest rates. The main reason for this is the massive amount of U.S. government debt held by the Japanese government and Japanese investors. The Bank of Japan (BOJ) alone holds nearly $900 billion worth of U.S. Treasury debt. If U.S. interest rates begin to fall, the prices of U.S. government bonds rise, increasing the USD-value of Japan's U.S. debt holdings. To offset, or hedge, their larger USD-long currency exposure, Japanese reserve managers need to sell more USD. This causes USD/JPY to closely track U.S. Treasury yields, as seen in Figure 8-2 which shows the USD/JPY rate and the yield on two-year U.S. Treasury notes on a monthly basis over ten years.

Long-term traders can take advantage of U.S. interest rate cycles via USD/JPY, buying the pair when U.S. rates are set to rise and selling when rates have peaked and begin to decline.

It's politically sensitive to trade

USD/JPY is the most politically sensitive currency pair among the majors. Japan remains a heavily export-oriented economy, accounting for more than 40 percent of overall economic activity. This means the JPY is a critical policy lever for Japanese officials to stimulate and manage the Japanese economy — and they aren't afraid to get involved in the market to keep the JPY from strengthening beyond desired levels.

A weak currency makes a nation's exports cheaper to foreigners and, all other things being equal, creates a competitive advantage to gain market share. On the flip side, a JPY that's too strong makes Japanese exports more expensive and may hurt the export sector and squeeze corporate profitability. That's one reason Japanese stock markets typically decline when the JPY strengthens sharply (USD/JPY lower).

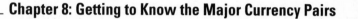

Figure 8-2:
USD/JPY
exchange
rate and
yields
on two-
year U.S.
Treasury
notes over
ten years on
a monthly
basis. USD/
JPY closely
follows the
track of U.S.
Treasury
yields due
to asset
manager
hedging
operations.

Source: Bloomberg, FOREX.com

The Ministry of Finance is routinely involved in the forex market

Currency intervention is usually a last resort for most major national governments. Instead, the Japanese Ministry of Finance (MOF) engages in routine
verbal intervention to influence the level of the JPY. The chief spokesman
on currencies is, of course, the Minister of Finance, but the Vice Finance
Minister for International Affairs is the more frequent commentator on forex
market developments.

As I mention earlier, the Japanese government has a history of intervening
to prevent excessive or run-away JPY strength, usually on a unilateral basis
(see Chapter 3 for more on official intervention). Typically, the JPY needs to
be appreciating quite substantially and quickly before intervention, and MOF
rhetoric will usually heat up in advance. The MOF orders intervention, and
the BOJ executes as the government's agent in the market. Most recently in
March 2011, in the wake of the earthquake/tsunami/nuclear disaster in Japan,
the Japanese government asked the G7 to support them in preventing further
JPY appreciation. The G7 agreed and undertook coordinated intervention
for the first time in more than a decade, weakening the JPY after it surged to
new all-time highs below 80.00 against the USD. The JPY had been gaining on
speculation Japanese insurers and investors would bring money home by
selling foreign assets and buying JPY, a process called *repatriation.*

As an alternative to direct market intervention, the MOF has been known to utilize covert intervention through sizeable market orders by the pension fund of the Japanese Postal Savings Bank, known as Kampo. This is sometimes referred to as semiofficial intervention in various market commentaries and can provide valuable trading information.

Japanese asset management trends

Due to historically high saving rates, Japanese asset managers and investors control trillions of dollars' worth of assets, mostly invested in bonds. With exceptionally low rates available in Japan, Japanese assets are frequently looking abroad for better yielding returns. When the risk environment is calm (see Chapter 5 for more on risk sentiment), they tend to be regular sellers of JPY against most other currencies. But if the risk environment deteriorates suddenly, those JPY are quickly bought back and JPY-crosses can collapse.

Japanese financial institutions also tend to pursue a highly collegial approach to investment strategies. The result for forex markets is that Japanese asset managers frequently pursue similar investment strategies at the same time, resulting in tremendous asset flows hitting the market over a relatively short period of time. This situation has important implications for USD/JPY price action (see the next section).

Important Japanese data reports

Keep in mind that government officials' (MOF) comments are quite frequent and can shift market sentiment and direction as much as, or more than, the fundamental data. The key data reports to focus on coming out of Japan are

- Bank of Japan policy decisions, monthly economic assessments, and Monetary Policy Committee (MPC) member speeches
- Tankan Report (a quarterly sentiment survey of Japanese firms by the BOJ — the key is often planned capital expenditures)
- Industrial production
- Machine orders
- Trade balance and current account
- All-Industry Index and Tertiary Industry (service sector) Index

Price action behavior of USD/JPY

Earlier in this chapter, I note that USD/JPY seems to have an on/off switch when compared to the other major currency pairs. Add to that the fact that USD/JPY liquidity can be similarly fickle. Sometimes, hundreds of millions of USD/JPY can be bought or sold without moving the market noticeably; other times, liquidity can be extremely scarce.

This phenomenon is particularly acute in USD/JPY owing to the large presence of Japanese asset managers. As I mentioned earlier, the Japanese investment community tends to move en masse into and out of positions. Of course, they're not the only ones involved in USD/JPY, but they do tend to play the fox while the rest of the market is busy playing the hounds.

Prone to short-term trends, followed by sideways consolidations

The result of this concentration of Japanese corporate interest is a strong tendency for USD/JPY to display short-term trends (several hours to several days) in price movements, as investors pile in on the prevailing directional move. This tendency is amplified by the use of standing market orders from Japanese asset managers.

For example, if a Japanese pension fund manager is looking to establish a long position in USD/JPY, he's likely to leave orders at several fixed levels below the current market to try to buy dollars on dips. If the current market is at 83.00, he may buy a piece of the total position there, but then leave orders to buy the remaining amounts at staggered levels below, such as 82.75, 82.50, 82.25, and 82.00. If other investors are of the same view, then they'll be bidding below the market as well.

If the market begins to move higher, the asset managers may become nervous that they won't be able to buy on weakness and raise their orders to higher levels, or buy at the market. Either way, buying interest is moving up with the price action, creating a potentially accelerating price movement. Any countertrend move is met by solid buying interest and quickly reversed.

Such price shifts tend to reach their conclusion when everyone is onboard — most of the buyers who wanted to buy are now long. At this point, no more fresh buying is coming into the market, and the directional move begins to stall and move sideways. The early buyers may be capping the market with profit-taking orders to sell above, while laggard buyers are still buying on dips. This leads to the development of a consolidation range, which can be as narrow as 40 to 50 pips.

Short-term traders can usually find trading opportunities in such consolidation ranges, but medium and longer-term traders may want to step back and wait for a breakout of the consolidation and a fresh directional movement.

Technical levels are critical in USD/JPY

So if you're a regular trader or investor and you don't work at a Japanese bank, how can you know where the orders are? Simple: Focus on the technical levels.

Perhaps no other currency pair is as beholden to technical support and resistance as USD/JPY. In large part, this has to do with the prevalence of substantial orders, where the order level is based on technical analysis. USD/JPY displays a number of other important trading characteristics when it comes to technical trading levels:

✔ **USD/JPY tends to respect technical levels with far fewer false breaks.** This situation is typically due to the presence of substantial order interest at the technical level. If trend-line analysis or daily price lows indicate major support at 82.20, for example, sizeable buying orders are likely to be located around there. The bank traders watching the order may buy in front of it, preventing the level from ever being touched, or tested. If the selling interest is not sufficient to fill the buying order, the level will hold. On the other hand, if the technical level is breached, it's a clear indication the selling interest is far greater and is likely to continue.

✔ **USD/JPY's price action are usually highly directional (one-way traffic) on breaks of technical support and resistance.** When technical support or resistance is overcome, price movements tend to be sharp and one-sided, with minimal pullbacks or backing and filling (prices coming back to test the breakout level). This situation is the result of strong market interest overcoming any standing orders, as well as likely stop-loss orders beyond the technical level.

Spike reversals (sharp — 20 to 50 pip — price movements in the opposite direction of the prior move) from technical levels are important signals. Spike reversals are evidence of a significant amount of market interest in the opposite direction and frequently define key highs and lows. They're also evidence that the directional move that was underway has probably ended. If the extreme point of the spike reversal is later exceeded, the prior directional move is likely resuming.

✔ **Japanese traders focus on Ichimoku levels and candlestick charts.** They're not alone as those approaches are increasingly popular with traders globally. Be aware of Ichimoku price levels for key support and resistance and if any prominent candlestick patterns are evident. (See Chapter 11 for more.)

✔ **Orders frequently define intraday highs and lows and reversal points.** Japanese institutional orders also tend to be left at round-number prices, such as 84.00, 84.25, 84.50, and so on. When you look at charts involving JPY, always note tops/bottoms close to round-number price levels because there could be significant orders there.

Tactical trading considerations in USD/JPY

Earlier, I note USD/JPY's tendency to either be active directionally or consolidating — the on/off switch. As such, I like to approach USD/JPY on a more strategic, hit-and-run basis — getting in when I think a directional move is happening and standing aside when I don't. I look for breaks of trend lines, Ichimoku levels, spike reversals and candlestick patterns, as my primary clues for spotting a potential directional move.

On the tactical level, USD/JPY is generally a cleaner trading market than most of the other majors, so I like to approach it with generally tighter trading rules. The idea is that if I'm right, I'll be along for the ride. But if I'm wrong, I jump off the bus at the next stop.

Actively trading trend-line and price-level breakouts

One of my trigger points for jumping into USD/JPY is breaks of trend lines and key price levels, such as hourly, daily or weekly highs/lows. I note earlier that it usually takes a significant amount of market interest to break key technical levels. I look at the actual breaks as concrete evidence of sizeable interest, rather than normal back-and-forth price action.

Jumping on spike reversals

After USD/JPY has seen a relatively quick (usually within two to three hours) move of more than 70 to 80 pips in one direction, I'm on alert for any sharp reversals in price. Spike reversals of 30 to 40 pips that occur in very short timeframes (5 to 20 minutes) are relatively common in USD/JPY. I look at them as an indication that the prior move has ended and it's now time to exit. Spike reversals are short-term phenomena and, if you can't be in front of your trading screen, using a 30 to 40 point trailing stop loss order is one way to guard against rapid reversals. Take a look at Figure 8-3 to see how spike reversals can frequently indicate significant turning points.

Figure 8-3:
Hourly USD/JPY chart highlighting spike reversals (circled areas). Quick 20 to 30 point reversals can be an important signal that a directional move has ended and may be reversing.

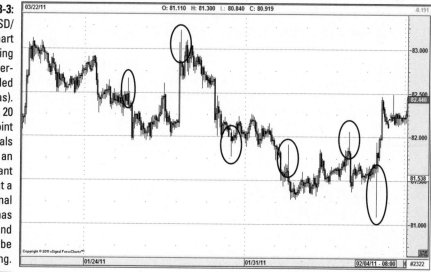

Source: www.eSignal.com

Monitoring EUR/JPY and other JPY crosses

USD/JPY is heavily influenced by cross flows and can frequently take a back seat to them on any given day. In evaluating USD/JPY, I always keep an eye on the JPY crosses and their technical levels as well. A break of important support in GBP/JPY, for instance, could unleash a flood of short-term USD/JPY selling, because GBP/JPY is mostly traded through the dollar pairs.

EUR/JPY is the most actively traded JPY cross and its movements routinely drive USD/JPY on an intraday basis. Be alert for when significant technical levels in the two pairs coincide, such as when both USD/JPY and EUR/JPY are testing a series of recent daily highs or lows. A break by either can easily spill into the other and provoke follow-through buying/selling in both.

The Other Majors: Sterling and Swissy

The other two major currency pairs are GBP/USD (affectionately known as sterling or cable) and USD/CHF (called Swissy by market traders). These two are counted as major currency pairs, but their trading volume and liquidity are significantly less than EUR/USD or USD/JPY. As a result, their trading characteristics have many elements in common. In this section, I look at their individual trading fundamentals separately and then discuss their trading behavior and tactical trading considerations together.

The British pound: GBP/USD

Trading in cable presents its own set of challenges, because the pair is prone to sharp price movements and seemingly chaotic price action. But it's exactly this type of price behavior that keeps the speculators coming back — when you're right, you'll know very quickly, and the short-term results can be significant. A good rule of thumb to remember comes from a former chief dealer of mine, a Brit no less: "The cable trader makes the most money and loses the most money."

Trading fundamentals of GBP/USD

The UK economy is the second largest national economy in Europe, after Germany, and the pound is heavily influenced by cross-border trade and mergers and acquisitions (M&A) activity between the United Kingdom and continental Europe. Upwards of two-thirds of UK foreign trade is conducted with EU member states, making the EUR/GBP cross one of the most important trade-driven cross rates.

The 2010 BIS survey of foreign exchange turnover showed that GBP/USD accounted for 9 percent of global daily trading volume, making cable the third most active pairing in the majors. But you may not believe that when you start trading cable, where liquidity seems always to be at a premium. Relatively lower liquidity is most evident in the wider bid-offer spreads, which are usually 3 to 5 pips compared to 2 to 3 pips in EUR/USD and USD/JPY.

Trading sterling by the numbers

GBP/USD is quoted in terms of the number of dollars it takes to buy a pound, so a rate of 1.5515 means it costs $1.5515 to buy £1. The GBP is the primary currency in the pair and the USD is the secondary currency. That means

- ✔ **GBP/USD is traded in amounts denominated in GBP.** In online currency trading platforms, standard lot sizes are £100,000, and minilot sizes are £10,000.

- ✔ The pip value, or minimum price fluctuation, is denominated in USD.

- ✔ **Profit and loss accrues in USD.** For one standard lot position size, each pip is worth $10; for one minilot position size, each pip is worth $1.

- ✔ **Margin calculations are typically calculated in USD in online trading platforms.** Because of its high relative value to the USD, trading in GBP pairs requires the greatest amount of margin on a per-lot basis. At a GBP/USD rate of 1.5500, to trade a one minilot position worth £10,000, it'll take $310 in available margin (based on 50:1 leverage). That calculation will change over time, of course, based on the level of the GBP/USD exchange rate. A higher GBP/USD rate will require more USD in available margin collateral, and a lower GBP/USD rate will need less USD in margin.

Trading alongside EUR/USD, but with a lot more zip!

Cable is similar to the EUR/USD in that it trades inversely to the overall USD. But while EUR/USD frequently gets bogged down in tremendous two-way liquidity, cable exhibits much more abrupt volatility and more extreme overall price movements. If U.S. economic news disappoints, for instance, both sterling and EUR/USD will move higher. But if EUR/USD sees a 60-point rally on the day, cable may see a 100+ point rally.

This goes back to liquidity and a generally lower level of market interest in cable. In terms of daily global trading sessions, cable volume is at its peak during the UK/European trading day, but that level of liquidity shrinks considerably in the New York afternoon and Asian trading sessions. During those off-peak times, cable can see significant short-term price moves simply on the basis of positioning (for example, shorts getting squeezed out).

Another important difference between cable and EUR/USD comes in their different reactions to domestic economic/news developments. Cable tends to display more explosive reactions to unexpected UK news/data than EUR/USD does to similar Eurozone news/data. For example, if better than expected Eurozone data comes out, EUR/USD may only politely acknowledge the data and move marginally higher. But if surprisingly strong UK data is reported, GBP/USD can take off on a moonshot.

Important UK data reports

Cable tends to react sharply to UK economic reports, especially when the data is in the opposite direction of expectations, or when the data is contrary to current monetary policy speculation. For example, if the market is expecting that the next rate move by the Bank of England (BOE) will be higher, and a monthly inflation report is released indicating a drop in price pressures, then GBP/USD is likely to drop quickly as interest rate bets are unwound.

Key UK data reports to watch for are:

✔ BOE Monetary Policy Committed (MPC) rate decisions, speeches by MPC members and the BOE governor

✔ BOE MPC minutes (released two weeks after each MPC meeting)

✔ Inflation gauges, such as CPI, PPI, and the British Retailers Consortium (BRC) shop price index

✔ Retail sales and the BRC retail sales monitor

✔ Royal Institution of Chartered Surveyors (RICS) house price balance

✔ Industrial and manufacturing production

✔ BOE quarterly inflation report

Safe haven or panic button: USD/CHF

The Swiss franc is frequently referred to as a *safe-haven* currency, meaning investors flock to it during times of geo-political tensions or uncertainty. That reputation is largely a relic of the Cold War. More recently, however, in the aftermath of the GFC and the Eurozone debt crisis of 2009–2010, the Swiss franc has emerged as a perceived safer alternative to the other major currencies (USD, EUR, GBP, and JPY), all of which are burdened by troubled economic outlooks and high debt levels. But there's nothing magically safe about CHF, as other currencies like AUD and CAD have similarly outperformed the beleaguered majors.

Trading fundamentals of USD/CHF

In terms of overall market volume, USD/CHF only accounts for 4 percent of global daily trading volume according to the 2010 BIS survey (and was eclipsed by AUD/USD [6 percent] and USD/CAD [5 percent]). With such a small share of market turnover, you'd be right in wondering why it's considered a major pair in the first place. And that's probably the key takeaway from this section: In terms of liquidity, Swissy is not a major.

Trading USD/CHF by the numbers

USD/CHF is quoted in terms of the number of CHF per USD. At a USD/CHF rate of 0.9800, it costs CHF 0.9800 to buy $1. USD/CHF trades in the overall direction of the U.S. dollar and inversely to the CHF. If the USD/CHF rate moves higher, the USD is strengthening and the CHF is weakening. The USD is the primary currency in the pairing, and the CHF is the secondary currency. That means

- ✔ **USD/CHF is traded in amounts denominated in USD.** In online currency trading platforms, standard lot sizes are $100,000, and minilot sizes are $10,000.

- ✔ The pip value, or minimum price fluctuation, is denominated in CHF.

- ✔ **Profit and loss accrues in CHF.** For one standard lot position size, each pip is worth CHF 10; for one minilot position size, each pip is worth CHF 1. To convert those amounts to USD, divide the CHF amount by the USD/CHF rate. Using 0.9800 as the rate, CHF 10 = $10.20 and CHF 1 = $1.02. The pip value will change over time as the level of the USD/CHF exchange rate fluctuates, with a lower USD/CHF rate giving a higher pip value in USD terms, and vice versa.

- ✔ **Margin calculations are typically calculated in USD.** So it's a straightforward calculation using the leverage rate to see how much margin is required to hold a position in USD/CHF. At 50:1 leverage, $200 of available margin is needed to open a minilot position of 10,000 USD/CHF.

Keeping the focus on Europe

When looking at economic fundamentals, its worth remembering that Switzerland conducts the vast share (about 80 percent) of its foreign trade with the Eurozone and remaining EU countries. So when it comes to the value of the CHF, the Swiss are most concerned with its level against the EUR as opposed to the USD.

The Swiss National Bank (SNB), the Swiss central bank, tends to get involved in the forex market only when the Swiss franc is either too strong or too weak against the euro. If the CHF is too weak, it can import inflation (higher CHF prices for the same goods), upsetting the SNB's carefully laid plans to tame inflation. If the CHF is too strong, it can hurt Swiss exports (more euros needed to buy the same Swiss goods) and undermine the economic outlook. More recently in 2010, CHF strength was also seen as contributing to the risks of deflation (negative inflation rates), potentially destabilizing the longer-term economic outlook.

The European debt crisis came to the fore in late 2009 and the EUR began to weaken sharply against CHF, falling below the key 1.5000 EUR/CHF level. The SNB began ratcheting up its rhetoric opposing CHF strength relative to the EUR, but the market forces were simply too great — the EUR was being dumped and CHF embraced. The SNB felt compelled to undertake unilateral intervention to stem CHF strength, but was ultimately overwhelmed and EUR/CHF fell to below 1.2500 despite nearly $200 bio being spent on intervention. This is another example of unilateral intervention proving ineffective, at least in the medium term. A longer-term shift in EUR/CHF will require a more positive outcome to the European debt crisis. Still, the SNB is unlikely to ever completely relent on efforts to limit CHF strength.

Important Swiss economic reports

Swiss data tends to get lost in the mix of data reports out of the United States and the Eurozone, with many in the market looking at Switzerland as a de facto Eurozone member. In that sense, market reactions to Swiss data and events primarily show up in EUR/CHF cross rates. The important Swiss data to keep an eye on are

- SNB rate decisions and speeches by directorate members
- KOF Leading Economic Indicator
- Retail sales
- Trade balance
- PPI and CPI
- Unemployment rate

Price action behavior in GBP/USD and USD/CHF

I group these two currency pairs together because they share similar market liquidity and trading interest, which are the main drivers of price action. The more liquid a market is, the more smoothly prices will move; the thinner the market, the more erratically prices will move. In both pairs, liquidity and market interest tend to be the thinnest among the majors, especially outside of European trading hours. As a result, both pairs typically trade with wider 3- to 5-pip prices relative to narrower spreads in EUR/USD and USD/JPY.

The most important trading characteristics of sterling and Swissy are as follows:

- **Price action tends to be jumpy, even in normal markets.** Cable and Swissy are like long-tailed cats in a room full of rocking chairs — extremely nervous. In a relatively calm market, you can see prices in these two pairs jump around by routine 2- to 3-pip increments (say, from 20/25 to 22/27 or 23/28, back to 21/26, and then 24/29).

When prices are moving in response to news or data, those price jumps can be even more pronounced, frequently changing by 3 to 5 pips between prices. Online traders are also likely to get more "rates changed" responses when trying to deal on the current market price. That response means the price changed by the time your trade request was received and the attempted trade was not completed. The subsequent price may be 2 to 3 pips higher or lower than where you first tried to deal.

✔ **Price action tends to see one-way traffic in highly directional markets.** When news or data move the market, the price changes in Swissy and cable are apt to be the most abrupt. If a data report sends EUR/USD higher by a quick 20 to 30 pips, cable and Swissy are likely to see prices move by 30 to 40 pips or more. On top of that, cable and Swissy will remain highly directional and tend to see minimal pullbacks or backing and filling.

✔ **Look at cable and Swissy as leading indicators for EUR/USD.** One of the ways that experienced traders judge the level of buying or selling interest, how *bid* or *offered* a market is, during a directional move is by looking at how cable and Swissy are trading. For example, if bids in USD/CHF keep appearing in a relatively orderly fashion, say every 1 to 2 pips on a downswing, it's a sign that the move is not especially extreme. On the other hand, if the prices are dropping by larger increments and displaying very few bounces, it's a strong indication that a larger move is unfolding.

✔ **False breaks of technical levels occur frequently.** Cable and Swissy also have a nasty habit of breaking beyond technical support and resistance levels, only to reverse course and then trade in the opposite direction. And I'm not talking about just a few points beyond the level here, but more like 25 to 30 pips in many cases. The frequency of false breaks is a result of the relatively lower level of liquidity and market interest in these pairs. Instead of having a selling order at technical resistance, which you may reasonably expect in EUR/USD or USD/JPY, there may only be a stop-loss buying order beyond the resistance in cable and Swissy.

✔ **Spike reversals are very common.** The tendency of cable and Swissy to overshoot in extreme directional moves and to generate false breaks of technical levels means that spike reversals appear frequently on short-term charts. Though the size of the spikes will vary depending on the market circumstances and current events, spike reversals of more than 30 to 40 points on an hourly closing basis should alert you to a potentially larger reversal taking place. The bigger the spike reversal (and it's not uncommon to see 50- to 70-pip spikes in cable and Swissy), the more significance it holds for the future direction.

Tactical trading considerations in GBP/USD and USD/CHF

The routine short-term volatility of cable and Swissy suggest several important tactical trading refinements. The overarching idea here is to adjust your trading strategies to weather the erratic price action and higher overall volatility in these pairs in comparison to the larger EUR/USD.

It may help to think of sailing a boat on a lake. When the wind is calm, you need to tighten up the sails to catch all the wind you can. But when the wind starts gusting, you need to let the sails out or you're liable to get blown over. The same is true when trading cable and Swissy.

Reducing position size relative to margin

This first consideration is especially important in cable, due to its higher relative value to the USD. With GBP/USD trading around 1.60 to the dollar (£1 = $1.60), a single minilot position (£10,000) eats up $320 in required margin at 50:1 leverage. A similar-size position in EUR/USD (at 1.30) requires only $260 in margin. If you're going to trade in cable, you'll need more margin than if you stayed with EUR/USD, USD/JPY, or Swissy.

Cable and Swissy's higher volatility also argue for overall smaller position sizes. A smaller position will allow you to better withstand their short-term volatility and give you greater staying power relative to margin. If you're willing to risk $500 in capital on a particular trade, that equates to 50 pips in EUR/USD and GBP/USD. But the chances of an adverse move of 50 pips in GBP/USD are greater than a 50-pip move in EUR/USD.

Allowing a greater margin of error on technical breaks

If you're basing your trades on technical levels of support and resistance, you need to anticipate that those levels will be tested at the minimum. In sterling and Swissy, tests of technical levels frequently result in false breaks as stops are triggered. If your stop loss is too close to the technical level, it's ripe for the picking by the market. Factoring in a margin of error when placing stop-loss orders can help — it allows you to withstand any short-term false break. Using a margin of error may also require you to reduce your position size to give you greater flexibility and margin staying-power. For a guide, I use a 25 to 30 pip margin of error in cable and Swissy versus 10 to 15 pips in EUR/USD.

Anticipating overshoots and false breaks for position entry

When you're looking to enter a position by selling on rallies or buying on dips, you're probably focused on selling at resistance and buying on support. You can take advantage of cable and Swissy's tendency to overshoot or make false breaks of technical levels by placing your limit order behind the technical level (above resistance, below support). If cable and Swissy break through the level, you'd be able to enter at a better price than you would have if you'd adhered to the technical level alone.

Alternatively, you can enter a portion of your desired position at the technical level and enter the rest at better prices if the level is breached, improving the average rate of your position. Worst-case scenario, the market only fills you for half of your desired position and then reverses. Best-case scenario, you establish your full desired position at a better rate than you expected and the market reverses. If the market keeps going against you, your average position rate is still better than if you'd stuck to the technical level alone.

Being quick on the trigger

Cable and Swissy tend to move very quickly and may not spend a lot of time around key price levels. This favors traders who are decisive and quick on the trigger in terms of entering and exiting positions. That's why it helps to have a disciplined trading plan in place before you enter the market. Above all, avoid being distracted from your plan by the sharper price movements.

Another way you can take advantage of the short-term volatility of cable and Swissy is by using resting orders to get in and out. You may not be in front of your trading screen, or your click-and-deal trade may not have made it through on a rapid price fluctuation. A standing limit order will accomplish the same trade — only automatically and instantly if the price deals. Trailing stops are especially useful when you have a position that's moving the right way.

Resisting the contrarian urge following large directional moves

After an extended directional price move, many traders may feel inclined to trade in the opposite direction, if only for a short-term correction. Maybe you missed the big move and think it's ripe for a pullback. Or maybe it looks like the move has gone too far, too fast. Resist that urge in cable and Swissy.

On days with large directional price moves of more than 100 pips, cable and Swissy often finish out the trading day at the extremes of the price move (meaning at the highs on an up-move and at the lows on a decline). So even if you sell the high of a move up, you're unlikely to get any joy on the day.

Picking your spots wisely

Instead of simply jumping into sterling or Swissy, the way you may in EUR/USD, you're going to need to do a fair amount of watching and studying to get a handle on where appropriate entry points may be. Short-term volatility in cable and Swissy make for treacherous short-term trading conditions. You'll greatly improve your chances of catching a favorable move if you step back and look at the medium and longer-term pictures (four-hour and daily) instead of getting caught up in the short-term volatility.

Chapter 9

Minor Currency Pairs and Cross-Currency Trading

*T*rading in the major currency pairs accounts for the lion's share of overall currency market volume, but speculative trading opportunities extend well beyond just the four major *dollar pairs* (currency pairs that include the USD). For starters, three other currency pairs — commonly known as the *minor* or *small* dollar pairs — round out the primary trading pairs that include the U.S. dollar. Still more trading options are available in the currencies of Scandinavian nations that haven't adopted the EUR, referred to as the *Scandies.* Then there are the *cross-currency* pairs, or *crosses* for short, which pit two non-USD currencies against each other.

In this chapter, I take a closer look at the minor currency pairs, Scandies, and cross-currency pairs to see how they fit into the overall market and offer an additional array of speculative trading opportunities. Although the USD is frequently the focus of the currency market, you're going to want to know where the opportunities are when the spotlight isn't on the greenback.

Trading the Minor Pairs

The minor dollar pairs are USD/CAD (the U.S. dollar versus the Canadian dollar), AUD/USD (the Australian dollar versus the U.S. dollar), and NZD/USD (the New Zealand dollar versus the U.S. dollar). The minor currency pairs are also commonly referred to as *commodity currencies.*

The *commodity currencies* reference stems from the key role that oil, metals, agricultural and mining industries play in the national economies of Canada, Australia, and New Zealand. See the nearby sidebar "The (not just) commodity currencies" for important qualifications about the commodity relationship. USD/CAD and AUD/USD account for 5 and 6 percent of global daily trading volume, respectively, according to the 2010 Bank for International Settlements (BIS) survey of forex market volumes. NZD/USD accounts for less than 2 percent each of spot trading volume. But these three pairs offer more than ample liquidity to be actively traded and can offer significant trading opportunities, both for short-term traders and medium- to longer-term speculators.

Trading fundamentals of USD/CAD

The Canadian dollar (nicknamed the *Loonie* after the local bird pictured on the dollar coins) trades according to the same macroeconomic fundamentals as most other major currencies. That means you'll need to closely follow Bank of Canada (BOC) monetary-policy developments, current economic data, inflation readings, and political goings-on, just as you would any of the other majors.

A key element to keep in mind when looking at USD/CAD is that the trajectory of the Canadian economy is closely linked to the overall direction of the U.S. economy. The United States and Canada are still each other's largest commercial trading partners, and the vast majority of Canadians live within 100 miles of the U.S./Canadian border. Even the BOC regularly refers to the U.S. economic outlook in its economic outlooks. So I don't think it's an overgeneralization to say that as goes the U.S. economy, so goes the Canadian economy. But it's a long-term dynamic, making for plenty of short-term trading opportunities, especially when U.S. and Canadian outlooks diverge.

The sharp rise in commodity demand from China and other rapidly developing economies in recent years has heightened the sensitivity of CAD to overall commodity price developments. In this light, be sure to factor in the global economic outlook when evaluating the Canadian outlook.

Geography also plays a role when it comes to U.S. and Canadian economic data, because both countries issue economic data reports around the same time each morning or only a few hours apart. At one extreme, the result can be a negative USD report paired with strong Canadian data, leading to a sharp drop in USD/CAD (selling USD and buying CAD). At the other end, strong U.S. data and weak Canadian numbers can see USD/CAD rally sharply. Mixed readings can see a stalemate, but it always depends on the bigger picture.

The (not just) commodity currencies

I don't want to leave you with the impression that the so-called commodity currencies' trading behavior is strictly a function of what's happening to commodity prices. To be sure, recent years' price movements in those pairs are generally highly correlated to movements in underlying commodities, like gold, silver and oil. But correlation is not causation. What that means is that just because two assets may move together in a statistically significant relationship, the movement of one is not necessarily causing movement in the other.

More typically, they may both be responding to broader fundamental developments that affect each similarly, such as the strength of global demand as seen in Chinese growth data. China is a tremendous consumer of raw materials, and Australia is a leading exporter of metals, coal, and grains. Market perceptions of strong demand could see prices move higher for such commodities. Gains in commodity prices may improve profitability at Australian mining and agricultural firms, attracting global investors who need AUD to buy such Australian stocks. In this scenario, it would not be surprising to see the AUD gain alongside commodity prices.

But there are also plenty of scenarios that could see such relationships break down, especially in the short run, and see prices diverge. Carrying on with the previously mentioned China/Australia relationship, strong growth and commodity demand could see the Reserve Bank of Australia (RBA), the Australian central bank, indicate that interest rates may need to be raised, reinforcing the positive correlation and tending to support AUD. But if the RBA later postpones raising rates due to unforeseen events, such as happened after massive floods in early 2011, currency market expectations may be disappointed and the AUD could weaken, even as commodity prices maintain gains, but now on production disruptions. I hope you get the idea that correlations between currencies and commodities are not carved in stone.

To give you a more concrete picture, the following tables show the historical correlations (*correlation coefficients*) between these currencies and individual commodities over a two-year and ten-year period ending in February 2011, respectively, based on weekly data and percentage changes. A *correlation coefficient* is a statistical measure of how closely two securities values change relative to each other. Coefficients can range from +1.00 to –1.00, with a coefficient of +1.00 meaning the two assets are perfectly positively correlated (meaning, a 1 percent gain in one would see a 1 percent gain in the other). A coefficient of –1.00 would mean the two are perfectly negatively correlated (meaning, a rise of 1 percent in the first would see a decline of 1 percent in the second). A coefficient of zero means there is no statistically identifiable relationship, and the two are said to be non-correlated. As a rough benchmark, a correlation of +0.7/–0.7 or more is considered a pretty strong relationship. But remember, correlations exist over time. What's closely correlated today may not be so closely correlated tomorrow, or next month. Medium and longer-term traders may find such correlations more useful than short-term, intraday traders, where individual market news is more likely to cause a breakdown in the observed relationship.

(continued)

(continued)

Two-Year Correlations	CRB	OIL	GOLD	SILVER
AUD/USD	0.94	0.96	0.84	0.81
NZD/USD	0.89	0.94	0.78	0.74
USD/CAD	−0.86	−0.95	−0.79	−0.70
USD Index	−0.56	−0.55	−0.19	−0.30

Ten-Year Correlations	CRB	OIL	GOLD	SILVER
AUD/USD	0.80	0.87	0.82	0.86
NZD/USD	0.85	0.78	0.63	0.69
USD/DAD	−0.84	−0.88	−0.81	−0.84
USD Index	−0.82	−0.81	−0.73	−0.73

Note the higher level of correlations over the more recent two-year period compared to the longer ten-year time frame. Also, over the longer period, the USD index is about as highly correlated to the commodities as the so-called commodity currencies themselves. So instead of thinking of these currencies as strictly commodity-price driven, think of commodity price movements as just one factor affecting these currencies.

Trading USD/CAD by the numbers

The standard market convention is to quote USD/CAD in terms of the number of Canadian dollars per USD. A USD/CAD rate of 1.0200, for instance, means it takes CAD 1.02 to buy USD 1. The market convention means that USD/CAD trades in the same overall direction of the USD, with a higher USD/CAD rate reflecting a stronger USD/weaker CAD and a lower rate showing a weaker USD/stronger CAD.

USD/CAD has the USD as the primary currency and the CAD as the counter currency. This means

✔ **USD/CAD is traded in amounts denominated in USD.** For online currency trading platforms, standard lot sizes are USD 100,000, and minilot sizes are USD 10,000.

✔ **The *pip value*, or minimum price fluctuation, is denominated in CAD.**

✔ **Profit and loss registers in CAD.** For a standard lot position size, each pip is worth CAD 10, and each pip in a minilot position is worth CAD 1. Using a USD/CAD rate of 1.0200 (which will change over time, of course), that equates to a pip value of USD 9.80 for each standard lot and USD 0.98 for each minilot.

✔ **Margin calculations are typically based in USD, so to see how much margin is required to hold a position in USD/CAD, it's a simple calculation using the leverage ratio.** At 50:1 leverage, for instance, $2,000 of available margin is needed to trade 100,000 USD/CAD, and $200 is needed to trade 10,000 USD/CAD.

USD/CAD is unique among currency pairs in that it trades for spot settlement only one day beyond the trade date, as opposed to the normal two days for all other currency pairs. The difference is due to the fact that New York and Toronto, the two nations' financial centers, are in the same time zone, allowing for faster trade confirmations and settlement transfers. For spot traders, the difference means that USD/CAD undergoes the extended weekend (three-day) rollover after the close of trading on Thursdays, instead of on Wednesdays like all other pairs, assuming no holidays are involved.

Canadian events and data reports to watch

On top of following U.S. economic data to maintain an outlook for the larger economy to the south, you'll need to pay close attention to individual Canadian economic data and official commentaries. CAD can react explosively when data or events come in out of line with expectations. In particular, keep an eye on the following Canadian economic events and reports:

✔ Bank of Canada speakers, rate decisions, and economic forecasts

✔ Employment report

✔ Gross domestic product (GDP) reported monthly

✔ International securities transactions

✔ International merchandise trade

✔ Wholesale and retail sales

✔ Consumer price index (CPI) and BOC CPI

✔ Manufacturing shipments

✔ Ivey Purchasing Managers Index

Trading fundamentals of AUD/USD

The Australian dollar is commonly referred to as *Aussie* (pronounced *aw*-zee), or even just *Oz* for short. These terms refer to both the AUD/USD pair and Australian dollar cross pairs. Aussie trading volume accounts for a little over 5 percent of daily global spot turnover, but it's still a regular mover, both against the U.S. dollar and on the crosses, so it makes an active currency pair for speculators.

In trading AUD/USD, you need to factor in all the usual macroeconomic suspects, like monetary policy outlooks, interest-rate levels, and all the domestic economic data that determine them. Comments by officials from the Reserve Bank of Australia (RBA), the central bank, and the finance minister can move Aussie sharply.

The boom in Asian regional growth over the past decade has supported the Australian economy in recent years. Those high levels of growth have brought with them higher levels of inflation, prompting the RBA to generally maintain higher interest rates than the major central banks. In addition to commodity prices and the outlook for global demand, the interest-rate outlook is especially critical to the value of the Aussie.

Aussie trading is also heavily influenced by cross trading, especially against the yen, because the AUD/JPY cross captures one of the highest interest differentials between major currencies. AUD/JPY has been a favorite among traders pursuing the carry trade, so you'll want to monitor important AUD/JPY technical levels.

Aussie trading is also regularly influenced by New Zealand economic data, but the flow is usually more significant in the opposite direction, where Aussie data will exert a larger pull on NZD prices, given the larger size of the Australian economy. Still, when trading Aussie, it helps to be aware of upcoming NZD data, because data surprises in NZ can trigger sharp swings in the AUD/NZD cross rate, with implications for AUD/USD.

Australian events and data reports to watch

Australian data and events regularly transpire during the New York late afternoon or early evening, which is early morning the next day in the land down under. Keep an eye on the following:

- ✔ RBA and Treasury speakers, RBA rate decisions and monetary policy statements, and the minutes of RBA meetings

- ✔ Trade balance (monthly) and current account balance (quarterly)

- ✔ Employment report (full-time/part-time)

- ✔ Westpac consumer and NAB business confidence indices

- ✔ CPI and producer price index (PPI) reports

- ✔ Retail sales and housing market data

Trading fundamentals of NZD/USD

The New Zealand dollar is nicknamed the *Kiwi*, as are most things New Zealand, after the indigenous bird of the same name; the term *Kiwi* refers to both the NZD and the NZD/USD pair. (What is it with birds and currency nicknames, anyway?) Given the relatively small size of the New Zealand economy, Kiwi is among the most interest-rate sensitive of all currencies.

The New Zealand economy has undergone a major transformation over the past two decades, moving from a mostly agricultural export orientation to a domestically driven service and manufacturing base. The rapid growth has seen disposable incomes soar; with higher disposable incomes have come generally high levels of inflation. As a result, the Reserve Bank of New Zealand (RBNZ), the central bank, has frequently been among the more hawkish central banks.

I put Kiwi in the commodity currency grouping, but there is an important distinction to note. New Zealand is primarily an agricultural-commodity-producing economy (dairy products and meat in particular), as opposed to the metals and energy commodities of Canada and Australia. As such, Kiwi displays a weaker relationship than CAD and AUD to the prices of gold, silver, and oil, as seen in the two tables in the previous sidebar.

In addition to all the standard New Zealand economic data and official pronouncements you'll need to monitor, Kiwi trading is closely tied to Australian data and prospects, due to a strong trade and regional relationship.

No set formula exists to describe the currencies' relationship, but a general rule is that when it's a USD-based move, Aussie and Kiwi will tend to trade in the same direction as each other relative to the USD. But when Kiwi or Aussie news comes in, the AUD/NZD (Aussie/Kiwi) cross will exert a larger influence. For example, disappointing Aussie data may see AUD/USD move lower, which will tend to drag down NZD/USD as well. But Aussie/Kiwi cross selling (selling AUD/USD on the weaker data and buying NZD/USD for the cross trade) will typically reduce the extent of NZD/USD declines relative to AUD/USD losses. A similar effect will play out when New Zealand data or news is the catalyst.

New Zealand events and data reports to watch

RBNZ commentary and rate decisions are pivotal to the value of Kiwi, given the significance of interest rates to the currency. Finance ministry comments are secondary to the rhetoric of the independent RBNZ but can still upset the Kiwi cart from time to time. Additionally, keep an eye on the following:

- Consumer prices, housing prices, and food prices
- Retail sales and electronic-card spending (debit and credit)
- Westpac and ANZ consumer confidence indices
- Quarterly GDP and monthly trade balance
- National Bank of New Zealand (NBNZ) business confidence survey

Trading Aussie and Kiwi by the numbers

AUD/USD and NZD/USD are both quoted in the same way, so I've put them together to look at the numbers. AUD/USD and NZD/USD rates reflect the number of USD per AUD or NZD. For example, a NZD/USD rate of 0.7000 means it costs USD 0.70 (or 70¢) to buy NZD 1. Aussie and Kiwi trade in the opposite direction of the overall value of the USD, so a weaker USD means a higher Aussie or Kiwi rate, and a lower Aussie or Kiwi rate represents a stronger USD.

AUD and NZD are the primary currencies in the pairs, and the USD is the counter currency, which means

- **AUD/USD and NZD/USD are traded in position sizes denominated in AUD or NZD.**
- **The pip values are denominated in USD.**
- **Profit and loss accrues in USD.** On a 100,000 NZD/USD position, each pip is worth USD 10; on a 10,000 Aussie position size, each pip is worth USD 1.
- **Margin calculations are typically based in USD on margin trading platforms.**

Using an NZD/USD rate of 0.7000 and a leverage ratio of 50:1, a 100,000 Kiwi position requires USD 1400 in margin, while a 10,000 NZD/USD position would need only USD 140 in margin. AUD/USD has risen to around parity with the USD as of early 2011, meaning an AUD/USD rate of 1.0000. At those levels, a 100,000 AUD/USD position requires $2,000 of available margin and a 10,000 AUD/USD position needs $200.

Tactical trading considerations in USD/CAD, AUD/USD, and NZD/USD

I group these three currency pairs together because they share many of the same trading traits and even travel as a pack sometimes — especially Aussie and Kiwi, given their regional proximity and close economic ties. Whether they're being grouped as the commodity currencies or just smaller regional currencies versus the U.S. dollar, they can frequently serve as a leading indicator of overall USD market direction.

Liquidity and market interest are lower

One of the reasons these pairs tend to exhibit leading characteristics is due to the lower relative liquidity of the pairs, which amplifies the speculative effect on them. If sentiment is shifting in favor of the U.S. dollar, for example, the effect of speculative interest — the fast money — is going to be most evident in lower-volume currency pairs.

When a hedge fund or other large speculator turns around a directional bet on the U.S. dollar (for example, from short to long), it's going to start buying U.S. dollars across the board (meaning against most all other currencies). A half-billion EUR/USD selling order (650 million USD equivalent at 1.3000 EUR/USD) is relatively easily absorbed in the high-volume, liquid EUR/USD market and may move it only a few points (say, 10 to 20 pips, depending on the circumstances). However, a proportionately smaller order to sell Aussie, sell

Kiwi, or buy USD/CAD (large speculators will typically allocate smaller position sizes to less-liquid currency pairs), amounting to only 100 million or 200 million in notional terms, may generate a 20- to 40-pip movement in these currency pairs, depending on the time of day and overall environment.

In general, you need to be aware that overall liquidity and market interest in these pairs is significantly lower than in the majors. On a daily basis, liquidity in these pairs is at its peak when the local centers (Toronto, Sydney, and Wellington) are open. London market makers provide a solid liquidity base to bridge the gap outside the local markets, but you can largely forget about USD/CAD during the Asia/Pacific session, and the Aussie and Kiwi markets are problematic after the London/European session close until their financial centers reopen a few hours later. The net result is a concentration of market interest in these currency pairs among the major banks of the currency countries, which has implications of its own (see the "Technical levels can be blurry" section, later in this chapter).

Price action is highly event driven

As a result of the overall lower level of liquidity in these currency pairs, in concert with relatively high levels of speculative positioning (at times), you've got the ultimate mix for explosive reactions after currency-specific news or data comes out. A dovish statement from a previously hawkish Bank of Canada governor can trigger a sea change in sentiment against the CAD. If expectations are running high for an NZD interest-rate hike, and a key inflation report contradicts that outlook (it's lower than expected), we've got a relatively small market, probably overpositioned in one direction (long NZD/USD), that's all heading for the exit (selling) at the same time.

The bottom line in these currency pairs is that significant data or news surprises, especially when contrary to expectations and likely market positioning, tends to have an outsized impact on the market. Traders positioning in these currencies need to be especially aware of this and to recognize the greater degree of volatility and risk they're facing if events don't transpire as expected. It's one thing if Eurozone CPI comes in higher than expected, but it's another thing entirely if Australian CPI surprises to the upside.

A data or event surprise typically leads to a price gap when the news is first announced. If the news is sufficiently at odds with market expectations and positioning, subsequent price action tends to be mostly one-way traffic, as the market reacts to the surprise news and exits earlier positions. If you're caught on the wrong side after unexpected news in these pairs, you're likely better off getting out as soon as possible than waiting for a correction to exit at a better level. The lower liquidity and interest in these currency pairs mean you're probably not alone in being caught wrong-sided, which tends to see steady, one-way interest, punctuated by accelerations when additional stop-loss order levels are hit.

All politics (and economic data) is local

Most of my discussion of market drivers centers on economic data and monetary policy, but domestic political developments in these smaller-currency countries can provoke significant movements in the local currencies. National elections, political scandals, and abrupt policy changes can all lead to upheavals in the value of the local currency. The effect tends to be most pronounced on the downside of the currency's value (meaning, bad news tends to hurt a currency more than good news — if there ever is any in politics — helps it). Of course, every situation is different, but the spillover effect between politics and currencies is greatest in these pairs, which means you need to be aware of domestic political events if you're trading them.

In terms of economic data, these currency pairs tend to participate in overall directional moves relative to the U.S. dollar until a local news or data event triggers more concentrated interest on the local currency. If the USD is under pressure across the board, for instance, USD/CAD is likely to move lower in concert with other dollar pairs. But if negative Canadian news or data emerges, USD/CAD is likely to pare its losses and may even start to move higher if the news was bad enough. If the Canadian news was CAD-positive (say, a higher CPI reading pointing to a potential rate hike), USD/CAD is likely to accelerate to the downside, because USD selling interest is now amplified by CAD buying interest.

Technical levels can be blurry

The relatively lower level of liquidity and market interest in these currency pairs makes for sometimes-difficult technical trading conditions. Trend lines and retracement levels in particular are subject to regular overshoots. Prices may move beyond the technical level — sometimes only 5 to 10 pips, other times for extensive distances or for prolonged periods — only to reverse course and reestablish the technical level later.

The basic reason behind this tendency to overshoot technical levels is that market interest is concentrated in fewer market-makers for these pairs — usually the local banks of the currency country. The result is a concentration of market interest in fewer hands, which can result in order levels being triggered when they may not be otherwise. For example, if you're an interbank market-maker watching a stop-loss order for 5 million AUD/USD, it's not a big deal, because 5 million Aussie is transacted easily. But if you have a stop loss for 50 million or 100 million AUD/USD, you're going to need to be fast (and, likely, preemptive) to fill the order at a reasonable execution rate.

If the price break of a technical level is quickly reversed, it's a good sign that it was just a position-related movement. If fresh news is out, however, you may be seeing the initial wave of a larger directional move.

Trading the Scandies: SEK, NOK, and DKK

A few of the Scandinavian, or Nordic, countries chose not to join the monetary union that led to the euro, namely Sweden, Norway, and Denmark. Trading volumes in the Scandies are generally light, but sufficient enough to offer additional speculative trading opportunities depending on the circumstances. Most of the trading in the Scandies is done versus EUR, driven by intra-European divergences in either growth or interest rate outlooks. Generally speaking, trading the USD versus the Scandies tends to mimic EUR/USD, but in mirror image due to quoting conventions.

Swedish krona — "Stocky"

The Swedish krona is affectionately referred to as Stocky after the capital Stockholm, and its currency code is SEK. Trading volumes in USD/SEK (dollar/Stocky) and EUR/SEK (euro/Stocky) each amounted to 1 percent of daily global volume, according to the 2010 BIS survey of forex markets. The Swedish central bank, *Sveriges Riksbank* in Swedish, is independent and is the key actor in setting interest rates and maintaining currency stability.

In addition to following the economic data coming out of Sweden, pay close attention to comments from the governor and other Riksbank officials. The Riksbank follows an *inflation target,* a desired level of inflation, so CPI reports are also critical inputs to the outlook for interest rates and SEK. The Swedish central bank also has a history of speaking out on the value of the krona itself, especially when it's either too strong or weak relative to EUR, where most of Swedish trade is conducted. EUR/SEK can become especially active when the Riksbank and the ECB are seen to be on divergent interest rate paths.

Technically speaking, after joining the European Union in 1995, Sweden is obliged to adopt the euro at some point in the future, but has effectively opted out and shows no signs of joining the euro.

Norwegian krone — "Nokkie"

The Norwegian krone (NOK) is nicknamed Nokkie after its currency code and in symphony with Stocky. USD/NOK and EUR/NOK trading volumes didn't get broken out on the 2010 BIS survey, so they're likely sub-1 percent of daily global volume. Still, liquidity in NOK is more than sufficient, especially during European trading hours. Norway's central bank, *Norges Bank,* is independent and pursues a traditional policy of maintaining price stability. Keep an eye out for guidance from the governor and other central bank officials, as Norges Bank policy may frequently diverge from ECB policy.

Norway is exceptionally wealthy owing to its large energy reserves, mainly North Sea oil, which has given it a large sovereign wealth fund, making it an important global asset manager. More importantly for day-to-day trading, Norway is the world's tenth largest oil producer, and NOK tends to trade as a petro-currency, similar to CAD, strengthening as oil prices rise and vice versa. Norway is not a member of the EU and so is unlikely to ever adopt the euro.

Danish krone — "Copey"

The Danish krone (DKK) is sometimes called Copey in reference to the capital of Copenhagen. Rather than pursuing currency independence like Sweden and Norway, Denmark opted to enter into a cooperative exchange rate agreement with Eurozone members, and the Danish krone is linked to the euro at a fixed exchange rate of 7.46038 +/–2.25%. Within this arrangement, the Danish central bank (Danmarks Nationalbank) effectively sets interest rates according to ECB decisions. The result is that the USD/DKK pair trades in mirror opposite fashion to EUR/USD and that the EUR/DKK pair trades in a very narrow band, typically about 0.25 percent, around the fixed rate. As such, there is little incentive for trading DKK, as EUR/USD offers better liquidity and EUR/DKK doesn't move. In early 2011, the Danish government indicated it hoped to hold another referendum on joining the euro later in 2011, so Copey's days may be numbered.

Cross-Currency Pairs

A *cross-currency pair* (or *cross,* for short) is any currency pair that does not have the U.S. dollar as one of the currencies in the pairing. (Turn to Chapter 4 for a list of all the different cross pairs.) But the catch is that cross rates are derived from the prices of the underlying USD pairs. For example, one of the most active crosses is EUR/JPY, pitting the two largest currencies outside the U.S. dollar directly against each other. But the EUR/JPY rate at any given instant is a function (the product) of the current EUR/USD and USD/JPY rates.

The most popular cross pairs involve the most actively traded major currencies, like EUR/JPY, EUR/GBP, and EUR/CHF. According to the 2010 BIS survey of foreign-exchange market activity, direct cross trading accounted for a relatively small percentage of global daily volume — around 10 percent for the major crosses combined.

But that figure significantly understates the amount of interest that is actually flowing through the crosses, because large interbank cross trades are typically executed through the USD pairs instead of directly in the cross markets. If a Japanese corporation needs to buy half a billion EUR/JPY (*half a yard,* in market parlance), for example, the interbank traders executing the order will alternately buy EUR/USD and buy USD/JPY to fill the order. Going directly through the EUR/JPY market would likely tip off too many in the market and drive the rate away from them. (I look at how large cross flows can drive the dollar pairs in the "Stretching the legs" section, later in this chapter.)

For individual traders dealing online, however, the direct cross pairs offer more than ample liquidity and narrower spreads than can be realized by trading through the dollar pairs. Additionally, most online platforms do not net out positions based on overall dollar exposure, so you'd end up using roughly twice the amount of margin to enter a position through the dollar pairs to create the same position you'd have if you'd gone through the direct cross market. The advances in electronic trading technology even make relatively obscure crosses like NZD/JPY and GBP/CHF easily accessible to individual online traders.

Why trade the crosses?

Cross pairs represent entirely new sets of routinely fluctuating currency pairs that offer another universe of trading opportunities beyond the primary USD pairs. Developments in the currency market are not always a simple bet on what's happening to the U.S. dollar. Crosses are the other half of the story, and their significance appears to be increasing dramatically as a result of electronic trading. Years ago, if you wanted a price in a cross pair, a human would have to push the buttons on a calculator to come up with the cross quote. Today's streaming price technology means that cross rates are as fluid as the dollar pairs, making them as accessible and tradable as USD/JPY or EUR/USD.

In particular, cross trading offers the following advantages:

- **You can pinpoint trade opportunities based on news or fundamental trends.** If the outlook and data for the UK is steadily deteriorating, you may be looking to sell GBP. But against what? If the USD is also weakening, buying USD and selling GBP may not yield any results. Selling GBP against another currency with better immediate prospects (such as selling GBP/CAD or GBP/NOK) may yield a more appreciable return.

- **You can take advantage of interest-rate differentials.** Selling low-yielding currencies against higher-yielding currencies is known as a *carry trade* (see Chapter 10). Carry trades seek to profit from both interest-rate differentials and spot price appreciation, and can form the basis of significant trends.

- **You can exploit technical trading opportunities.** The majors may be range bound or showing no actionable technical signals, but a cross rate may be set to stage a directional price breakout. Survey charts of cross rates to spot additional technical trading setups.

✔ **You can expand the horizon of trading opportunities.** Instead of looking at only four to seven dollar pairs, cross rates offer another dozen currency pairs that you can look to for trading opportunities.

✔ **You can go with the flow.** Speculative flows are ever-present in the currency market, but they don't always involve the dollar pairs. Today's speculative flow may be focused on the JPY crosses or selling CAD across the board on the back of surprisingly weak CAD data. The more attuned you are to cross-currency pairs, the more likely you are to identify and capitalize on the speculative move du jour.

Stretching the legs

A lot of interbank cross-trading volume does not go through the direct cross market, because institutional traders have a vested interest in hiding their operations from the rest of the market. In many cases, too, standing liquidity is simply not available in less-liquid crosses (GBP/JPY or NZD/JPY, for example). So they have to go through the legs, as the dollar pairs are called with respect to cross trading, to get the trade done. They also have an interest in maximizing the prices at which they're dealing — to sell as high as possible and to buy as low as possible.

One of the ways they're able to do that is to alternate their trading in the dollar legs. For instance, if you have to sell a large amount of EUR/JPY, you can alternate selling EUR/USD, which may tend to drive down EUR/USD but also push USD/JPY higher (because U.S. dollars overall are being bought). You now (you hope) have a higher rate at which to sell the USD/JPY leg of the order. But selling USD/JPY may push USD/JPY lower or cap its rise, leading EUR/USD to stop declining and recover higher, because U.S. dollars are now being sold. Now you have a slightly better EUR/USD rate to keep selling the EUR/USD leg of the order. By alternating the timing of which U.S. dollar leg you're selling, you have (you hope) executed the order at better rates than you could have directly in the cross and likely managed to obscure your market activity in the more active dollar pairs.

Of course, it doesn't always work out as neat and clean as what I just described. The net result in the market is a steady directional move in the cross rate, while the USD pairs remain relatively stagnant or within recent ranges. Be alert for such dollar-based movement, and consider that it may be a cross-driven move and a potential trading opportunity.

Cross-rate movements can also have a pronounced effect on how individual dollar pairs move in an otherwise dollar-based market reaction. Let's say some very USD-positive news or data has just been released, and the market starts buying USD across the board. (I focus on buying USD/JPY and selling EUR/USD in this example.) If USD/JPY happens to break a key technical resistance level, it may accelerate higher and prompt EUR/JPY to break a similarly significant resistance level, bringing in EUR/JPY buyers. The net effect in this case is that EUR/USD will not fall as much or as rapidly as USD/JPY will rally, because of the EUR/JPY cross buying. If you went short EUR/USD on the positive U.S. news, you may not get as much joy. But the legs also tend to move in phases, and continued EUR/USD selling may eventually break through support, sending EUR/JPY lower and capping USD/JPY in the process.

As you can see, crosses can affect the market in virtually limitless ways, and there's no set way these things play out.

When the U.S. dollar is not the primary focus of the market's attention, or if major U.S. news is approaching (like a nonfarm payrolls [NFP] report or a Federal Open Market Committee [FOMC] decision in a few days), sending market interest to the sidelines, speculative interest frequently shifts to the crosses. Always consider that the market's focus may be cross-driven rather than centered on the USD or any other single currency. Some days it's a dollar market, and other days it's a cross market. GBP may be weakening across the board on weak UK data, but if the USD is similarly out of favor, the pound's weakness is likely to be most evident on the crosses.

When looking at cross-trade opportunities, you may be tempted to translate the cross idea into a USD-based trade. You may think that AUD/JPY is forming a top, for example. If you're right, you may be thinking that one of two moves is likely — USD/JPY will move lower or AUD/USD will move lower — and you may be tempted into selling one of the legs (AUD/USD or USD/JPY) because you don't want to get involved in a cross. But there's another possibility: One leg may go down precipitously while the other moves higher, still sending the cross lower as you expected. But if you went short the wrong leg, you missed the boat.

When you spot a trade opportunity in a cross, trade the cross. Don't try to outguess the market and pick which component will make the cross move. Trust that if your trade analysis is correct, the cross will move the way you expect.

Trading the JPY crosses

The JPY crosses constitute one of the primary cross families and basically pit the JPY against the other major currencies. EUR/JPY is the highest volume of the JPY crosses, but the prominence of the carry trade, where the low-yielding JPY is sold and higher-yielding currencies are bought, has seen significant increases in AUD/JPY and NZD/JPY trading volume. Those currencies offer the highest interest-rate differentials against the JPY.

JPY crosses have their pip values denominated in JPY, meaning profit and loss will accrue in JPY. The margin requirement will vary greatly depending on which primary currency is involved, with GBP/JPY requiring the greatest margin and NZD/JPY requiring the least.

In terms of JPY-cross fundamentals, risk sentiment (see Chapter 5) and over-all volatility tend to have the greatest impact, but as I caution earlier, trying to pin down which leg is going to cause the JPY crosses to move is a risky game. When trading in the JPY crosses, you need to keep an eye on USD/JPY in particular, due to its relatively explosive tendencies and its key place as an outlet for overall carry trade buying or selling. Be alert for similar technical levels between USD/JPY and the JPY crosses, as a break in either could spill over into the other.

Trading the EUR crosses

Outside of EUR/JPY, EUR cross action tends to be concentrated in EUR/GBP and EUR/CHF, where the cross direction is largely determined by changing outlooks between the Eurozone economy relative to the UK and Swiss econo-mies. Reactions to Eurozone and Swiss news or data are most likely to be felt in the EUR crosses as opposed to EUR/USD or USD/CHF, whereas UK news/ data is going to explode all over GBP/USD and EUR/GBP. Trading in EUR/SEK and EUR/NOK offers yet another way to exploit divergent economic or interest rate trajectories between continental Europe and the Scandinavian countries.

Sharp USD-driven moves will also affect these crosses, with the brunt of the USD move being felt in GBP/USD and USD/CHF, frequently biasing those legs to drive their EUR cross in the short run. That means frequently (but not always) that a sharp move higher in the USD will tend to see a higher EUR/CHF and EUR/GBP, while a rapid USD move lower will tend to see lower EUR/CHF and EUR/GBP.

The pip values of these EUR crosses will be denominated in either GBP or CHF, with GBP significantly more expensive on a pip basis than CHF (as of this writing). Typical daily ranges in the EUR crosses are relatively small on a pip basis — roughly 20 to 40 pips on average — but they're still substantial on a pip-value basis and roughly equivalent to daily EUR/USD ranges.

Part III

Developing a Trading Plan

The 5th Wave   By Rich Tennant

Defining your investment risk with the:
TOAST RETRIEVING RISK TOLERANCE TEST

LOW RISK | Waits for toast to pop up even though it's burning.

MODERATE RISK | Goes after toast with wooden toast prongs.

HIGH RISK | Goes after toast with all metal butter knife.

ULTRA HIGH RISK | Goes after toast with metal butter knife wearing a wet swim suit and a stainless steel colander on head.

In this part . . .

Sun Tzu famously observed that every battle is won or lost before it even begins. That same rationale applies to trading. And just as an army must know its strengths and weaknesses to succeed, you have to get to know yours, too. Here I look at various trading styles, provide tips to develop trading discipline, and offer a practical plan for analyzing markets with an eye to spotting trade opportunities. I also take a hard look at risks beyond just losing money, so you can be prepared for bumps in the road.

Chapter 10

Training and Preparing for Battle

*B*efore you get involved in actively trading the forex market, it's important to take a step back and think about how you want to approach the market. There is more to this than meets the eye, and I think it's one of the most important determinants of overall trading success.

Looking at the title of this chapter, you may think I'm exaggerating a bit with the reference to training and preparing for battle, but I'm really not. The Chinese military philosopher Sun Tzu famously observed that every battle is won or lost before it is ever fought. I can think of no better analogy when it comes to trading in financial markets in general or forex markets in particular.

In this chapter, I take you through the main points to consider as you seek to define your own approach to trading currencies. I review the characteristics of some of the most commonly applied trading styles and discuss what they mean in concrete terms. I also look at what constitutes trading discipline and some of the psychological and emotional hazards you're likely to experience. Last, and probably most important, I run you through the essential elements of developing and sticking to a trading plan.

Finding the Right Trading Style for You

I'm frequently asked, "What's the best way to trade the forex market?" For starters, that's a loaded question that suggests there's a right way and a wrong way to trade currencies. It also implies that there's some magic formula out there, and if you can just find out what it is, you'll be guaranteed trading success. Unfortunately, there is no easy answer. Better put, there is no *standard* answer — one that applies to everyone.

The forex market's trading characteristics have something to offer every trading style (long-term, medium-term, or short-term) and approach (technical, fundamental, or a blend). So in terms of deciding what style or approach is best suited to currencies, the starting point is not the forex market itself, but your own individual circumstances and way of thinking.

Real-world and lifestyle considerations

Before you can begin to identify a trading style and approach that works best for you, you need to give some serious thought to what resources you have available to support your trading. As with many of life's endeavors, when it comes to financial-market trading, there are two main resources that people never seem to have enough of: time and money. Deciding how much of each you can devote to currency trading will help to establish how you pursue your trading goals.

If you're a full-time trader, you have lots of time to devote to market analysis and actually trading the market. But because currencies trade around the clock, you still have to be mindful of which session you're trading, and of the daily peaks and troughs of activity and liquidity. (See Chapter 2 for trading-session specifics.) Just because the market is always open doesn't mean it's necessarily always a good time to trade.

If you have a full-time job, your boss may not appreciate you taking time to catch up on the charts or economic data reports while you're at work. That means you'll have to use your free time to do your market research. Be realistic when you think about how much time you'll be able to devote on a regular basis, keeping in mind family obligations and other personal circumstances.

When it comes to money, I can't stress enough that trading capital has to be risk capital and that you should never risk any money that you can't afford to lose. The standard definition of *risk capital* is money that, if lost, will not materially affect your standard of living. It goes without saying that borrowed money is *not* risk capital — you should never use borrowed money for speculative trading.

When you determine how much risk capital you have available for trading, you'll have a better idea of what size account you can trade and what position size you can handle. Most online trading platforms typically offer generous leverage ratios that allow you to control a larger position with less required margin. But just because they offer high leverage doesn't mean you have to fully utilize it. (I look at the risk and reward components of leverage in greater detail in Chapter 13.)

Making time for market analysis

In other chapters, I talk about the amount of data and news that flows through the forex market on a daily basis — and it can be truly overwhelming. That's one reason the major banks that are active in the forex market employ teams of economists, strategists, technical analysts, and traders. So how can an individual trader possibly keep up with all the data and news?

The key is to develop an efficient daily routine of market analysis. Thanks to the Internet and online currency brokerages, independent traders can access a variety of daily and intraday market reports, covering both technical and fundamental perspectives. Your daily regimen of market analysis should focus on

- ✔ **Overnight forex market developments:** Who said what, which data came out, and how the currency pairs reacted.

- ✔ **Daily updates of other major market movements over the prior 24 hours and the stories behind them:** If oil prices or U.S. Treasury yields rose or fell substantially, find out why.

- ✔ **Data releases and market events (for example, the retail sales report, Fed speeches, central bank rate announcements) expected for that day:** Ideally, you'll monitor data and event calendars one week in advance, so you can anticipate the outcomes along with the rest of the market.

- ✔ **Multiple-timeframe technical analysis of major currency pairs:** There is nothing like the visual image of price action to fill in the blanks of how data and news affected individual currency pairs.

- ✔ **Current events and geopolitical themes:** Stay abreast on issues of major elections, political scandals, military conflicts, and policy initiatives in the major currency nations.

Establishing a research routine will take some time at first. You'll have to read many different news stories and analysts' reports before you get a handle on which sources provide the best overnight summaries, which fundamental analysts are most focused on the forex market, and which technical analysts are focused on actionable trading strategies. I tend to focus on the mainstream financial news media, such as Bloomberg.com, Reuters.com, and MarketWatch.com.

Technical versus fundamental analysis

I look at fundamental analysis and technical analysis in greater depth in Chapters 7 and 11. I include them here as elements to consider as you develop your overall approach to the market. Ask yourself on what basis you'll make your trading decisions — fundamental analysis or technical analysis?

Followers of each discipline have always debated which approach works better. Rather than take sides, I suggest following an approach that *blends* the two disciplines. In my experience, macroeconomic factors, such as interest rates, relative growth rates, and market sentiment, determine the big-picture direction of currency rates. But currencies rarely move in a straight line, which means there are plenty of short-term price fluctuations to take advantage of — and some of them can be substantial.

Technical analysis can provide the guideposts along the route of the bigger price move, allowing traders to more accurately predict the direction and scope of future price changes. Most important, technical analysis is the key to constructing a well-defined trading strategy. For example, your fundamental analysis, data expectations, or plain old gut instinct may lead you to conclude that EUR/USD is going lower. But where exactly do you get short? Where do you take profit, and where do you cut your losses? I like to use technical analysis to refine trade entry and exit points, and to decide whether and where to add to positions or reduce them.

Sometimes forex markets seem to be more driven by fundamental factors, such as current economic data or comments from a central bank official. In those times, fundamentals provide the catalysts for technical breakouts and reversals. At other times, technical developments seem to be leading the charge — a break of trend-line support or recent daily lows may trigger stop-loss selling by market longs and bring in model systems that are selling based on the break of support. Subsequent economic reports may run counter to the directional breakout, but data be damned — the technical support is gone, and the market is selling.

Fundamental data and events are only one piece of the puzzle. Be aware that forex markets frequently ignore individual reports and do their own thing based on some larger theme or adjustment. That's why I always stress that the market reaction to data is more important than the data itself.

Approaching the market with a blend of fundamental and technical analysis will improve your chances of both spotting trade opportunities and managing your trades more effectively. You'll also be better prepared to handle markets that are alternately reacting to fundamental and technical developments or some combination of the two.

Different Strokes for Different Folks

After you've given some thought to the time and resources you're able to devote to currency trading and which approach you favor (technical, fundamental, or a blend), the next step is to settle on a trading style that best fits those choices.

There are as many different trading styles and market approaches in FX as there are individuals in the market. But most of them can be grouped into three main categories that boil down to varying degrees of exposure to market risk. The two main elements of market risk are time and relative price movements. The longer you hold a position, the more risk you're exposed to. The more of a price change you're anticipating, the more risk you're exposed to.

In the next few sections I detail the main trading styles and what they really mean for individual traders. My aim here is not to advocate for any particular trading style. (Styles frequently overlap, and you can adopt different styles for different trade opportunities or different market conditions.) Instead, my goal is to give you an idea of the various approaches used by forex market professionals so you can understand the basis of each style. I think this information will help you settle on a style that best fits your personality and individual circumstances. Equally important, you'll be able to recognize whether your style is drifting and generally maintain a more disciplined approach to the market.

Short-term, high-frequency day trading

Short-term trading in currencies is unlike short-term trading in most other markets. A short-term trade in stocks or commodities usually means holding a position for a day to several days at least. But because of the liquidity and narrow bid/offer spreads in currencies, prices are constantly fluctuating in small increments. The steady and fluid price action in currencies allows for extremely short-term trading by speculators intent on capturing just a few pips on each trade.

Short-term trading in forex typically involves holding a position for only a few seconds or minutes and rarely longer than an hour. But the time element is not the defining feature of short-term currency trading. Instead, the pip fluctuations are what's important. Traders who follow a short-term trading style are seeking to profit by repeatedly opening and closing positions after gaining just a few pips, typically 5 to 10 pips but also as little as 1 or 2 pips.

Jobbing the market pip by pip

In the interbank market, extremely short-term, in-and-out trading is referred to as *jobbing the market;* online currency traders call it *scalping.* (I use the terms interchangeably.) Traders who follow this style have to be among the fastest and most disciplined of traders because they're out to capture only a few pips on each trade. In terms of speed, rapid reaction and instantaneous decision-making are essential to successfully jobbing the market.

When it comes to discipline, scalpers must be absolutely ruthless in both taking profits and losses. If you're in it to make only a few pips on each trade, you can't afford to lose much more than a few pips on each trade. The overall strategy is obviously based on being right more often than being wrong, but the key is not risking more than a few pips on each trade. The essential motto is "Take the money and run" — repeated a few dozen times a day.

Jobbing the market requires an intuitive feel for the market. (Some practitioners refer to it as *rhythm trading*.) Scalpers don't worry about the fundamentals too much. If you were to ask a scalper for her opinion of a particular currency pair, she would likely respond along the lines of "It feels *bid*" or "It feels *offered*" (meaning, she senses an underlying buying or selling bias in the market — but only at that moment). If you ask her again a few minutes later, she may respond in the opposite direction.

Successful scalpers have absolutely no allegiance to any single position. They couldn't care less if the currency pair goes up or down. They're strictly focused on the next few pips. Their position is either working for them, or they're out of it faster than you can blink an eye. All they need is volatility and liquidity.

Adapting jobbing to online currency trading

Retail traders are typically faced with bid/offer spreads of between 1 and 4 pips. Although this makes jobbing slightly more difficult, it doesn't mean you can't still engage in short-term trading — it just means you'll need to adjust the risk parameters of the style. Instead of looking to make 1 to 2 pips on each trade, you need to aim for a pip gain at least as large as the spread you're dealing with in each currency pair. The other basic rules of taking only minimal losses and not hanging on to a position for too long still apply.

Here are some other important guidelines to keep in mind when following a short-term trading strategy:

✔ **Trade only the most liquid currency pairs, such as EUR/USD, USD/JPY, EUR/GBP, EUR/JPY, and EUR/CHF.** The most liquid pairs will have the tightest trading spreads and will be subject to fewer sudden price jumps.

✔ **Trade only during times of peak liquidity and market interest.** Consistent liquidity and fluid market interest are essential to short-term trading strategies. Market liquidity is deepest during the European session when Asian and North American trading centers overlap with European time zones — about 2 a.m. to noon eastern time (ET). Trading in other sessions can leave you with far fewer and less predictable short-term price movements to take advantage of.

✔ **Focus your trading on only one pair at a time.** If you're aiming to capture second-by-second or minute-by-minute price movements, you'll need to fully concentrate on one pair at a time. It'll also improve your feel for the pair if that pair is all you're watching.

✔ **Preset your default trade size so you don't have to keep specifying it on each deal.**

✔ **Look for a brokerage firm that offers click-and-deal trading so you're not subject to execution delays or re-quotes.** (See Chapter 13 for more on broker executions.)

✔ **Adjust your risk and reward expectations to reflect the dealing spread of the currency pair you're trading.** With 1- to 4-pip spreads on most major pairs, you probably need to capture 3 to 10 pips per trade to offset losses if the market moves against you.

✔ **Avoid trading around data releases.** Carrying a short-term position into a data release can be risky because prices may gap sharply after the release, blowing a short-term strategy out of the water. Markets are also prone to quick price adjustments in the 15 to 30 minutes ahead of major data releases as nearby orders are triggered. This can lead to a quick shift against your position that may not be resolved before the data comes out.

Keeping sight of the forest while you're in the trees

Trading a short-term strategy online also requires individual traders to invest more time and effort in analyzing the overall market, especially from the technical perspective.

If you pursue a short-term trading strategy online, where dealing spreads can equal profit targets, you need to be right by a larger margin. To give yourself a better chance of capturing slightly larger short-term moves, always know where you stand in longer charting timeframes. By all means, use tick, one-minute, and five-minute charts to refine your trade timing, entry, and exit. But be aware of the larger picture suggested by hourly, multihour, and daily charts because they're going to hold the keys to the larger directional movements.

Medium-term directional trading

If you thought short-term time frames were exceptionally brief, medium-term time frames aren't much longer. Medium-term positions are typically held for periods ranging anywhere from a few hours to a day or two, but usually not much longer. Just as with short-term trading, the key distinction for medium-term trading is not the length of time the position is open, but the amount of pips you're seeking/risking.

Where short-term trading looks to profit from the routine noise of minor price fluctuations, almost without regard for the overall direction of the market, medium-term trading seeks to get the overall direction right and profit from more significant currency rate moves. By the same token, medium-term traders recognize that markets rarely move in one direction for too long, so they approach the market with well-defined trade entry and exit strategies.

Almost as many currency speculators fall into the medium-term category (sometimes referred to as *momentum trading* and *swing trading*) as fall into the short-term trading category. Medium-term trading requires many of the same skills as short-term trading, especially when it comes to entering/exiting positions, but it also demands a broader perspective, greater analytical effort, and a lot more patience.

Capturing intraday price moves for maximum effect

The essence of medium-term trading is determining where a currency pair is likely to go over the next several hours or days and constructing a trading strategy to exploit that view. Medium-term traders typically pursue one of the following overall approaches, but there's also plenty of room to combine strategies:

- **Trading a view:** Having a fundamental-based opinion on which way a currency pair is likely to move. View trades are typically based on prevailing market themes, like interest rate expectations or economic growth trends. View traders still need to be aware of technical levels as part of an overall trading plan.

- **Trading the technicals:** Basing your market outlook on chart patterns, trend lines, support and resistance levels, and momentum studies. Technical traders typically spot a trade opportunity on their charts, but they still need to be aware of fundamental events, because they're the catalysts for many breaks of technical levels.

- **Trading events and data:** Basing positions on expected outcomes of events, like a central bank rate decision or individual data reports. Event/data traders typically open positions well in advance of events and close them when the outcome is known (also known as buy the rumor/sell the fact, or vice versa).

- **Trading with the flow:** Trading based on overall market direction (trend) or information of major buying and selling (flows). To trade on flow information, look for a broker that offers market flow commentary, like that found in FOREX.com's *Forex Insider* (www.forex.com/forex_research.html).

When is a trend not a trend?

When it's a range. A *trading range* or a *range-bound market* is a market that remains confined within a relatively narrow range of prices. In currency pairs, a short-term (over the next few hours) trading range may be 20 to 50 pips wide, whereas a longer-term (over the next few days to weeks) range can be 200 to 400 pips wide.

For all the hype that trends get in various market literature, the reality is that most markets trend no more than a third of the time. The bulk of the time they're bouncing around in ranges, consolidating, and trading sideways.

If markets reflect all the currently known information that's available, they're going to experience major trends or shifts only when truly new and unexpected information hits the market. On a day-to-day basis, incoming economic data and events usually result in an adjustment of prices only within a prevailing range, rather than a breakout, but that's enough for medium-term traders to take advantage of the opportunity.

Taking what you get from the market

Medium-term traders recognize that sizeable price movements and trends are more the exception than the rule. So rather than selling and holding in the case of a downtrend, for example, they're looking to capitalize on the 50- to 150-point price declines that make up the overall downtrend. The key here is that medium-term traders will take profit frequently and step back to reassess market conditions before getting back in.

Although medium-term traders are normally looking to capture larger relative price movements — say, 50 to 100 pips or more — they're also quick to take smaller profits on the basis of short-term price behavior. For instance, if a break of a technical resistance level suggests a targeted price move of 80 pips higher to the next resistance level, the medium-term trader is going to be more than happy capturing 70 to 80 percent of the expected price move. They're not going to hold on to the position looking for the exact price target to be hit. It goes without saying that it's better to catch 75 percent of *something* than 100 percent of *nothing*.

Long-term macroeconomic trading

Long-term trading in currencies is generally reserved for hedge funds and other institutional types with deep pockets. Long-term trading in currencies can involve holding positions for weeks, months, and potentially years at a time. Holding positions for that long necessarily involves being exposed to significant short-term volatility that can quickly overwhelm margin trading accounts.

With proper risk management, individual margin traders can seek to capture longer-term trends. The key is to hold a small enough position relative to your margin that you can withstand volatility of as much as 5 percent or more. Mini accounts, which trade in lot sizes of 10,000 currency units, are a good vehicle to take advantage of longer-term price trends.

For example, let's say you're of the view that the euro is going to weaken due to the high debt levels of some of the member countries and the potential for a sovereign bond default. EUR/USD is trading around 1.3500, for this example, and you think it's heading to 1.1000 or even lower. But if EUR/USD strengthens above 1.4500, you think the debt crisis will have been resolved and you'd want to exit the trade. In this case you're risking 1,000 pips to gain 2,500 pips.

For a 10,000 EUR trade size, that works out to a risk of losing $1,000 (10,000 × 0.1000 [1,000 EUR pips] = USD 1,000) or gaining $2,500 (10,000 × 0.2500 [2,500 EUR pips] = USD 2,500.)

Identifying the macro elements that lead to long-term trends

Long-term trading seeks to capitalize on major price trends, which are in turn the result of long-term macroeconomic factors. Before you embark on long-term speculation, you want to see how some of the following macroeconomic chips stack up:

- **Interest rate cycles:** Where are the two currencies' relative interest rates, and where are they likely to go in the coming months? Narrower interest-rate differentials will tend to help the lower-yielding currency and hurt the higher-yielding currency; wider interest-rate differentials will help the higher-yielding currency and hurt the lower-yielding one.

- **Economic growth cycles:** What's the outlook for relative growth over the next several months? An economy that is in an expansionary phase of growth is likely to see higher interest rates in the future, which would support that currency. An economy that is showing signs of slowing may see interest rate expectations lowered, hurting the currency in the process.

- **Currency policies:** Are the currencies considered to be excessively overvalued or undervalued by the major global trading powers? Is the G20 or national government/central bank agitating for changes in a currency's value?

- **Structural deficits or surpluses:** Do the currencies have any major structural issues that tend to see currencies weaken or strengthen, such as fiscal deficits/surpluses or trade deficits/surpluses?

Trading around a core position

Just because you're trading with a long-term view doesn't mean you can't take advantage of significant price changes when they're in your favor in the medium term. Trading around a core position refers to taking profit on a portion of your overall position after favorable price changes. You continue to hold a portion of your original position — the core position — and look to reestablish the full position on subsequent market corrections. *Remember:* It never hurts to take some money off the table when you're winning.

Taking partial profit on a long-term position works best when the currency pair you're trading is reaching significant technical levels, such as multiday or multiweek highs. If the trend of the currency pair you're holding is displaying a channel on the charts, taking partial profit near the top of the channel in an uptrend or near the channel bottom in a downtrend is one way of judging when to take partial profit.

The risk with trading around a core position is that the trend may not correct after you've taken partial profit, never giving you the chance to reestablish your desired full position. But you're still holding the core of your position, and because the market hasn't corrected, it means your core position is doing just fine.

Carry trade strategies

A *carry trade* happens when you buy a high-yielding currency and sell a relatively lower-yielding currency. The strategy profits in two ways:

- ✔ **By being long the higher-yielding currency and short the lower-yielding currency, you can earn the interest-rate differential between the two currencies, known as the *carry*.** If you have the opposite position — long the low-yielder and short the high-yielder — the interest-rate differential is against you, and it is known as the *cost of carry*.

- ✔ **Spot prices appreciate in the direction of the interest-rate differential.** Currency pairs with significant interest-rate differentials tend to move in favor of the higher-yielding currency as traders who are long the high yielder are rewarded, increasing buying interest, and traders who are short the high yielder are penalized, reducing selling interest.

So let me get this straight, you may be thinking: All I have to do is buy the higher-yielding currency/sell the lower-yielding currency, sit back, earn the carry, and watch the spot price move higher? What's the catch?

Right you are. There is a catch, and the catch is that downside spot price volatility can quickly swamp any gains from the carry trade's interest-rate differential. The risk can be compounded by excessive market positioning in favor of the carry trade, meaning a carry trade has become so popular that everyone gets in on it. When everyone who wants to buy has bought, why should the price continue to move higher? Even more daunting, if the price begins to reverse against the carry trade, it may trigger a panic exodus out of the trade, accelerating the price plunge. Take a look at Figure 10-1 to get an idea of the trends that can develop around carry trades as well as the sharp setbacks that can happen along the way.

Carry trades usually work best in low-volatility environments, meaning when financial markets are relatively stable and investors are forced to chase yield. Keep in mind that carry trades need to have a significant interest-rate differential between the two currencies (typically more than 2 percent) to make them attractive. And carry trades are definitely a long-term strategy, because depending on when you get in, you may get caught in a downdraft that could take several days or weeks to unwind before the trade becomes profitable again.

Figure 10-1: AUD/JPY trends higher in line with carry trade funda- mentals (Australia's interest rates are much higher than Japan's), but it meets sharp set- backs along the way.

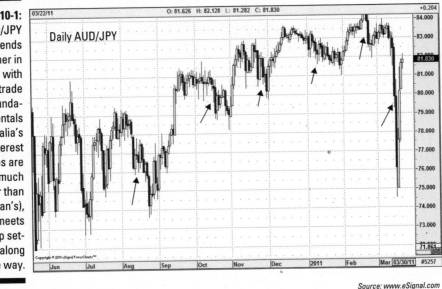

Source: www.eSignal.com

In the wake of the Great Financial Crisis of 2008–2009, major central banks slashed their benchmark interest rates to zero or nearly zero, and many of them are still around that level as of this writing. Near-zero interest rates have eliminated much of the appeal of carry trades in currencies, and it looks to be several years until interest rates are normalized and attractive differentials put carry trades back in vogue.

Trading on Auto-Pilot

Earlier in Chapter 3, I referred to algorithmic trading systems and indicated these were mainly the tools of hedge funds and other institutional players. The rapid growth of the online Forex market has spawned a diverse array of automated trading systems for individual traders, known as *Expert Advisors,* or EAs for short. EAs represent yet another trading approach and one that can blend many of those I outlined earlier.

EAs come in all shapes and sizes with varying complexity or number of rules. (EAs are also known as *rules-based trading systems,* meaning whenever the systems' rules are satisfied, a trade signal is generated.) Some are fully auto- mated (nondiscretionary), firing off trades whenever the rules of the program are met by market movements. Others generate trade alerts and require a manual confirmation by the user before executing a trade (discretionary). Some EAs can be bought off the shelf in a ready-to-go, black-box format, meaning you're using a trading model designed by someone else that usually doesn't allow for modifications. Other EAs come in a build-it-yourself format, allowing you to select the rules you'd like to apply to your trading.

Potential inputs to drive an EA system

There are literally unlimited inputs that can be combined to form the set of rules that go into an EA, but most of them are usually based on technical indicators or price developments. Here are some of the more popular inputs:

- **Crossovers:** These could be crossovers of anything from moving averages (like a 5 minute and 15 minute for a short-term EA, or 9 day and 21 day for a medium term EA) to momentum oscillators (like stochastics or MACD, again of any timeframe).

- **New price highs or lows:** Some trend-following models generate trade signals when new highs or lows are made, usually based on the close of a defined time period, like a new high on an hourly closing basis.

- **Time periods:** Some EAs will function only during specified time periods, say during peak liquidity hours in the London afternoon/NY morning. Still others will function only around specified data releases, when a directional move may be more likely.

- **Daily or weekly closes:** Longer-term systems may look for a daily close above/below a daily moving average, Ichimoku lines, or some other technical approach.

Because many EAs are based on a combination of rules, there's virtually a limitless number of possibilities. Here's an example of one possibility for the long side of a short-term EA: Buy EUR/USD (specify amount) on a new high 5 minute close, if 5 minute MACD is positive, and GBP/USD is also making new high 5 minute close, and 5 minute RSI is <80, and time is between 0600ET-1200ET, and day is between Tuesday and Thursday. The EA would also include something similar for the sell side and also a set of rules for exiting the trade. Note these rules are untested; I just wanted to give you an idea of how an EA might look.

Caveat emptor on models

EAs carry their own set of risks and limitations. Just as you wouldn't put on a blind fold and go for a Sunday drive, you shouldn't expect an EA to deliver a smooth ride all the time. EAs are all based on historical relationships between the various parameters, or rules. And as the ultimate risk disclaimer goes, "past performance is no guarantee of future results."

EAs rely on *back-testing* to evaluate their potential future trading results. Back-testing is a process where a set of rules is applied to historical price data to see how the system *would have* performed. The results are by definition hypothetical, and don't reflect real-world trading conditions (e.g., execution slippage, re-quoting, or price gaps, to mention just a few). To be sure, there is much to commend historical relationships, and I certainly employ them in my own mental models for forex trading. You need to be aware that they can break down, and factor that into your trading plan.

One important result of using an EA is that if you go with a nondiscretionary system, you're taking emotion out of the picture, and that may improve your trading discipline, which I look at next.

Developing Trading Discipline

No matter which trading style you decide to pursue, you need an organized trading plan, or you won't get very far. The difference between making money and losing money in the forex market can be as simple as trading with a plan or trading without one. A *trading plan* is an organized approach to executing a trade strategy that you've developed based on your market analysis and outlook.

Here are the key components of any trading plan:

- **Determining position size:** How large a position will you take for each trade strategy? Position size is half the equation for determining how much money is at stake in each trade.

- **Deciding where to enter the position:** Exactly where will you try to open the desired position? What happens if your entry level is not reached?

- **Setting stop-loss and take-profit levels:** Exactly where will you exit the position, both if it's a winning position (take profit) and if it's a losing position (stop loss)? Stop-loss and take-profit levels are the second half of the equation that determines how much money is at stake in each trade.

That's it — just three simple components. But it's amazing how many traders, experienced and beginner alike, open positions without ever having fully thought through exactly what their game plan is. Of course, you need to consider numerous finer points when constructing a trading plan, and I focus on them later in this chapter. But for now, I just want to drive home the point that trading without an organized plan is like flying an airplane blindfolded — you may be able to get off the ground, but how will you land?

And no matter how good your trading plan is, it won't work if you don't follow it. Sometimes emotions bubble up and distract traders from their trade plans. Other times, an unexpected piece of news or price movement causes traders to abandon their trade strategy in midstream, or midtrade, as the case may be. Either way, when this happens, it's the same as never having had a trade plan in the first place.

Developing a trade plan and sticking to it are the two main ingredients of *trading discipline*. If I were to name the one defining characteristic of successful traders, it wouldn't be technical analysis skill, gut instinct, or aggressiveness — though they're all important. Nope, it would be trading discipline. Traders who follow a disciplined approach are the ones who survive year after year and market cycle after market cycle. They can even be wrong more often than right and still make money because they follow a disciplined approach. Yet establishing and maintaining trading discipline is an elusive goal for many traders.

Taking the emotion out of trading

If the key to successful trading is a disciplined approach — developing a trading plan and sticking to it — why is it so hard for many traders to practice trading discipline? The answer is complex, but it usually boils down to a simple case of human emotions getting the better of them.

I may be dating myself here a bit, but I remember an episode of the TV sitcom *M*A*S*H,* in which Hawkeye Pierce (Alan Alda) observes that the three basic human emotions are greed, fear, and greed. Certainly, that's the case in financial market trading. When it comes to trading in any market, don't underestimate the power of emotions to distract and disrupt.

So exactly how do you take the emotion out of trading? The simple answer is: You can't. As long as your heart is pumping and your synapses are firing, emotions are going to be flowing. And truth be told, the emotional highs of trading are one of the reasons people are drawn to it in the first place. There's no rush quite like putting on a successful trade and taking some money out of the market. So just accept that you're going to be experiencing some pretty intense emotions when you're trading.

The longer answer is that because you can't block out the emotions, the best you can hope to achieve is an understanding of where the emotions are coming from, recognizing them when they hit, and limiting their impact on your trading. It's a lot easier said than done, but keep in mind some of the following, and you may find you're better able to keep your emotions in check:

- ✔ **Focus on the pips and not the dollars and cents.** Don't be distracted by the exact amount of money won or lost in a trade. Instead, focus on where prices are and how they're behaving. The market has no idea what your trade size is and how much you're making or losing, but it does know where the current price is.

- ✔ **It's not about being right or wrong; it's about making money.** At the end of the day, the market doesn't care if you were right or wrong, and neither should you. The only true measure of trading success is dollars and cents.

✔ **You're going to lose in a fair number of trades.** No trader is right 100 percent of the time. Taking losses is as much a part of the routine as taking profits. You can still be successful over time with a solid risk-management plan.

✔ **The market is not out to get you.** The market is going to do what it does whether you're involved in it or not, so don't take your trading results personally. Interpret them professionally, just as you would the results of any other business venture.

Managing your expectations

Currency trading is a relatively new opportunity for individual traders, and a lot of people have no frame of reference about what to expect when it comes to price movements. A frequent question asked by newcomers is "How much can I expect to make on this trade?" Whoa, Nelly. Talk about a loaded question.

Financial markets are not bank ATMs, and the forex market is certainly no exception. There are a lot of people speculating on which way various currency pairs are going to move; some of those people are going to be right, and some are going to be wrong. Some may also be right for a moment but suddenly end up on the wrong side of equation.

Before you get involved with trading currencies, you need to have a healthy sense of what to expect when it comes to trading outcomes. Many people choose to focus only on the upside prospects of currency trading, like the view expressed in that loaded question earlier. But losses are part of trading, too. Even the biggest and best traders have losing trades on a regular basis.

One of the keys to establishing trading discipline is to first accept that losses are inevitable. The second step is to dedicate yourself to keeping those losses as small as possible. Most experienced traders will tell you the hardest part of trading is keeping the money you've made and not giving it back to the market.

Imagining realistic profit-and-loss scenarios

The trading style that you decide to pursue will dictate the relative size of profits and losses that you can expect to experience. If you're trading on a short- to medium-term basis, look at average daily trading ranges to get a good idea of what to expect.

The *average daily trading range* is a mathematical average of each day's trading range (high to low) over a specified period. Keep in mind that this figure is just a statistical average — there will be days with larger ranges and days with narrower ranges. Also, average daily ranges will vary significantly by currency pair.

But the average daily trading range covers a full 24-hour trading session and tends to overstate what short- and medium-term traders can expect from intraday trading ranges. Generally speaking, you're better off anticipating more modest price movements of 30 to 80 pips rather than aiming for the home-run ball.

And no matter what any infomercial tells you, you're not going to retire based on any single trade. The key is to hit singles and stay in the game.

Balancing risk versus reward

Trading is all about taking on risk to generate profits. So one question is frequently posed: "How much should I risk in any given trade?" There is no easy answer to that question. Some trading books advise people to use a risk/reward ratio, like 2:1, meaning that if you risk $100 on a trade, you should aim to make $200 to justify the risk. Others counsel to never risk more than a fixed percentage of your trading account on any single trade. It's all a bit formulaic, if you ask me, and it also has no relation to the reality of the markets.

A better way to think about risk and reward is to look at each trade opportunity on its own and assess the outcomes based on technical analysis. This approach has the virtue of being as dynamic as the market, allowing you to exploit trade opportunities according to prevailing market conditions.

Another factor to consider in balancing risk and reward is the use of leverage (see Chapter 13). In online currency trading, generous leverage ratios of 50:1 or 100:1 are typically available. The higher the leverage ratio, the larger position you can trade based on your margin. But leverage is a double-edged sword because it amplifies profits *and* losses.

The key here is to limit your overall leverage utilization so you're not putting all your eggs in one basket. If you open the largest position available based on your margin, you'll have very little cushion left in case of adverse price movements. It may seem sexy to trade as large a position as possible, but whoever said prudent, risk-aware trading was supposed to be sexy? Keep your feet on the ground, and don't lose your head in the clouds of leverage.

Keeping your ammunition dry

The margin you're required to post with your forex broker is the basis for all your trading. The amount of margin you put up will determine how large a position you can hold and for how long (in pips) if the market moves against you. Unless you just won the lottery, your margin collateral is a precious, finite resource, so you have to use it sparingly.

If Hamlet were alive today and trading currencies, his famous soliloquy might begin "To trade or not to trade?" One of the biggest mistakes traders make is known as overtrading. *Overtrading* typically refers to trading too often in the market or trading too many positions at once. Both forms suggest a lack of discipline, and sound more like throwing darts at a board and hoping something sticks.

Keeping your ammunition dry refers to staying out of the market, watching and waiting, and picking your trades more selectively.

Opportunity lost or opportunity cost?

One of the more popular market aphorisms is "You've got to be in it to win it." Though it's obviously a truism, I would counter that trading discretion is the better part of trading valor. Holding open positions not only exposes you to market risk, but can also cost you market opportunities.

After you enter a position, your available margin is reduced, which in turn lowers the amount of new positions you can establish. If you're routinely involved in the market because you don't want to miss out on the next big move, you actually run the risk of missing out on the next big move because you may not have enough available margin to support a new position for the big move.

Don't be afraid about missing out on some trade opportunities. No one ever catches all the moves. Instead, focus on your market analysis and pinpoint the next well-defined trading opportunity. (I look at spotting trade setups in Chapter 12.)

Thinking clearly while you still can

Another virtue of trading less frequently is that your market outlook is not skewed by any of the emotional entanglements that come with open positions. If you ask a trader who's long EUR/USD what he thinks of EUR/USD, surprise, surprise — he's going to tell you he thinks it's going up. That's called *talking your book*.

But being out of the market, or being square, allows you to step back and analyze market developments with a clear perspective. That's when you can spot opportunities more clearly and develop an effective trade strategy to exploit them. All too soon, you'll be on to your next trade, and the emotional roller coaster will start all over again.

Chapter 11

Cutting the Fog with Technical Analysis

Saying that there is a lot of information to absorb in the forex market is an understatement of major proportions. To help make sense of all the information, a lot of which can be just noise — the fog of the market — professional traders focus on the one piece of information that is not subject to dispute or opinion: prices.

The field of technical analysis is huge, and there's no way I can cover it in its entirety in this single chapter. Literally hundreds of books have been written on technical analysis in general, as well as on specific approaches (such as the Elliott wave principle or candlestick analysis). In Chapter 20, I suggest several of my favorite books on technical analysis as additional reading. I strongly urge you to supplement the material in this chapter with further in-depth study.

In this chapter, I give you as rich a slice of the technical cake as possible, covering the main elements of technical analysis as they apply to the forex market. What's more, I approach it from a trader's perspective, focusing on the technical tools and approaches that I've found most useful in my own currency trading, as well as what it means for trade strategies and spotting trade setups. That approach may get me in trouble with some technical purists out there, but, hey, that's what makes a market — a difference of opinion.

The Philosophy of Technical Analysis

Calling technical analysis a philosophy is probably a bit of a stretch, but plenty of technical traders are almost cultish in their devotion to it. More than anything, technical analysis is a subjective approach aimed at bringing a sense of order to seemingly random price movements.

Traders use technical analysis to identify trade opportunities, refine their trading strategies (entry and exit levels), and manage their market risk.

Personally, I like to use fundamentals to guide my overall view of market direction, and refine that with technical analysis to identify entry and exit points for specific trades. But not infrequently, technical analysis will suggest a trade opportunity all by itself, even though it may be counter to my fundamental outlook (see the Tips in the "Candlestick patterns" section later in this chapter for more).

What is technical analysis?

In a nutshell, *technical analysis* is the study of historical price movements to predict future price movements. You're probably familiar with the standard disclaimer that "past performance is no guarantee of future results," a statement that tends to call into question the validity of using past price data to forecast future price developments.

But technical analysis is able to get *beyond* those concerns based on two main considerations:

- **Markets are made up of humans.** Human psychology and investing behavior haven't changed very much over the years, whether it's the Dutch tulip frenzy of the 1600s, the dot-com bubble of the 1990s, or the real estate bubbles of the last decade. The emotional forces that dictate buying and selling decisions are reflected in historical price patterns that appear over and over in all manner of financial markets. As long as humans are still making the decisions (or are writing the programs for the computers that make the decisions), you'll be able to look at past behavior as a guide to what is likely to happen in the future.

- **Technical analysis is widely practiced in all markets.** This is the self-fulfilling-prophecy aspect of technical analysis. The greater the number of traders who focus on technical analysis, the more likely their actions will reflect the interpretations of technical analysis, reinforcing the impact of that analysis. Believe me when I say that professional currency traders who do not practice some form of technical analysis are a rarity.

What technical analysis is not

Despite its name, technical analysis is not some engineer-designed, surefire, guaranteed method of market analysis. There are no such methods, period. Technical analysis involves a high degree of subjectivity where individual interpretations can vary significantly. Two technical traders looking at the same currency chart could reach opposite conclusions about the course of future prices. What's more, they could both be right, depending on their timing and specific strategies.

Technical analysis requires a great deal of patience, practice, and experimentation based on individual preferences and circumstances. Short-term traders focusing on the next few minutes and hours find certain tools and approaches more helpful than long-term traders do. Longer-term traders looking at multiday or multiweek trades use other tools and indicators entirely. Certain technical approaches work better in some currency pairs than others. Overall market conditions of volatility and liquidity also influence which technical approach works best. The key is to develop your own approach based on your particular circumstances — time frame, risk appetite, discipline (see Chapter 10 for more on this).

No single, magical technical indicator or approach always works. Be careful about becoming too reliant on any single indicator. A particular indicator may yield excellent signals in certain market environments but fail when market conditions begin to change. I suggest becoming familiar with several different approaches and indicators, using them to cross-check each other depending on market conditions. (I look at this idea in the "Waiting for confirmation" section, later in this chapter.)

Forms of technical analysis

Technical analysis can be broken down into three main approaches:

- **Chart analysis:** Visual inspection of price charts to identify price trends, ranges, support, and resistance levels. (I look at chart analysis in "The Art of Technical Analysis," later in this chapter.)

- **Pattern recognition:** Identifies chart formations or patterns that provide specific predictive signals, such as a reversal or a breakout. (I show you some of the most common traditional chart patterns and candlestick formations in the "Recognizing chart formations" section, later in this chapter.)

- **Momentum and trend analysis:** Looks at the rate of change of prices for indications of market sentiment regarding the price movement. Trend indicators seek to determine the presence of a trend and its strength. (I look at these indicators in "The Science of Technical Analysis," later in this chapter.)

Finding support and resistance

One of the basic building blocks of technical analysis is the concept of *support and resistance:*

- ✔ **Support:** A price level where buying interest overwhelms selling interest, causing a price decline to stop, bottom out, or pause. Think of support as a floor for prices in a downmove.

- ✔ **Resistance:** The opposite of support. Resistance is where selling interest materializes and slows or overpowers buying interest, causing prices to peak, stall, or pause in a price rally. Think of resistance as the ceiling in a price advance.

Support and resistance levels are identified based on prior price action, such as highs and lows and short-term (minutes to hours) *consolidation* or *congestion zones* (where prices get all stopped up and can't move one way or the other for a period of time). Support and resistance can also be determined by drawing trend lines. Still other forms of support and resistance come from Fibonacci retracement levels, *Ichimoku* lines, and moving averages, which I save for later in this chapter. Figure 11-1 shows some basic support and resistance levels from sloping and horizontal trend lines drawn off key highs and lows.

Sloping trend line support from key highs and lows

Figure 11-1:
Trend lines drawn off key highs and lows can be used to identify important support and resistance levels as well as illuminating unfolding pattern formations.

Horizontal support and resistance from prior lows and highs

One of the key concepts of support and resistance is that after a support or resistance level is broken, it shifts direction. In other words, after a support level is broken in a move to the downside, it becomes resistance in subsequent price attempts to rally. After a resistance level is broken to the upside, it may later act as support for further price gains.

Not all support and resistance are created equal

Support and resistance come in all shapes and sizes. Some support or resistance levels are stronger or weaker than others, and technical analysts typically refer to support as either minor or major. But those terms are subjective and difficult to quantify with any precision.

The best way to get a handle on the relative strength of a support or resistance level is to view it in the context of time and price significance.

- ✔ **The longer the time frame of the price point, the greater its significance.** A weekly high/low is more important than a daily high/low, which is more important than an hourly high/low, and so on, down the time scale.

- ✔ **Trend-line strength is also a function of time frame and durability.** A trend line based on daily charts tends to be stronger than a trend line based on hourly prices. A trend line that dates back six months has greater significance than one that's only a week or two old. Also, the more often a trend line is tested (meaning, prices touch the trend line but do not break through it, or break through it only very briefly and by small amounts), the more valid it is.

- ✔ **The strength of support or resistance levels during a retracement depends on the strength of the support or resistance during the prior directional move.** A retracement refers to a price movement in the opposite direction of a previous price advance or decline. The distance that prices reverse, or retrace, is called a *retracement.* For example, trend lines that were support in a downmove will act as resistance in any retracement higher. The strength of the trend-line support on the way down, such as how many attempts were needed to break below it, will give a good indication of its likely strength as resistance in the retracement.

Support and resistance are made to be broken

I don't want to leave you with the impression that support and resistance levels are immutable forces in the market that are never challenged or broken. Just the opposite: Forex markets spend much of the time testing support or resistance levels, looking for the weak side in which to push prices.

Different trading styles focus on different types of support and resistance:

✔ **Tests and breaks of short-term support or resistance levels are the meat and potatoes of intra-day trading.** Short-term traders focus on the nearest support or resistance levels (for example, 5- or 15-minute or hourly highs/lows and trend lines) as guides to the immediate direction of prices.

✔ **Tests and breaks of longer-term support and resistance levels are the fuel that fires longer-term trends or defines medium-term ranges.** Medium- to longer-term traders typically focus on longer-term support or resistance levels, such as daily/weekly highs/lows, and trend lines drawn off them, to guide their trading.

One of the keys to assessing the significance of a break of support or resistance levels is the strength of follow-through that occurs after the level is broken. *Follow-through* is the price action that takes place after technical support or resistance is broken. After resistance is broken, for example, prices should accelerate higher as shorts who sold in front of the resistance buy back their positions and new buyers enter the market, because resistance has been surpassed. The amount of follow-through buying or selling that materializes, or fails to materialize, after the break of a technical support or resistance level is an important indication of the strength of the underlying move.

Waiting for confirmation

I was tempted to title this section "Looking for confirmation," but I thought that sounded too proactive in the sense that if you go looking for something on a chart, odds are you can find it and rationalize it as confirmation. The more disciplined approach involves *waiting* for confirmation, letting market prices provide you with unambiguous signs of a change in direction or break of a chart pattern.

Confirmation refers to price movements that verify, or confirm, a technical observation that suggests a particular outcome. For example, certain chart patterns are useful predictors of a potential reversal in price direction. But note that the starting point in this case is that prices are moving in a trend or steady direction. Blindly following a pattern that suggests that a trend is about to end is very risky. After all, the trend is your friend, so why would you take the risk of going against the trend?

If you're patient and wait for price action to provide you with confirmation that a directional move or trend is indeed reversing, essentially confirming that the observed chart pattern is playing out as you expected, you're reducing the risks of being wrong-sided or premature in your trade. The trade-off is that you may sacrifice a better entry level for a higher degree of certainty in the overall trade setup. Looked at the other way around, you're reducing the risks of getting into a trade setup too soon and being wrong if the setup doesn't play out as you expected. The difference is not making as much money as possible or losing money outright. Which would you prefer?

Technical-based observations provide you with a heads-up alert that a price shift may soon take place — for example, prices may be stalling in a move higher, potentially setting up a reversal lower. Confirmation comes when prices break an established trend line, prior high or low, or other key technical levels of support or resistance. Be careful about looking for confirmation from multiple technical indicators, because they may be measuring the same thing, just in slightly different formats. *Price* is the key element of confirmation.

The Art of Technical Analysis

Chart analysis is at the heart of technical analysis. Don't become reliant on all the fancy indicators and technical studies on your charting system. The most powerful technical indicators you have are your eyes and what's behind them.

In this section, I show you the basics of drawing trend lines and look at some of the most common, yet significant, price patterns you'll encounter over and over again in your trading. In Chapter 12, I go into greater detail and suggest practical approaches to drawing and applying trend lines on a regular basis, as well as how to trade the chart formations you observe.

Bar charts and candlestick charts

In this section, I introduce the two main types of charts you'll likely be using as you pursue your own technical analysis.

Measuring markets with price bars

Most charting systems are set to default to show *bar charts,* probably the most widely used form of charting among Western traders. Bar charts are composed of price bars, which encompass the key points of each trading *period* — namely, the open, high, low, and close. A period is the time interval you've selected to analyze, such as 5 or 15 minutes for short-term traders, and 1 hour, 4 hour, daily, or weekly for longer-term traders (though short-term traders need to be aware of the longer periods, too). Each bar is displayed as a vertical line with a tick mark on each side of the bar. The tick mark on the left side of the price bar represents the open of the period; the tick mark on the right side is the close of the period; and the upper and lower levels of the bar are the period's highs and lows. For example, Figure 11-1 is a bar chart.

You can use bar charts to draw trend lines, measure retracement levels, and gauge overall price volatility. Each bar represents the trading range for the period; the larger the bar, the greater the range and the higher the volatility (and vice versa for smaller bars). Bar charts are best suited to relatively basic analysis, such as getting a handle on an overall trend.

Lighting the way with candlesticks

I put my favoritism right out front for everyone to see: I love using candlestick charts to spot trade setups, especially impending price reversals. I think candlesticks are among the more powerful predictive tools in the trader's arsenal, and I strongly recommend that you study them further. In particular, I highly recommend reading Steve Nison's *Japanese Candlestick Charting Techniques,* 2nd Edition (see Chapter 20 for more on Nison's book).

Candlestick charts are among the earliest known forms of technical analysis, dating back to trading in the Japanese rice markets in the 18th century. Candlestick charts, or just *candles* for short, provide a more visually intuitive representation of price action than you get from simple bar charts. They do this through the use of color and by more clearly breaking out the key price points of each trading day — open, close, high, and low.

Figure 11-2 shows the components of two candlesticks. Immediately, you can see that one candle is light, and the other is dark. What does that mean? Think of yin and yang, good and bad, up and down. The light candlestick indicates that the close was higher than the open — it was an up day. The dark candle indicates that the close was lower than the open — a down day.

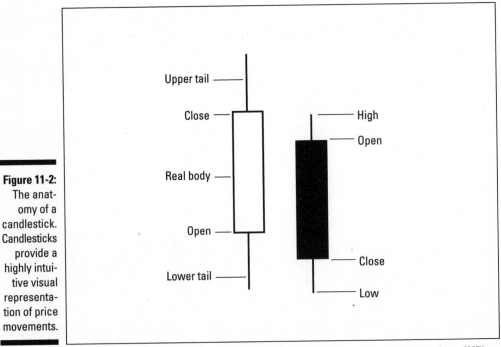

Figure 11-2:
The anatomy of a candlestick. Candlesticks provide a highly intuitive visual representation of price movements.

Source: FOREX.com

The light/dark portion in the middle of the candle is called the *real body* or just *body;* it displays the difference between the open and the close. The lines above and below the body are called *tails* (the term I'll use going forward), *shadows,* or *wicks;* these lines represent the high and low of the period. (I look more at candlesticks in the "Candlestick patterns" section, later in this chapter.)

Candlestick charts are best analyzed using daily or weekly periods rather than intra-day periods like 1 hour or 30 minutes. The philosophy behind candle stick analysis is that a full day or week of trading is needed before the market has rendered a verdict, potentially offering signals about future direction.

Drawing trend lines

Probably no exercise in technical analysis is more individualistic than identifying and drawing trend lines. Very often, it comes down to a matter of beauty being in the eye of the beholder. But in the case of chart analysis, beauty is order, and the trend lines you draw are the outlines of that order. Ultimately, drawing trend lines is not that complicated — with a bit of practice, you'll get the hang of it pretty quickly.

What is a trend line? Basically, a *trend line* is a line that connects significant price points over a defined time period on a price chart. The significant price points are usually the highs and lows of bars or candles, though in the case of candles you can also use the open or close levels of the candle's real body.

Connecting the dots

The starting point in drawing trend lines is looking at the overall price chart in front of you. What do you see? If it's your first time looking at a price chart, it probably looks like a jumble of meaningless bars or candles. The key is to turn that jumble into a meaningful visualization of what's happening to prices. (I offer several graphical representations of trend lines throughout Chapter 12.)

Scan the chart from left to right, starting in the past and looking into the present. What are prices doing? Are they moving up, down, or a little of both? (If you're looking at a currency chart, you can bet they're doing a little bit of both.) Draw your first trend lines to connect the highest highs (you need only two points to form a line) and the lowest lows, to capture the overall range in the observed period. Always use the extreme points of the price bars or candles when connecting price points (lows with lows, highs with highs).

Look at what's happening between those two trend lines. You'll invariably see a number of smaller, distinct price movements making up the whole. You can draw trend lines to connect the highs of price moves down and the lows of price moves up. Be sure to extend your trend lines all the way to the right edge of the chart, regardless of other bars or candles that later break it. Look for evenness, whether it's horizontal, sloping down, shooting steeply higher, or anything in between. Eventually, that evenness will be broken by price moves that break through the trend lines.

Your ultimate focus will be on the prices on the right side of the chart, because that's the most recent price action, and beyond lies future price developments. The idea is to winnow out trend lines from the past that appear to have little relevance (they're frequently broken), and keep the trend lines that have the most relevance (prices reverse course when they're hit, and they're largely unbroken) and extend them into the future. Those trend lines are going to act as support and resistance just as they did in the past and provide you with guidance going forward.

Looking for symmetry

When you're drawing trend lines, be alert for symmetrical patterns, such as parallel channels, sloping up or down, or simply horizontal. Look for horizontal tops and bottoms to be made where prior high and lows were reached. Note that a rising trend line may be heading for a falling trend line, forming a triangle. The two lines are set to intersect at some point in the future, and one of them will be broken, sparking a price reaction.

Charting systems usually have a trend-line function that allows you to draw a line parallel to another line, or copy an existing line and move it to a parallel position. Experiment with that tool, and you'll be surprised how frequently price points match up to it.

Recognizing chart formations

Pattern recognition, or the identification of chart formations, is another form of technical analysis that helps traders get a handle on what's happening in the market. In the following sections, I cover some of the most widely observed chart formations and what they mean from a trading standpoint. While you're looking through them, keep in mind that the formations can occur in different charting time frames (for example, 15 minutes, hourly, daily).

The key to trading on chart formations is to recognize the time period in which they're apparent and to factor that into your trade strategy. A reversal pattern that occurs on an hourly chart, for example, may constitute a reversal that lasts for only a few hours or a day and retrace a relatively smaller pip distance. A reversal pattern on a daily chart, in contrast, could signal a significant multiweek reversal spanning several hundred pips. Keep the formations you observe in the proper time-frame perspective.

Basic chart formations

Chart formations are part and parcel of trends. They're generally grouped into categories that reflect what they mean in the context of a trend. The two most common types of chart patterns are

- ✔ **Reversal patterns:** A reversal pattern indicates that the prior directional price movement is coming to an end. It does not necessarily mean that prices will actually begin to move in the opposite direction, though in many cases they will.

- ✔ **Consolidation and continuation patterns:** Consolidation and continuation patterns represent pauses in directional price moves, where prices undergo a period of back-and-forth consolidation before the overall trend continues.

Double tops and double bottoms

Double tops and *double bottoms* are typically considered among the most powerful chart formations indicating a reversal in the direction of an overall trend. Double tops form in an uptrend, and double bottoms form in a downtrend. Figure 11-3 shows a double-bottom pattern on a daily AUD/USD chart, and Figure 11-1 shows a double top on a four-hour AUD/USD chart (not labeled, but you can see the two highs).

In terms of market dynamics, the idea behind both is that a directional move (up or down) will make a high or low at some point. After a period of consolidation, the market will frequently test the prior high or low for the trend. If the trend is still intact, the market should be able to make a new high or low beyond the prior one. But if the market is unable to surpass the prior high or low, it's taken as a signal that the trend is over, and trend followers begin to exit, generating the reversal.

As with most chart formations, double tops and bottoms rarely form perfectly. The second high or low may come up short of the prior high/low; that inability even to retest the prior high/low can create a more rapid and volatile reversal. Other times, the first low may be surpassed by a brief amount and for a brief time (possibly due to stops at the prior low being triggered), as in Figure 10-3, only to be rejected, leading to the reversal.

Head and shoulders and inverted head and shoulders

Head-and-shoulders (H&S) formations are another form of reversal pattern, sometimes referred to as a *triple top*. The H&S top formation develops after an uptrend, and an *inverted H&S* comes after a downtrend. Figure 11-4 shows a classic example of an inverted H&S formation, signaling the end of the EUR's decline after the Eurozone debt crisis. In the case of an uptrend, a high is made at some stage followed by a pullback lower, creating the left shoulder. A subsequent new high is made, generating the head, followed by yet another correction lower. A third attempt to move higher fails to reach the second or highest high and may surpass, equal, or fall short of the left shoulder. Failure to reach the prior high typically triggers selling, and confirmation of a reversal is received when prices fall below the *neckline,* which is formed by connecting the lows seen after each pullback from the shoulder and the head.

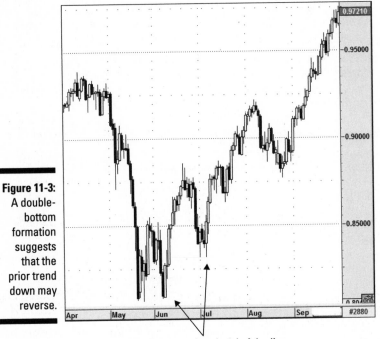

Figure 11-3: A double-bottom formation suggests that the prior trend down may reverse.

Double bottoms signal end of declines

Source: www.eSignal.com

The standard *measured move objective* (the price move suggested by a chart pattern) in an H&S pattern is the distance from the top of the head to the neckline. When the neckline is broken, prices should subsequently move that distance.

Flags

Flags are consolidation patterns that typically form in a counter-trend direction. For example, if prices have moved higher (the trend is up) and run into resistance above, for a flag to form, prices will begin to consolidate in a downward (counter-trend) channel. The formation suggests that the flag consolidation channel will eventually break out in the direction of the prior trend, and the directional move will resume. Perhaps somewhat confusingly, a *bull flag* actually slopes downward, but it's called a bull flag because after it breaks, the bullish trend resumes. A *bear flag* slopes upward, but after it breaks to the downside, the bearish trend resumes.

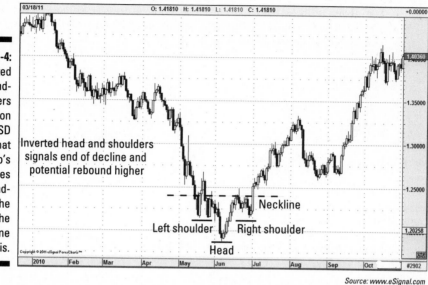

Figure 11-4:
An inverted head-and-shoulders formation in EUR/USD signals that the euro's declines may be ending after the worst of the Eurozone debt crisis.

If the opposite side of the flag channel is broken (the lower end of a bull flag/upper end of a bear flag), the pattern is invalidated and it may signal a larger reversal.

Flags have a measured move objective based on the *flagpole,* or the distance of the prior move that ultimately stalled, resulting in the formation of the flag. When the flag is broken, the price target is usually equal to the length of the flagpole projected from the flag break, as shown in Figure 11-5.

Triangles

Triangles are another type of consolidation pattern, and they come in a few different forms:

- ✓ **Symmetrical triangles:** These formations have downward-sloping upper edges and upward-sloping lower edges, resulting in a triangle pointing horizontally. Symmetrical triangles are mostly neutral for the direction of the ultimate breakout, but they have a slightly greater tendency to break out in the direction in which they entered the triangle consolidation, meaning the trend is resuming.

- ✓ **Ascending triangles:** These formations have a flat or horizontal top and an upward-sloping lower edge (see Figure 11-6). Ascending triangles typically break out to the upside after resistance on the top is overcome. The rising lower edge signifies that buyers keep coming back at ever-higher levels to push through the horizontal top. The minimum measured move objective on a breakout is equal to the distance between the rising bottom and where the flat top is first reached.

✔ **Descending triangles:** These formations are the inverse of ascending triangles, where the horizontal edge and the expected direction of the breakout are to the downside.

Figure 11-5:
A break of
a bear flag
consolida-
tion pattern
on an hourly
chart of
NZD/USD
signals that
the move
down is
resuming.

Bear flag consolidation pattern
break sees downmove continuation
measured move objective equal to
length of flagpole

Flagpole

Flag projection from channel
break gives a price target

Source: www.eSignal.com

Candlestick patterns

Candlestick patterns are some of the most powerful predictors of future price direction. Candlesticks have little predictive capacity when it comes to the size of future price movements, so you need to look at other forms of technical analysis to gauge the extent of subsequent price moves. But if you can get the direction right, you're more than halfway there. (I look more at using candles to develop trade strategies in Chapter 12.)

Candlestick formations come in two main forms:

✔ **Reversal patterns:** Where a preceding directional move stops and changes direction

✔ **Continuation patterns:** Where a prior directional move resumes its course after a period of consolidation

I like to look at candlestick patterns primarily for reversal signals because they're among the most reliable of the candlestick patterns.

The key to interpreting a candle formation as a reversal indicator is that there has to be an identifiable directional move in the preceding days. The directional price move may be part of an extended uptrend or downtrend, or simply a day or two of a clear directional move higher or lower, as shown by relatively large real bodies.

Literally dozens of different candlestick reversal patterns exist, but I focus on the most common patterns in the following sections. Keep in mind that some candle reversal formations consist of a single candle, whereas others depend on two or three candles to constitute the pattern. Look closely, and you'll see that many of them are variations on the same theme (namely that a directional move is losing force, increasing the potential for a price reversal). A good source of candlestick reference can be found for free at www.candlesticker.com.

Doji

Doji are among the most significant of the candlestick patterns because their basic shape forms the basis for many other candlestick patterns. A doji occurs when the close is the same as the open, generating a candlestick with no real body — simply a vertical line with a cross on it.

Figure 11-6: The break of the flat top in an ascending-triangle formation signals an upside breakout. Note that the top of the triangle subsequently acted as support.

Ascending triangle signals upmove
is resuming when flat top is broken

Source: www.eSignal.com

On days when the close is only a few points apart from the open, generating a candle with an extremely small real body, you can take some artistic license and consider it a potential doji depending on the preceding candles. If the prior days' candles were composed of long real bodies, that increases the likelihood that the very small real body should be viewed as a doji (or a spinning top, which I cover later in this section). Figure 11-7 is a good example of this — the open and close were only 5 pips apart. Whenever you spot a doji after a daily close, you should note it and consider that the preceding directional move may be ending or set for a reversal.

Figure 11-7:
After a move higher in AUD/USD, a doji signals the gains may be about to reverse.

Source: www.eSignal.com

Doji are significant because they represent indecision and uncertainty. When viewing a doji, think of buyers and sellers fighting to a draw. In the case of a preceding decline lower, for example, it signals that sellers are losing power and buyers have emerged. Figure 11-7 shows a classic doji, where the open and close are the same and about in the middle of the day's trading range. The longer the upper and lower tails are in a doji, the greater the sense of uncertainty displayed by the market and the more likely the prior trend is to be ending.

A double doji occurs when two doji appear in successive periods. The increased uncertainty associated with a double doji tends to signal that the subsequent price move will be more significant after the market's indecision is resolved. A long-legged doji, one with larger tails, is another indication that the market's uncertainty may resolve with a more pronounced move.

On its own, a doji is considered neutral. You need to wait for subsequent price action, such as a trend-line break, to confirm that the doji is signaling a reversal.

Hammers and shooting stars

Hammers and *shooting stars* are single-candle formations that indicate a reversal may be in store. Hammers appear after a decline and are notable for a long lower tail (at least twice the height of the real body) and a small real body at the upper end of the candle (akin to a doji or spinning top). A shooting star is the mirror image after a move higher — a long upper tail and a small real body at the bottom of the day's range. The color of the candle can be either light or dark. In both cases the market dynamic is the same: After a price rise, in the case of a shooting star, buyers attempted to extend the advance, but by the end of the day were beaten back by sellers, and vice versa with hammers.

The size of the tails is an important indication of the strength of the signal — the larger the tail, the greater the opposing force to the prior move and the more likely prices are to reverse course. Figure 11-8 shows a shooting star signaling recent gains may be set to reverse. (See Figure 11-10 for a hammer as part of another candle pattern.)

Hammers and shooting stars are one of my major alerts for price reversals. They're a signal to exit or at least reduce positions in the direction of the prior trend, and a good basis to establish a position in the opposite direction. If the high of a shooting star or the low of a hammer is exceeded, then the signal is negated and you have to get out. (See more in Chapter 12 for trading tactics using candles.)

Spinning tops

A *spinning top* (see Figure 11-9) is a single-candle formation that has a small real body and typically short tails, sort of like a fatter version of a doji, but with larger tails. (Larger tails may signify a greater potential price move; however, the size of the tails is secondary.) The formation gets its name because it resembles a child's toy top. A spinning top frequently appears in pairs, similar to a double doji. The significance of a spinning top is that it has a small real body, which represents a drop in directional momentum after a series of up or down candles, which may signal a directional move is stalling and is ripe for a correction. Spinning tops require confirmation by subsequent candles, but be on alert for potential reversals if you spot a spinning top.

Figure 11-8:
A shooting star signals a price peak and potential for a downside reversal. The bullish engulfing line suggests a decline is over and a rebound may follow. Note the white candle's body completely engulfs the prior candle's body.

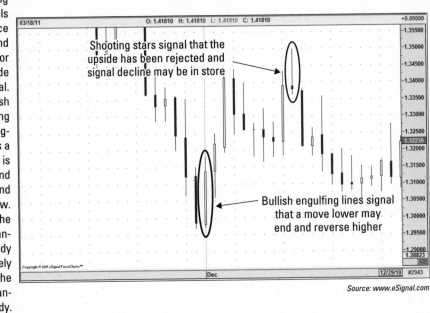

Shooting stars signal that the upside has been rejected and signal decline may be in store

Bullish engulfing lines signal that a move lower may end and reverse higher

Source: www.eSignal.com

Figure 11-9:
Spinning tops are similar to doji both in shape and in that they suggest uncertainty and a potential reversal of the prior directional move.

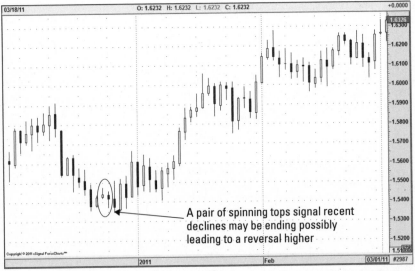

A pair of spinning tops signal recent declines may be ending possibly leading to a reversal higher

Source: www.eSignal.com

Engulfing lines

Engulfing lines are two-candlestick patterns that can be either bullish or bearish, depending on whether they come after a downmove or an upmove:

- ✔ **Bullish engulfing line:** The first candle is dark, followed by a large light candle, the body of which completely engulfs the body of the dark candle, seen in Figure 11-8. The smaller the body of the first candle (think spinning top — see the preceding section), the more significant the reversal signals.

- ✔ **Bearish engulfing line:** The first candle is light, followed by a long dark-colored candle that engulfs the body of the first candle, as shown in Figure 11-10 as part of another candle pattern.

Engulfing lines also rank among my favorite candlestick patterns and are a sufficient basis to establish a position in the opposite direction of the preceding price move. If the high/low of the candle preceding the engulfing candle is exceeded, the pattern is negated and you need to exit.

Tweezers tops and tweezers bottoms

Tweezers formations are two-candlestick patterns that get their name because they resemble the pincer end of a pair of tweezers. Tweezers tops and bottoms (shown in Figure 11-10) correspond to double tops and bottoms in traditional chart analysis, and they mean the same thing — a reversal after failing to make new highs or lows. Tweezers tops and bottoms are characterized by long tails on the bottom after a move down, similar to a hammer, and long tails above after a move higher, like shooting stars. The extremes of the tails should ideally be equal, but if the tails are sufficiently long, I'd take notice.

Hopefully you noticed that many of the candlestick patterns I discuss have two things in common — long tails and small bodies. As part of your technical analysis routine (see Chapter 12), I strongly suggest reviewing daily candle charts after each day's close (5 p.m. ET), and on the weekends for weekly candles, to see if any patterns are evident. They can be powerful signals about where prices are heading in the next trading day or week.

Fibonacci retracements

A *retracement* is a price movement in the opposite direction of the preceding price move. For instance, if EUR/USD rises by 150 pips over the course of two days and declines by 75 pips on the third day, prices are said to have retraced half the move higher, or made a 50 percent retracement of the move up. (Fifty percent is not technically a Fibonacci retracement, but I include it here because many traders watch it, too, because of its clean, halfway demarcation.)

Figure 11-10:
A tweezers
top and
bottom
formation
signals that
an upmove
is set to
reverse
and that a
decline may
be ending.
Note the
doji in the
days prior
to the twee-
zers top
suggesting
that upside
sentiment
was already
uncertain.

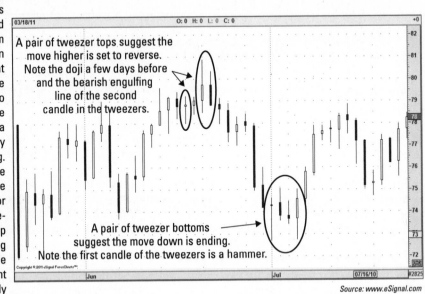

A pair of tweezer tops suggest the move higher is set to reverse. Note the doji a few days before and the bearish engulfing line of the second candle in the tweezers.

A pair of tweezer bottoms suggest the move down is ending. Note the first candle of the tweezers is a hammer.

Source: www.eSignal.com

Fibonacci retracements come from the ratios between the numbers in the Fibonacci sequence, a nearly magical numerical series that appears in the natural world and mathematics with regularity. The most important Fibonacci retracement percentages are 38.2 percent and 61.8 percent, with 76.4 percent as a secondary, but still important, level.

Most charting systems contain an automatic Fibonacci retracement drawing tool. All you need to do is click the starting point of a directional price move (the low for an upmove; the high for a downmove) and drag the cursor to the finishing point of the movement. The charting system will then display lines that correspond to 38.2 percent, 50 percent, 61.8 percent, 76.4 percent, and 100 percent.

Currency traders routinely calculate Fibonacci retracement levels to deter-mine support and resistance levels, and Fibonacci retracement levels are strong examples of self-fulfilling prophecies in technical analysis. Figure 11-11 provides a good illustration of how Fibonacci retracement levels can act as resistance in a correction higher following a price decline. You can see the 38.2 percent retracement level put up a pretty good fight for a while, but after it broke above, prices blew right past the 50 percent point and quickly moved to the 61.8 percent level, even exceeding it briefly before a pullback. That pullback was nicely contained by the 38.2 percent level. Prices went on to surpass the 61.8 percent level and then tested 76.4 percent, which also held for a time and sent prices back to the 61.8 percent point. From there they rallied higher and finally broke the 76.4 percent level, setting up potential for a 100 percent retracement of the prior decline.

Figure 11-11: You can identify future support and resistance levels by drawing Fibonacci retracements of prior directional price moves on your charting system.

Source: www.eSignal.com

The Science of Technical Analysis

Relax. Nothing is especially scientific or particularly complicated about technical analysis. Many in the market use the term *science* to describe the mechanics of various technical tools, but in my opinion technical analysis is far more art than science.

Each tool in technical analysis has a number of concrete elements that I need to outline before you can start interpreting what they mean. Unless you're developing your own systematic trading model, you don't need to get too caught up in the math or the calculations behind various indicators. Far more important is understanding what the indicators are measuring and what their signals mean and don't mean.

Momentum oscillators and studies

Momentum refers to the speed at which prices are moving, either up or down. Momentum is an important technical measurement of the strength of the buying or selling interest behind a movement in prices. The higher the momentum in a downmove, for example, the greater the selling interest is thought to be. The slower the momentum, the weaker the selling interest.

Currency traders use momentum indicators to gauge whether a price movement will be sustained, potentially developing into a trend, or whether a directional move has run its course and is now more likely to reverse direction. If momentum is positive and rising, it means prices are advancing, suggesting that active buying is taking place. If momentum begins to slow, it means prices are advancing more slowly, suggesting that buying interest is beginning to weaken. If buying interest is drying up, selling interest may increase.

Momentum takes on added significance in currencies because there's no viable way of assessing trading volume on a real-time basis. In stock and futures markets, volume data is an important indicator of the significance of a price move. For example, a sharp price movement on high volume is considered legitimate and likely to be sustained, while a similarly sharp move on low volume is discounted and viewed as more likely to reverse.

Momentum indicators fall into a group of technical studies known as *oscillators,* because the mathematical representations of momentum are plotted on a scale that sees momentum rise and fall, or oscillate, depending on the relative speed of the price movements. A variety of different momentum oscillators exist, each calculated by various formulas, but they're all based on the relationship of the current price to preceding prices over a defined period of time.

Momentum oscillators are typically displayed in a small window at the bottom of charting systems, with the price chart displayed above, so you can readily compare the price action with its underlying momentum.

Overbought and oversold

Momentum oscillators have extreme levels at the upper and lower ends of the oscillator's scale, where the upper level is referred to as *overbought* and the lower level is referred to *oversold.* No hard definitions of *overbought* and *oversold* exist, because they're relative terms describing how fast prices have changed relative to prior price changes. The best way to think of overbought and oversold is that prices have gone up or down too fast relative to prior periods.

Many momentum indicators suggest trading rules based on the indicator reaching overbought or oversold levels. For example, if a momentum study enters overbought or oversold territory, and subsequently turns down or up and moves out of the overbought or oversold zone, it may be considered a sell or buy signal.

Just because a momentum indicator has reached an overbought or oversold level does not mean that prices have to reverse direction. After all, the essence of a trend is a sustained directional price movement, which could see momentum remain in overbought or oversold territory for a long period of time as prices continue to advance or decline in the trend. Breaking news or data may be behind the price move, lending a fundamental urgency to price adjustments that defy momentum analysis. Momentum is only an indicator. The key is to wait for confirmation from prices that the prior direction or trend has, in fact, changed.

Divergences between price and momentum

Another useful way to interpret momentum indicators is by comparing them to corresponding price changes. In most cases, momentum studies and price changes should move in the same direction. If prices are rising, for example, you would expect to see momentum indicators rising as well. By the same token, if momentum begins to stall and eventually turn down, you would expect to see prices turn lower, too. But relatively frequently, especially in shorter, intraday time frames (15 minutes, 1 hour, or 4 hours), prices *diverge* from momentum (meaning, prices may continue to rise even though momentum has started to move lower).

When prices move in the opposite direction of momentum, it's called a *divergence*. Divergences are relatively easy to spot — new price highs are not matched by new highs in the momentum indicator, or new price lows are not matched by new lows in the momentum study. When a new price high or low is made, and momentum fails to make a similar new high or low, the price action is not confirmed by the momentum, suggesting that the price move is false and will not be sustained. The expectation, then, is that the price will change direction and eventually follow the momentum.

When prices make new highs, and momentum is falling or not making new highs, it's called a *bearish divergence* (meaning, prices are expected to shift lower — move bearishly — in line with the underlying momentum). When prices are making new lows, but momentum is rising or not making new lows, it's called a *bullish divergence* (meaning, prices are expected to turn higher — bullish — in line with momentum). (In Chapter 12, I show an example of a bearish divergence.)

Divergences are great alerts that something may be out of kilter between prices and the underlying strength or momentum of the price move. Whenever you spot a divergence between price and momentum, you should start looking more closely at what's happening to prices. Are stop-loss levels being run in thin liquidity conditions? Or has some important news just come out that has sent prices moving sharply, and momentum will eventually catch up?

In a trending environment, prices may continue to move in the direction of the trend (that's what a trend is), but at a slower pace, causing momentum to diverge. To know for certain, you need to wait for confirmation from prices before you enter a trade based on a divergence.

Using momentum in ranges and trends

Momentum indicators work best in range environments, where price movements are relatively constrained and no trend is evident or has moved into consolidation. As buying drives prices toward the upper end of a range, for example, selling interest comes in, slowing the price advance and turning momentum lower. As the buyers turn around, the selling interest increases and momentum begins to accelerate lower, confirming the change in direction. At the bottom of the range, the same thing happens, but in the opposite direction.

Momentum studies frequently give off incorrect signals during breakouts and trending markets. This is especially the case when using shorter time frames, such as hourly and shorter periods. The key to understanding why this happens is to recognize that momentum studies are backward-looking indicators. All they can do is quantify the change in current prices relative to what has come before. They have little predictive capacity, which is why you always need to wait for confirmation from prices before trading based on a momentum signal.

Some of the most extreme price moves typically occur when momentum readings are in overbought or oversold territory. Divergences in shorter time frames also appear frequently, especially during breakouts, where rapid price moves are not reflected quickly enough in momentum studies. By the time the momentum indicator has caught up with the price breakout, prices may already have peaked or bottomed, again causing momentum to signal a divergence. Just because momentum is overbought or oversold doesn't mean prices can't continue to move higher or lower.

Here are the main momentum oscillators used by currency traders:

- **Relative Strength Index (RSI):** A single-line oscillator plotted on a scale from 0 to 100, based on closing prices over a user-defined period. Common RSI periods are 9, 14, and 21. RSI compares the strength of up periods to the weakness of down periods — hence, the label *relative strength*. RSI readings over 75 are considered overbought; readings below 25 are considered oversold. RSI signals are given when the indicator leaves overbought or oversold territory and on divergences with price.

- **Stochastic:** A two-line oscillator plotted on a scale of 0 to 100. The two lines are known as *%K* (fast stochastic) and *%D* (slow stochastic). Stochastics are also based on closing prices of prior periods. The basic theory behind stochastics is that the strength of a directional move can be measured by how near the close is to the extreme of a period.

In an uptrend, a close near the highs for the period signifies strong momentum; a close in the middle or below signals that momentum is weakening. In a downtrend, the close of a period should be nearer to the lows for momentum to strengthen. As momentum shifts, the %K line will cross over the slower-moving %D line. Crossovers in overbought or oversold territory are considered sell or buy signals. Overbought is above 80, and oversold is below 20.

✔ **Moving Average Convergence/Divergence (MACD):** Not really a momentum oscillator, but a complex series of moving averages. (It functions similarly to momentum studies, so I include it here.) MACD fluctuates on either side of a zero line and has no fixed scale, so overbought or oversold are judged relative to prior extremes. MACD also consists of two lines: the MACD line (based on two moving averages) and the signal line (a moving average of the MACD line). Trading signals are generated if the MACD line crosses up over the signal line while below the zero line (buy) or crosses down below the signal line while above the zero line (sell). MACD tends to generate signals more slowly than RSI or stochastics due to the longer periods typically used and the slower nature of moving averages. The result is that it takes longer for MACD to cross over, generally preventing fewer false signals.

Trend-identifying indicators

One of the market's favorite sayings is "The trend is your friend." The idea is that if you trade in the direction of the prevailing trend, you're more likely to experience success than if you trade against the trend. Now, how can you argue with logic like that?

The hard part for us mortals is to determine whether there's a trend in the first place. The question becomes more complex when you look at multiple time frames, because trends can exist in any time frame. On a daily time frame, the market may be largely range bound. But in a shorter time frame, such as hourly or 30 minutes, there may be a trending movement that presents an opportunity for short-term traders.

Determining whether a trend is in place is also important when it comes to deciding whether to follow the signals given by momentum indicators. Momentum studies are great in relatively range-bound markets, but they tend to give off bad signals during trends and breakouts. The key is to determine whether a trend is in place.

In the following sections, I look at a few technical studies you can use to identify whether a trend is in place and how strong it may be.

Directional Movement Indicator system

The Directional Movement Indicator (DMI) system is a set of quantitative tools designed to determine whether a market is trending. The DMI is based on the idea that when a market is trending, each period's price extremes should exceed the prior price extremes in the direction of the trend. For example, in an uptrend, each successive high should be higher than the prior period's high. In a downtrend, the opposite is the case: Each new low should be lower than the prior period's low. That's the essence of a trend.

The DMI system is composed of the ADX line (the average directional movement index) and the DI+ and DI– lines (which refer to the directional indicators for up periods [+] and down periods [–]). The ADX is used to determine whether a market is trending (regardless if it's up or down), with a reading over 25 indicating a trending market and a reading below indicating no trend. The ADX is also a measure of the strength of a trend — the higher the ADX, the stronger the trend. Using the ADX, traders can determine whether a trend is operative and decide whether to use a trend-following system or to rely on momentum oscillator signals.

As its name would suggest, the DMI system is best employed using both components. The DI+ and DI– lines are used as trade-entry signals. A buy signal is generated when the DI+ line crosses up through the DI– line; a sell signal is generated when the DI– line crosses up through the DI+ line. Wilder suggests using the *extreme-point rule* to govern the DI+/DI– crossover signal. The rule states that when the DI+/DI– lines cross, you should note the extreme point for that period in the direction of the crossover (the high if DI+ crosses up over DI–; the low if DI– crosses up over DI+). If that extreme point is exceeded in the next period, the DI+/DI– crossover is considered a valid trade signal. If the extreme point is not surpassed, the signal is not confirmed.

The ADX can also be used as an early indicator of the end or pause in a trend. When the ADX begins to move lower from its highest level, the trend is either pausing or ending, signaling that it's time to exit the current position and wait for a fresh signal from the DI+/DI– crossover.

Moving averages

One of the more basic and widely used indicators in technical analysis, moving averages can verify existing trends, identify emerging trends, and generate trading signals. Moving averages are simply an average of prior prices over a user-defined time period displayed as a line overlaid on a price chart. There are two main types of moving averages:

✔ **Simple moving average** gives equal weight to each historical price point over the specified period.

✔ **Exponential moving average** gives greater weight to more recent price data, with the aim of capturing directional price changes more quickly than the simple moving average.

In terms of defining a trend, when prices are above the moving average, an uptrend is in place; when prices are below the moving average, a downtrend is in place.

Traders like to experiment with different periods for moving averages, but a few are more commonly used in the market than others, and they're worth keeping an eye on. The main moving average periods to focus on are 21, 55, 100, and 200. Shorter-term traders may consider looking at the 9- and 14-period moving averages.

Another way moving averages are used is by combining two or more moving averages and using the crossovers of the moving averages as buy or sell signals based on the direction of the crossover. For example, using a 9- and 21-period moving average, you would buy when the faster-moving 9-period average crosses up over the slower-moving 21-period average, and vice versa for a crossover to the downside.

Trading with clouds — Ichimoku charts

Ichimoku Kinko Hyo, or "one-glance equilibrium," charts are another technical analysis approach imported from Japan that is gaining widespread popularity in forex (and other financial) markets. Often referred to as *cloud charts* because of the central feature of the system (the cloud, or *kumo* in Japanese), Ichimoku is basically a trend-following system. But Ichimoku lines can also define significant support and resistance levels not identified by more traditional technical approaches.

The key components of Ichimoku charts are five lines shown in Figure 11-12:

✔ **Tenkan line.** The faster moving average based on the average of the high and low of the prior nine days.

✔ **Kijun line.** The slower moving average based on the average of the high and low from the prior 26 days.

✔ **Senkou span A (leading span A).** The average of the Tenkan and Kijun lines from the prior 26 days, projected 26 days into the future.

✔ **Senkou span B (leading span B).** The average of the high and low of the prior 52 days projected 26 days into the future. The cloud is the space between the two leading spans.

✔ **Chikou span (lagging span).** Today's closing price reflected 26 days into the past.

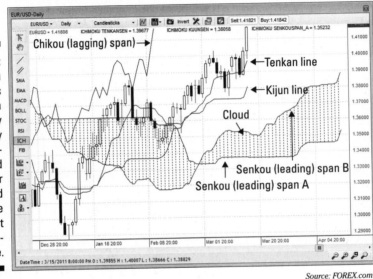

Figure 11-12: Ichimoku charts provide a quick way to identify trend direction and also offer support and resistance levels not found elsewhere.

Source: FOREX.com

A few points to note here: Ichimoku is a daily-based chart approach (weekly views can also be used) making it a tool for longer-term traders. Most importantly, intra-day breaks of Ichimoku lines are relatively common, but it's only the daily close that matters, reinforcing it as a medium/longer-term trading tool.

Ichimoku trading signals are based on the position of the current price relative to the lines as well as crossovers of the lines themselves. In the simplest form, the trend is up when prices are above the cloud and down when prices are below. Buying and selling signals also come from crossovers of the Tenkan and Kijun lines, but the strength of the signal depends on the position of price relative to the cloud. A crossover of the Tenkan below the Kijun line (bearish crossover) with price above the cloud is a weak sell signal. If price is inside the cloud, it's a medium strength sell signal. If prices are below the cloud, it's a strong sell signal. The same applies in bullish crossovers, but in reverse. The Chikou span is also used to gauge the validity of the trade signals, based on where current prices are relative to prior periods. The idea is that if an uptrend is in place, for example, current price should be above those of prior periods, as seen by the lagging span.

Earlier I indicated that intra-day breaks of Ichimoku lines are common, but they also have an uncanny way of acting as formidable support and resistance, too. In particular, the slower moving Kijun line can be used as a level to re-enter a prevailing trend, buying a downside retracement in an uptrend or selling rebounds higher in a downtrend. I always make a point of noting the Ichimoku levels as part of my daily technical analysis routine.

Chapter 12

Identifying Trade Opportunities

. . . .

In This Chapter

▶ Organizing market analysis to spot trade setups

▶ Locating pivotal support and resistance levels

▶ Using momentum to spot trades and fine-tune entry and exits

▶ Trading on candlestick patterns

▶ Constructing a real-time trade strategy

. . . .

S potting trade opportunities and applying a trading plan are what it all boils down to. Traders and speculators spend the time and energy to follow the market and know what's going on. They analyze and strategize, persistently scanning the market for trade opportunities, or *setups,* and waiting for the right time to step in and commit their money. And when they step in, they have a well-defined trade plan to guide them through whatever the market throws at them.

There's certainly no shortage of opinions and ideas being voiced by market analysts and commentators, but in the end the trades you make are your decision. In this chapter, I go through the key steps to spotting trade opportunities and putting together a risk-aware trading plan to exploit the setup. In this chapter, I draw on many of the technical analysis concepts I outline in Chapter 11.

Developing a Routine for Market Analysis

The first step is to commit to making time for market analysis. The more regular your analysis, the greater the feel you'll develop for where the market has been and where it's likely to go. Also, the more regularly you update yourself on the market, the less time it'll take to stay up to speed. It's a lot easier updating yourself every day than it is trying to catch up on several days' worth of market news, data, and price developments.

Give some long, hard thought to how much time you can realistically afford to devote to market analysis before committing yourself to a specific routine. You may find you're able to devote only a relatively short amount of time each day, so focus your energies on only one or two currency pairs. If you have the time, you can more effectively follow and analyze multiple currency pairs.

At the minimum, you should be prepared to devote at least an hour every day to looking at the market and keeping tabs on upcoming data and events. I like to follow a routine that focuses on:

✓ Multiple-time-frame technical analysis to identify support and resistance levels and to track overall price developments

✓ Candlestick and Ichimoku analysis after each daily and weekly close

✓ Reading economic data reports that have come out overnight to update our fundamental model (see Chapter 7)

✓ Assessing the likely market impact of upcoming data reports and events

✓ Reviewing market commentaries to stay on top of major themes and overall market sentiment

This may seem like a lot to squeeze into a single hour, but with time and practice, you'll get your charting and market information sources all lined up so you can streamline the entire routine.

Performing Multiple-Time-Frame Technical Analysis

Look closely at the charts in Figures 12-1, 12-2, and 12-3. Notice anything similar about them? Don't be surprised if you don't — they all look extremely different. But that's the point. They're all charts of the same currency pair, but viewed in three different time frames. As you can see, viewing the forest through the trees takes on a whole new meaning when it comes to chart analysis.

Multiple-time-frame technical analysis is nothing more complicated than looking at charts using different time frames of data. The basic idea is to look at the big picture first to identify the key longer-term features and then drill down into shorter data time frames to pinpoint short-term price levels and trends. My own preference is to focus on daily, four-hour, and hourly time frames, but you can use whichever time frames you think best match your trading style. Short-term traders, for instance, may want to focus on 2-hour, 30-minute, and 5-minute charts to better reflect the narrower time frames of their trading.

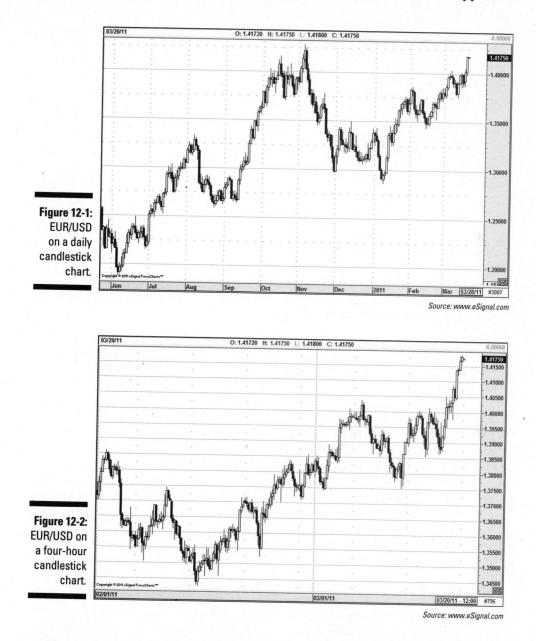

Figure 12-1:
EUR/USD
on a daily
candlestick
chart.

Source: www.eSignal.com

Figure 12-2:
EUR/USD on
a four-hour
candlestick
chart.

Source: www.eSignal.com

Whichever time frames you end up working with, I strongly recommend that you include longer time frames, like daily and weekly, so you can get a sense of where the most significant price levels are. The strength and significance of support and resistance levels are a function of the time frame in which they're evident, with longer-term technical levels holding greater meaning than shorter ones. You don't want your focus to become so narrow that you lose sight of the big picture and go with a break of short-term resistance, for instance, when major daily or weekly resistance is just beyond.

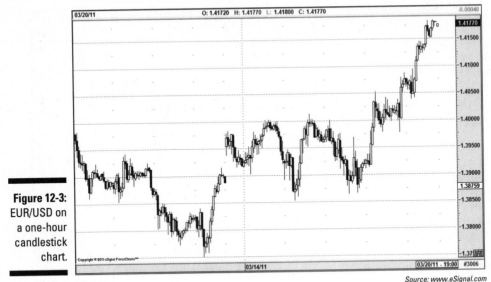

| 03/20/11 | | O: 1.41720 H: 1.41770 L: 1.41800 C: 1.41770 | | .0.00040 |

Figure 12-3:
EUR/USD on
a one-hour
candlestick
chart.

Copyright © 2011 eSignal ForexCharts™

| 03/14/11 | | | 03/20/11 - 19:00 | #3006 |

Source: www.eSignal.com

The good thing about daily and weekly charts is that the technical levels don't change quite as frequently as shorter time frames, so you can probably make do with updating the daily and weekly charts much less often.

In Figures 12-4, 12-5, and 12-6, I reproduce the same charts as the ones shown in Figures 12-1, 12-2, and 12-3, but this time I include my trend lines. I start by looking at the daily chart to identify the big levels and draw in longer-term trend lines. Then I drill down to the four-hour chart, where I take a fresh look based on what I'm seeing in that time frame and draw in more trend lines to encapsulate any price patterns or trends. To finish, I go down one more level to the hourly charts for a close-up view of the market's most recent price action.

Make sure the charting system you're using has the ability to save trend lines across time frames, meaning that a trend line you draw on a daily chart should also appear on the four-hour and hourly charts, and vice versa. Also, make sure the charting system has the ability to save the entire chart so you don't have to redraw the trend lines every time you pull up the same chart.

On subsequent updates, keep the trend lines that still appear to be valid (meaning, price action has not broken through them), and erase trend lines that are no longer active or have been broken. But don't be in too great a rush to erase broken trend lines, because they'll often continue to act as support or resistance, but in the opposite direction.

When support is broken, it becomes resistance, and vice versa.

Figure 12-4:
Start out by drawing trend lines on longer-term charts, like weekly and daily (shown here), to identify major technical levels.

Source: www.eSignal.com

Figure 12-5:
Drill down from a longer-term view to a medium-term time frame, such as four hours (shown here) or two hours, to identify key medium-term support and resistance levels.

Source: www.eSignal.com

Over time, you'll get an idea of how good you are at spotting meaningful trend lines by the frequency with which you have to discard old trend lines. The longer the trend line contains price action or the longer prices react substantially when a trend line is broken, the more significant the trend line was. In Figures 12-4, 12-5, and 12-6, I keep in some of my older trend lines to give you an idea of how to draw them, as well as to show that some broken trend lines can still be valid.

Figure 12-6:
Focus in
on shorter
time frames
using 1-hour
(shown
here),
30-minute,
15-minute,
and shorter
time frames
to identify
short-term
support and
resistance.

Identifying Support and Resistance Levels

Multiple-time-frame technical analysis is your early-warning radar system. It alerts you to key support and resistance levels that, if broken, are likely to lead to larger directional breakouts and potential trading signals. Of course, the flip side is that if the support or resistance levels hold, price direction is likely to reverse course.

Now that you've gone through and analyzed a currency pair with trend lines in multiple time frames, you're well on the way to identifying key technical support and resistance levels. But while trend lines are one of the simpler yet more powerful technical tools, there are still plenty of other sources of support and resistance to take note of. In Figure 12-7, I provide a chart showing support and resistance derived from the methods I outline in the following sections.

Trend lines

You didn't think you were done with trend lines yet, did you? Believe me when I say that trend lines are the gifts that keep on giving, as long as you keep drawing and redrawing them.

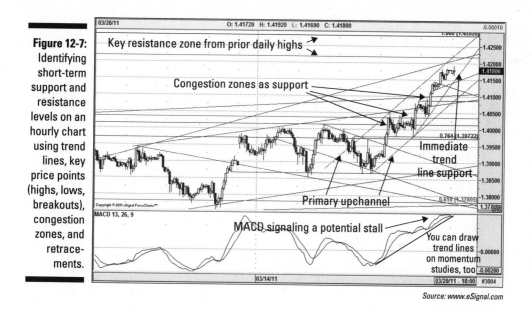

Figure 12-7: Identifying short-term support and resistance levels on an hourly chart using trend lines, key price points (highs, lows, breakouts), congestion zones, and retracements.

Source: www.eSignal.com

To determine support and resistance levels that correspond to the trend lines you've drawn, you simply need to place the cursor of your charting system on the trend line at the current time period. Your charting system should display the price value of the cursor placement on the right side of the chart; if not, you may have to use the crosshairs tool of the charting system to see the value. Keep in mind that trend-line price values will shift over time based on the slope of the trend line. If you've identified a trend line that's sloping steeply higher, for instance, its price value will be higher in later periods. You can run the cursor up the trend line and note the price level and time interval to gauge how much it will change over time.

Note the price levels of the trend lines you observe and use them for placing orders based on your fundamental or technical view. Breaks of trend lines are signals for short-term traders to go with the break. I suggest using a relatively tight stop loss of 20 to 30 points from the trend line in case the break is not sustained (a false break). You can also use trend lines as entry points in trending moves, buying on pullbacks of up moves and selling on rebounds in downtrends. Depending if any chart pattern is evident, the breakout may have a target, or measured move objective (see Chapter 11), which you can use to establish you're take-profit order. Again, allow for a margin of error in case the target level is not quite reached. It's better to capture 80 percent of something than 100 percent of nothing.

Breaks of sloping trend lines always have an immediate hurdle to climb, namely the prior high of a move up in the case of a break of downward sloping trend lines, or the prior low in the case of upward sloping trend lines. Some technical traders disregard sloping trend lines altogether and focus only on breaks of recent highs or lows, which I discuss next. (By the way, you can probably tell I'm not one of them. I'll leave it to you to judge the importance of sloping trend lines based on the charts in this book.)

Highs and lows

After trend lines, markets tend to place the greatest amount of emphasis on period highs and lows as points of support and resistance, frequently referred to as *horizontal* support/resistance. You can pinpoint support or resistance levels from highs and lows by simply noting the price high or low, but give yourself a few pips of latitude (5 to 10 pips), because different charting systems have different data feeds, which may have slightly different high/ low readings.

When you're looking at a daily chart, you can pretty easily identify the relevant high or low. But when you're looking at charts in shorter time frames, it's not always clear which high/low you should use. A general rule is to look for significant price reactions from recent prior highs and lows.

The more sharply prices move away from a high or low, the more significance that high or low carries as support or resistance. The more slowly or less dramatic the price movement off the high or low, the less significance that high or low usually carries. Look for long tails on shorter-term candlestick charts, like 30-minute or hourly time frames, for indications that a prior high is acting as resistance or a prior low is giving support.

Lots of algorithmic trading systems are based on breaks of period highs and lows. To use such breaks as trade signals, prices need to finish the period beyond the break of the high/low. For example, a short-term system will need to see the break of a recent hourly high sustained on an hourly close basis before going long. A longer-term model will want to see the break of a daily low sustained on a daily close below it before going short. You can use such period closes as confirmation the break is valid, but always have a stop in place in case that level is subsequently breached on another similar period close.

Congestion zones

Congestion zones are price bands in which prior price action gives way to *consolidation,* or a period of sideways price action (see Figure 12-7 for some examples). Most congestion zones are roughly 30 to 50 pips wide, but they may be larger in more volatile pairs, like GBP/USD and USD/CHF, or the JPY crosses. Unfortunately, there's no easy recipe when it comes to deciding whether the top or bottom of a congestion zone will act as support or resistance, so you need to factor in the whole zone as a potential source of support/resistance. Prices moving higher, for instance, may stall at the base of a congestion zone, or they may make it all the way to the top. If the zone is cleared, however, prices are likely to move on to the next resistance level.

Fibonacci Retracements

Fibonacci retracements should be drawn after significant directional price moves when it's clear (or as clear as it can be) that the directional movement has stopped and reversed direction. (For more on Fibonacci levels, see Chapter 11.) You can draw the retracements by using the Fibonacci retracement drawing tool that's standard in most charting systems. Figure 12-7 contains a Fibonacci retracement based on the most recent decline, and with prices currently above them they serve as potential support levels in any pullbacks.

Breaks of Fibonacci levels on a daily close basis are considered significant by traders. (See Chapter 11 for a discussion of how breaks of Fibonacci levels can be a trading signal.) You can also use Fibonacci levels as targets for price moves, placing take profits based on them or using them as stop loss exit levels.

The 76.4 percent mark is sort of the forgotten Fibonacci level, but it's often the key turning point in more volatile currency pairs, like USD/CHF and GBP/USD. Just when you think that the 61.8 percent level failed, and it looks like the market is going for a 100 percent retracement, it pulls up short at 76.4 percent.

Fibonacci retracements can be drawn for almost any discernible price movement, but their significance is closely related to the size of the main directional move. The larger the primary directional price move, the more significance the support or resistance from the Fibonacci retracements will be. Generally speaking, don't get caught up calculating retracements of moves of less than 200 points. Instead, focus on daily charts to spot the most significant price moves, and calculate the potential retracements based on them.

Ichimoku levels

Ichimoku, or cloud charts, are an important source of support and resistance levels you won't find anywhere else. I discuss the basics of Ichimoku charts in Chapter 11. The key to spotting trade opportunities with Ichimoku charts are daily closes above/below the various Ichimoku lines (Tenkan, Kijun, and the leading spans that make up the top and bottom of the cloud). On an intraday basis, those levels may be exceeded, but it's only on a daily close basis that trading signals should be taken. After a move higher, for instance, a daily close below the Tenkan line should be taken as a cue to exit the prior trend, or potentially to go short.

For intra-day trading, Ichimoku levels can provide actionable trading levels, providing seemingly unseen support or resistance levels to buy or sell on in extreme price moves. But if those levels are exceeded on a daily close basis, you should exit the trade. For longer-term traders, those with a wait-and-see attitude, daily closes above/below Ichimoku levels offer a potentially longer-term trading signal. I like to use pullbacks or rebounds to the Kijun line as potential entry opportunities when a trend is evident.

Looking for Symmetry with Channels

If you're new to chart analysis you may be thinking that the array of bars or candles on a price chart looks like the ultimate in randomness. Sometimes that's true, but more often than not, you'd be surprised how frequently symmetrical formations appear. By *symmetrical formations,* I mostly mean *price channels,* but also other chart patterns that I illustrate and cover in detail in Chapter 11.

Drawing price channels

A *price channel* is nothing more complicated than a series of parallel trend lines that encapsulate price action over a discernible period. Channels will form in all time frames, with long-term channels on a daily chart highlighting multiday or multiweek trading ranges, and short-term channels on an hourly chart revealing steady buying or selling during a trading session. Price channels can also form in any direction, from horizontal to steeply sloping up or down and anything in between.

The way to identify price channels is through visual inspection, using your eyes and imagination, as well as a fair amount of trial and error. Drawing channels is made much easier by the Copy a Line and Parallel Line functions, which are standard in most charting systems. To begin looking for and drawing potential channels, you need only one trend line to start with — the *primary* trend line. (In Figure 12-7, the lower trend line in the primary upchannel is the primary trend line.)

If the primary trend line is below the price bars or candles (support), look up at the tops of the price action to see if there is any parallel symmetry to the primary support trend line. If you're not sure, simply copy the support trend line and drag it to the tops of the price bars to see if it captures the highest highs. If the copied trend line fits neatly onto the tops of the price action, you've found yourself a price channel.

That said, the parallel side (the upper channel line based on upward-sloping primary trend lines, and the lower channel line for downward-sloping primary trend lines) never behaves quite as neatly as the primary side. For example, during an uptrend most people are looking to buy; that's why the price action often goes exactly to the primary channel support and then bounces higher. However, on rallies during an uptrend, there usually aren't as many traders looking to sell and price action frequently exceeds the upper channel line. The same happens with the base of channels during declines, where fewer buyers are involved.

When you're looking for channels, especially if prices have just changed direction and a new move is just beginning, keep in mind that you may have only one or two price points opposite the primary trend line to connect the parallel channel line. When that happens, go ahead and draw the parallel channel line — it'll extend into empty space for the time being — but consider it only a tentative channel top or bottom until more price action confirms its validity.

The whole point of looking for and drawing channel lines, of course, is to highlight additional sources of support or resistance. Directional price moves rarely go from Point A to Point B in a straight line. More typically, for example, prices will move higher for a period of time before short-term buying interest fades or encounters heavier selling interest, sending prices back down to the trend-line support. When this pattern repeats itself several times, a channel is formed.

You can use channels as part of your trading strategy to guide both position entry and exit. Short-term traders in particular like to use channels to trade around a core position, for example, selling short on trend-line resistance and buying a portion of the position back if prices drop to channel support. If the channel continues to hold, they'll resell on gains back toward trend-line resistance, reestablishing their core short position. When channels break, it's also a sign that prices are either accelerating in the direction of the trend, as shown by the channel, or that the trend is reversing and prices break out of the channel in the opposite direction.

Listening to Momentum

In Chapter 11, I look at various momentum indicators, like Relative Strength Index (RSI) and stochastics, and what they mean. As part of your routine of multiple-time-frame technical analysis, I strongly suggest that you incorporate two technical studies into your regimen of analysis.

Factoring momentum analysis into your routine

The first study to include in your analysis is a momentum oscillator like RSI or stochastics. I also recommend Moving Average Convergence/Divergence (MACD) — it's not technically a momentum indicator, but it certainly acts like one. In fact, I prefer MACD over the more traditional momentum studies because MACD tends to change direction and generate crossovers more slowly than the other momentum studies. The result is fewer false signals, but the trade-off is that the signal may be delayed, giving you a less advantageous price entry level. In reality, though, the generally slower MACD signals are well suited to the forex market's tendency to push a directional move as far as it will go for as long as possible.

The second study I recommend that you include in your analysis routine is the Directional Movement Indicator (DMI) system (which I also look at in greater detail in Chapter 11). The DMI serves as a double check on the momentum study. The Average Directional Index (ADX) component of the DMI is a trend identification signal that tells you whether the market is trending, regardless of direction. Relying solely on a momentum study can lead to serious problems when the market sets off on an extended trending movement.

Momentum studies typically register overbought and oversold readings after an extensive directional move, potentially signaling that the market is ripe for a correction in the opposite direction. Worse, shorter-term momentum studies routinely cross over as price movements inevitably slow in the course of a directional, potentially trending movement, giving a signal to trade in the opposite direction. But if a trend is, in fact, taking hold, those momentum readings can be highly misleading.

The key is to double-check momentum readings with the ADX level to see if trending conditions are in place. If the ADX is above 25, you should discount what the momentum studies are indicating. Don't completely ignore what the momentum study is showing — just defer to the ADX reading while it's above 25. When the ADX tops out and turns down, you have a second indicator signaling that the directional move is likely coming to an end. If the ADX is below 25, defer to what the momentum indicators are signaling.

Most charting systems will allow you to save charts including multiple technical studies, such as MACD, RSI, stochastics, and ADX/DMI. I suggest layering the studies so only one is visible at a time, leaving the maximum amount of space to display the price chart, which is always the primary focus. You can then toggle between different studies at your convenience.

Looking at momentum in multiple time frames

Just as you were presented with starkly differing images by looking at the same price chart in different time frames, so will you be confronted with vastly different momentum readings across time frames. At any given moment, daily momentum readings may be negative and moving lower; four-hour momentum may be nearing overbought territory; and hourly momentum may have topped and turned lower.

Which one should you listen to? Simply put, all of them. The trick, however, is to keep each reading in perspective according to its time frame. Daily momentum readings develop over many days and weeks. Shorter-term readings play out in correspondingly shorter time frames.

The key is to view each period's momentum indication in line with the time frame of the study. An hourly reading that has bottomed out and turned higher suggests that prices may stop declining for a few hours and possibly begin to move higher — but it's no sure thing. Look next to the longer time frames to put the shorter-term readings into perspective. For example, if the hourly has bottomed out and started to move higher, and the four-hour reading is bottoming out in oversold territory, you may just have the makings of a larger turnaround to the upside. But if the four-hour reading is still in neutral territory and pointed lower, the hourly reading may suggest just a short-term bounce in a continuing move lower.

I like to focus on four-hour momentum readings as the principal gauge of the durability of a directional price move. Shorter-term studies, such as hourly or 90-minute, are good as early-warning indicators and guides to short-term timing, but they can be quickly overwhelmed by strong directional price moves. Daily studies tend to be too slow to give off timely signals for short- and medium-term trading, generally confirming larger directional shifts well after the fact. The four-hour period is a solid compromise that's long enough to capture intraday and multiday mini-trends without generating too many false signals, while being just short enough to give timely indications of a pending reversal.

Trading on divergences between price and momentum

In Chapter 11, I introduce the idea of bullish/bearish divergences between price and momentum. In a nutshell, a bullish divergence occurs when prices make new lows, but momentum is not making similar new lows; a bearish divergence occurs when prices make new highs, but momentum is not making similar new highs.

Figure 12-8 shows an example of a bullish divergence between price and MACD. Because momentum is an underlying gauge of the speed of a directional move and, therefore, an indication of the level of market interest behind the move, a divergence between price and momentum typically signals that the latest price movement is false or unlikely to be sustained and will eventually reverse course in the direction of the momentum. So a bullish divergence tends to signal a price rebound after fresh selling makes new lows, and a bearish divergence typically signals a price decline after last-ditch buying makes a new high.

The key to trading off divergences is to be patient and wait for confirmation. The latest rally in prices, for example, may be the start of a new wave higher, and the momentum study may eventually turn around or catch up and confirm the latest gains, negating the apparent divergence. Also, prices can diverge from momentum for many hours or days. By all means, always take note of divergences when you spot them, but keep them in context:

✔ **Has *new* information (data, comments, and so on) come into the market?** If it's new news, it may generate a fresh wave of directional buying or selling and overwhelm the divergence. If it's old news, like reiterated comments or as-expected data that's already been discounted, it could make for an ideal divergence setup.

✔ **Are prices making *significant* new highs or lows?** If prices have broken below a key daily low or trend-line support, for example, fresh selling interest may be coming into the market that creates a new wave lower. But if prices are pushing only below recent hourly lows, and longer-term support is still some distance off, the divergence will tend to correctly reflect that the price move down is invalid.

Figure 12-8: A bullish divergence is created when new price lows are not matched by new lows in momentum, suggesting that the latest price decline may not be sustained.

A bullish divergence occurs when new price lows are not matched by new lows in momentum studies, suggesting the price decline may reverse higher.

Source: www.eSignal.com

The safest way to trade off divergences is to wait for confirmation that prices are indeed reversing course in the direction of the momentum divergence. In most cases, there will be a key trend line that is guiding prices higher or lower while prices are diverging with momentum. When that trend line is broken by a price reversal, such as in Figure 12-8, you can consider it confirmation that the divergence is beginning to play out.

Using momentum for timing entry and exit

You can also use momentum studies to refine the timing of your trade entry and exit. If your analysis has led you to conclude that a long position is the way to go, for instance, and you've identified key trend-line support on which to buy, you can look at various time frames of momentum to determine the likelihood of prices actually reaching that support. If hourly momentum has turned up from oversold levels, and four-hour momentum is showing signs of bottoming out, but prices are still 50 pips away from your trend-line entry level, you may consider stepping in ahead of the trend-line support and buying sooner.

Alternatively, if daily and four-hour studies are both solidly negative, and hourly momentum has just gone through a short-term bounce higher but is now turning negative again, you can likely afford to wait for prices to reach your desired price level. (You may even rethink the overall strategy in light of such bearish momentum readings.) You can use momentum studies in the same way to gauge the likelihood of reaching your take-profit targets.

Momentum is only a gauge of the relative speed of price movements and not always a leading indicator of changes in direction. Although you should always listen to what momentum studies are saying, so you can anticipate and prepare for alternative outcomes, you should always wait for confirmation from prices themselves. Even then, markets and events have a way of throwing curve balls at you, but at least you minimized the risks by waiting for price confirmation.

Trading on Candlestick Patterns

Candlestick formations are among my favorite trade identification tools; I highlight some of the most common reversal patterns to look for in Chapter 11. There are lots more patterns where those came from, with others signaling trend continuation or consolidation. Obviously, I like to home in on the reversal patterns because I think they give me the most price bang for my analysis buck.

Most trading books say that you can analyze candles in any time frame, but I like to focus exclusively on daily and weekly candles. My thinking is that a full day's or week's price action carries more weight than a few hours or other intraday periods. Besides, a candlestick pattern that presents itself on a daily or weekly chart typically portends a larger price movement (hundreds of pips) over the next few days or weeks rather than smaller price moves signaled by intraday candle analysis.

The other neat feature of candlesticks is that most formations offer a clearly defined price level that negates the scenario suggested by the pattern. Clarity is a rare commodity in the forex market, so when you have a tool that offers generally clearly defined scenarios, it's well worth making it a standard part of your analysis routine.

The catch with candlesticks is that the formations offer only a general directional signal, such as a recent price move higher that looks set to reverse. Even the term *reverse* doesn't necessarily mean prices will move lower — only that they're likely to stop going up. But this is the forex market, where prices are always moving, so when they stop going in one direction, they usually start going in the other direction. The other trick with candlestick formations is that they typically don't suggest tactical price levels to enter or exit. As a result, trading based on a candle formation can be a leap of faith, as in "The pattern suggests prices should move lower in coming days but doesn't indicate how high prices may go first."

One way to trade candlestick reversal patterns is to leave orders to sell at higher levels in the case of a bearish reversal pattern, or to buy at lower levels in the case of a bullish reversal formation. The selling level would be on the approach to the highs for the preceding move up, with a stop placed a margin of error above those highs, which should not be surpassed if the pattern is valid. A similar approach could be used to buy on a bullish reversal pattern. The idea is that the market may still try again in the direction of the prior move, providing you better levels at which to enter your position based on the candlestick formation.

Alternatively, or in tandem with the above strategy on an either/or basis, you can identify a key support/resistance level in the direction suggested by the candlestick pattern and place a stop loss order to enter on the other side, in case the market moves directly as the pattern suggests. I outline a similar strategy in more detail in the following section.

Building a Trade Strategy from Start to Finish

If you've read any other trading books, you've undoubtedly seen numerous chart illustrations where the authors can point to a chart pattern and say, "See, the pattern indicates a price top," and sure as shootin', the rest of the chart shows that prices move lower. Don't you just hate that? Well, hindsight is 20/20. Don't get me wrong; I'm guilty of the same thing in this book. It's largely unavoidable to get the point across.

In the real market, you're never going to have the benefit of hindsight in advance. On every chart you look at, the future is going to be blank. And that's the eternal struggle — basing decisions in the here and now on events that have yet to happen, all the while putting your money at risk.

To make amends, I do something a bit strange here and depict a trade opportunity in real time, or as real as I can make it in a book. Who knows? The trade may blow up in my face, and I'll have a bad trade recommendation preserved in book form for posterity. The point of this exercise, however, is not to show you how good or bad I am at spotting trades. It's to give you an insight into how you may analyze the market and construct a trade strategy on a regular basis, using many of the approaches I outline in this chapter.

Follow along with Figures 12-9 and 12-10, which show some of the key daily and hourly price points I use to define my trade strategy for EUR/USD from March 21, 2011. In Chapter 11, I indicate my preference to use fundamental elements to determine the overall direction a currency pair should move, and then apply technical analysis to refine entry and exit levels.

So, how do the fundamentals for EUR/USD stack up? At the moment, pretty good in my view. European leaders have reached agreement on a long-term debt relief mechanism, and the market seems to find it credible, reducing fears of financial instability. The ECB has strongly indicated it plans to raise rates at its next meeting in a few weeks' time, while the Fed has signaled rates will stay low for the foreseeable future, giving EUR an advantage over the USD on the monetary policy outlook. Also, one week ago the G7 intervened for the first time in more than a decade to support Japanese efforts to restrain JPY strength in the aftermath of the earthquake/tsunami/nuclear disaster earlier in March. That action saw the ECB buy EUR/JPY, giving EUR/USD, and risk assets in general, a boost in the process. And the USD is generally quite weak.

As such, my expectation is to see EUR/USD strengthen further (currently 1.4230) to the 1.4450 to 1.4500 area initially, with potential to around 1.4680 based on the measured move objective of the broken bull flag last month. A look at daily Ichimoku charts shows price well above the cloud and above the Tenkan and Kijun, signs of a solid trend higher.

But I'm also wary that EUR/USD has *already* gained ground on the fundamental factors I cite earlier, so I'm reluctant to buy at current levels. I also note the highs from November 2010 at about 1.4250/1.4280 as a potentially significant resistance point. I definitely don't want to get long 50 points below a major daily high.

Instead, I'll look to get long at better levels. Looking at the daily chart in Figure 12-9, the break above the 1.4000/50 level stands out as the most recent acceleration in the trend higher. Maybe I'll get a chance to buy a retest of the break?

The hourly chart in Figure 12-10 shows prices potentially set to drift out of the primary channel, another cautionary sign. The hourly MACD is showing a bearish divergence on the newest highs, but it could also be basing out above the zero line, potentially signaling another move higher. Cross-checking with the ADX, it based out above the 25 trending level, and is currently above, but only barely. All in all, I think I have a reasonable basis to expect a pullback lower while the 1.4280 highs hold. If they don't, I'll have a strategy for that scenario.

My strategy then is to buy a pullback at 1.4070 for a single lot of 100,000 EUR/USD, placing my if-done/then-OCO limit buying order just above the key 1.4000/50 break level in case it's not reached. I'll place my stop below that zone, allowing for a 20-pip margin of error, at 1.3980, for a total risk of about 90 pips, or $900. My take profit order will be to sell at 1.4420, just below what I think will be key round number resistance in the 1.4450/4500 area, possibly on some option-related selling interest, too, for a potential gain of around 350 pips or $3,500. I'll raise the stop loss to 1.4200 if the 1.4280/85 highs are tested, to lock in some profit in case of a failure.

In case prices move directly higher, I'm prepared to step up and buy on a stop loss basis at 1.4310, which would represent a clear break of both the 1.4280 highs and the 1.4300 level. But if it's triggered, I won't hang on for too long in case the break ultimately fails. I'll leave my stop at 1.4240 for a risk of around 70 pips, or $700. The take profit will be the same at 1.4420 for a potential gain of around 110 pips. Depending on the strength of any follow-through buying above 1.4280, I may opt for a trailing stop loss of 70 pips and see how the 1.4450/4500 area reacts.

Figure 12-9:
Daily EUR/USD analysis suggests potential price targets based on the broken bull flag, but key daily highs loom just above current prices.

Source: www.eSignal.com

03/21/11   O: 1.41720 H: 1.42400 L: 1.41390 C: 1.42247   +0.00437

Hourly EUR/USD

Congestion zone

Break above 1.4030/50
sees gains extend

Figure 12-10:
Hourly EUR/
USD shows
some
signs of a
potential
stall in
recent gains
as seen in
a bearish
divergence
in MACD.

Possible bearish divergence

Daily channel support

MACD 13, 26, 9

but ADX is above 25, just barely

ADX/DMI 14

03/14/11   03/22/11 - 01:00   #3010

Source: www.eSignal.com

So how'd the trade turn out? Surprise, surprise, it went well, but I changed what was a medium-term strategy into a short-term trade based on market developments. First, EUR/USD tried higher one more time on Tuesday, but stopped short of 1.4250 with a high at 1.4249, before turning lower. A combination of weaker Eurozone data, better U.S. data and escalating concerns over Portuguese debt (the government collapsed on Wednesday night) saw EUR/USD drop to as low as 1.4054 (which is where the Ichimoku Tenkan line was on that day), triggering my limit entry order at 1.4070 on Thursday morning in European trading. A disappointing U.S. durable goods report later in the New York morning saw EUR/USD rebound quickly above 1.4120, eventually triggering stop loss orders at 1.4150/70 and jumping as high as 1.4220.

With the quick bounce from the key 1.4000/50 support area identified earlier, I felt quite confident in the overall strategy. But I was also mindful of the key resistance up at 1.4250/80, which now appeared to be drawing sellers in below it. I decided to protect my profits, so I narrowed my order to a stop loss at 1.4145 (locking in 75 pips profit), just below the break-up level at 1.4150 earlier in the morning and lowering my take profit to 1.4230. The rest of Thursday traded between those levels, and I finished out the day still long one lot from 1.4070. Looking ahead, I considered headlines coming from the EU debt summit could send EUR/USD lower in a flash, and also that the German IFO survey due out on Friday morning was forecast to decline, also potentially sending EUR/USD back down. Shortly after the New York close, I decided to exit the trade and sold at 1.4175, for a gain of 105 pips, or $1,050.

What did I do right and what did I do wrong in the trade? First, I took time to analyze key price levels and identify an opportunistic entry level, placing my order just above key support, in case it wasn't reached. Second, I aggressively protected my profits, adjusting my stop loss order based on unfolding price movements. Third, I stayed flexible regarding exiting the trade, taking into account technical levels and developing fundamental events. Last and most important, I took profit. EUR/USD could've gone to the moon on Friday (it didn't, but that's another story) and I might've missed out as my ultimate view of a higher EUR was realized. But the bottom line is that I developed a trade strategy, stuck to it, and have something to show for it. You can't go broke taking profit.

What did I do wrong? In hindsight, I could have been more aggressive and sold short above 1.4200, keeping a tight stop over 1.4250 or 1.4280, for a well-defined and relatively minimal risk. But that would have been contrary to my fundamental expectations, and I would have regretted it if it failed. I also may have then become gun-shy and reluctant to get long at even higher levels. So maybe it wasn't such a bad thing after all.

I hope this example gives you a practical idea of how to put it all together, drawing on fundamentals, chart formations, and technical analysis to identify a trade setup and construct the trading plan to exploit it. In Chapters 13, 14, and 15, I look at considerations and strategies for entering positions, managing positions, and exiting trades in much greater detail.

Chapter 13

Risk-Management Considerations

. . . .

In This Chapter

▶ Understanding the different types of risk

▶ Managing leverage and inflated expectations

▶ Setting up trade plans in terms of risk

▶ Planning for the unexpected

. . . .

Trading is all about risk, yet it's frequently the last thing many individual traders think about. Too often, they're fixated on the expectation of positive trading results, as in "How much can I make?" To a large extent, that's basic human nature. Why would anyone speculate in anything unless he believed he could win?

I think traders should approach the forex market with eyes wide-open when it comes to the risks they're taking. And I'm not talking about some simple risk formula that comes out to dollars and cents. I'm looking at it from the perspective of an overall risk-taking enterprise philosophy. The more aware you are of the risks you face in the forex market, the more likely you'll be able to avoid them — and the more likely your success.

Managing Risk Is More Than Avoiding Losses

On the most basic level, *risk* in currency trading is the same as trading in any other financial market — the risk is that you'll lose money. But risk comes in many different forms and from many different sources. Sometimes the biggest risks are the ones that you never knew existed.

I believe forewarned is forearmed. In this section, I look at some of the main sources of risk that may not be readily apparent or that are easily overlooked.

Leverage amplifies gains and losses — and expectations

Leverage refers to the multiple applied to your available margin collateral, which translates into the maximum size of your market position. Leverage is typically expressed as a multiplier rate (like 10 times or 20 times) or a ratio (like 10:1 or 20:1) If the leverage rate is 10-times/ratio is 10:1, for example, and you have $1,000 of available margin, you're able to hold a maximum position equal to $10,000.

Online currency trading firms typically offer higher leverage ratios than you may be familiar with from trading stocks on margin. Leverage ratios among currency brokers are typically on the order of 100:1 for standard-size accounts (100,000 trade-lot size) and 200:1 for mini-accounts (10,000 trade-lot size). Recent regulatory changes around the world have limited maximum leverage ratios to lower levels, such as 20:1 in Hong Kong or 50:1 in the United States, which I think is more than sufficient for individual traders.

Be wary of forex brokerage firms that offer super-sized leverage. I've seen some offering up to 400-times leverage, or 400:1. I strongly discourage you from employing that much leverage. As well, regulatory limits on leverage have seen some traders go jurisdiction shopping, looking for the highest leverage available, but ending up in dodgy locales that may carry additional risks.

Leverage is a great trading tool, allowing traders with less capital to participate in markets that they couldn't trade otherwise. But leverage is still just a tool. As with any other tool (think of a chainsaw here), if you learn how to use it properly, you'll be able to get the job done faster and easier. But if you don't learn how it works, and respect it, you're asking for trouble.

Most people see only the upside benefits of leverage — the larger the position on a profitable trade, the larger the profit, right? Yes, leverage will magnify your gains, but it'll also magnify your losses — the larger the position on a losing trade, the larger the loss you'll experience. You need to have a healthy respect for the downside risk in trading, or you won't last very long.

Take an example of a $100,000/lot-size account with $10,000 in initial margin deposited at a 50:1 leverage ratio. That margin balance translates into a maximum position size of $500,000, or five lots. If you were to take a position in USD/JPY at 90.00 using the maximum position size available, every pip change in USD/JPY is worth about $55.55 ([$500,000 × 0.01 pips] ÷ 90.00 = $55.55). But USD/JPY is regularly subject to 50- to 100-pip price swings in a single day (or more). If you're positioned the wrong way, you could lose around $2,778 to $5,555 in the course of a normal, run-of-the-mill trading day. That's about 28 percent to 55 percent of your trading capital in just one trade!

The key here is to avoid being seduced by leverage. Just because you're able to get 100:1 leverage doesn't mean you have to use it all. Trading a larger position may seem sexy, but no one ever said prudent, risk-aware trading was supposed to be sexy. Use leverage as a tool to facilitate your trading strategies, not as an ego booster.

Knowing your margin requirements

Online forex brokers require margin posted as collateral to cover any losses on your trading account. To protect themselves from client losses eating up the entire margin (or going negative) in adverse market movements, online brokers typically require you to have 100 percent of available margin for any open positions.

For example, at 50:1 leverage, if you're holding a $100,000 position in USD/CHF, you'll need to have at least $2,000 of available margin to hold the position ([$100,000 ÷ 100] × 0.50 = $500). If your available margin balance falls below $2,000 at any time, even for a second or just by pip, your broker has the right to liquidate your position, which is a fancy way of saying it closes out your position for you. Your losses are locked in, and your available margin balance is reduced.

Margin balances are typically monitored by computer programs based on current market prices. If a price move causes your available margin to fall below the required level, the position will be closed — no margin call, no notification to you, just a liquidated position. You may think that's unfair, but the reality is that brokers need to liquidate losing positions at some point, or your loss will become theirs.

As a trader, it's your responsibility to read the fine print and to know the minimum margin requirements and liquidation policies before you start trading. Regulated forex brokers must disclose their policies in your customer account agreement.

Liquidation policies can vary among brokers with some closing all open positions at once (in the case of multiple open positions) and others closing the largest losing position first until the minimum requirement is met to close remaining open positions.

From a trader's perspective, you never want to be in the situation where your positions are liquidated due to insufficient margin. It means you're trading too large a position for your available margin or you've let the losses run for too long relative to your available margin. Each trade plan needs to factor in the minimum margin requirement, and it should never even come close, or you're better off with a smaller position size. I look at the critical relationship between position size and margin later in this section.

Market liquidity, volatility, and gap risk

The forex market is routinely described as the most liquid financial market in the world, and that's true. But it doesn't mean that currencies are not subject to varying liquidity conditions.

Liquidity refers to the amount of market interest (the number of active traders and the overall volume of trading) present in a particular market at any given time. From an individual trader's perspective, liquidity is usually experienced in terms of the volatility of price movements. A highly liquid market will tend to see prices move very gradually and in smaller increments. A less liquid market will tend to see prices move more abruptly and in larger price increments.

Shifting liquidity conditions can increase volatility

Forex market liquidity will vary throughout each trading day as global financial centers open and close in their respective time zones. Reduced liquidity is first evident during the Asia-Pacific trading session, which accounts for only about 21 percent of global daily trading volume. Japanese, Chinese, or Australian data or comments from regional finance officials may provoke a larger-than-expected or more-persistent reaction simply because there is less trading interest to counteract the directional move suggested by the news.

Peak liquidity conditions are in effect when European and London markets are open, overlapping with Asian sessions in their morning and North American markets in the European afternoon. Following the close of European trading, liquidity drops off sharply in what is commonly referred to as the *New York afternoon market*.

During these periods of reduced liquidity and interest, currency rates are prone to drift in narrow ranges, but are also subject to more sudden and volatile price movements. The catalyst could be a news event or a rumor, and the reduced liquidity sees prices react more abruptly than would be the case during more liquid periods.

Another common source of erratic price moves during less liquid periods is short-term market positioning. A classic example is a strong rally in a currency pair during the North American morning/European afternoon. As Europe heads home, the currency pair typically settles into a consolidation range near the upper end of the day's rally. If sufficient short positions have been established on the rally, further price gains may force some shorts to buy and cover. With reduced liquidity, prices may jump abruptly, provoking a flood of similar buying from other shorts, resulting in a *short squeeze* higher.

The same phenomenon can occur following market declines, where market longs are forced to exit in a rush on further price declines. Still another variation on this theme is sharp price reversals of an earlier rally, where longs take profit in thin conditions and the resulting price dip brings out selling by other longs rushing to preserve profits. After a sell-off, profit-taking on short positions can provoke a sharp *short-covering reversal.*

There's no way to predict with any certainty how price movements will develop in such relatively illiquid periods, and that's the ultimate point in terms of risk. The bottom line is that if you maintain a position in the market during these periods of thin liquidity, you're exposed to an increased risk of more volatile price action.

Liquidity is also reduced by market holidays in various countries and seasonal periods of reduced market interest, such as the late summer and around the Easter and Christmas/New Year holidays.

Typically, holiday sessions result in reduced volatility as markets succumb to inertia and remain confined to ranges. The risks also increase for sudden breakouts and major trend reversals. Aggressive speculators, such as hedge funds, exploit reduced liquidity to push markets past key technical points, which forces other market participants to respond belatedly, propelling the breakout or reversal even further. By the time the holiday is over, the market may have moved several hundred points and established an entirely new direction.

Just because you're enjoying an extended holiday weekend doesn't mean you're not exposed to risk from higher volatility in holiday markets. You are — and you need to factor liquidity conditions into your overall trading plan.

Getting a handle on volatility

Volatility is a statistical term referring to average price fluctuations (standard deviation) relative to the average price over a specified period of time. Volatility is what makes the trading world go 'round, and without it, speculators would have a lot of time on their hands.

But not all volatility is created equal, and you need to be aware of two main types of volatility that can alter the currency playing field:

✔ **Market volatility:** Market volatility is the overall level of price volatility in various financial markets at any given time. The VIX S&P 500 volatility index is a good overall barometer of market volatility. Market volatility typically increases during periods of uncertainty or unexpected economic data or monetary policy developments. If you're trading on a short-term basis or using a model that relies on relatively low volatility (for example, mean reverting systems, moving averages, or regression channels), you need to be aware that increased volatility can quickly swamp such strategies. Better to stay on the sidelines and sit out the upheavals than jump in with a strategy unsuited to higher volatility.

 ✓ **Currency-pair volatility:** Different currency pairs trade with different volatility characteristics, both in the short and long term. Before you go with a trade setup in a currency pair you've spotted on a chart, make sure you're aware of the pair's relative volatility. (I discuss individual currency-pair volatility and other trading characteristics in greater detail in Chapters 8 and 9.)

Minding the gap

Gap risk refers to the potential for prices to *gap,* or jump from one price level to another with no tradeable prices in between. Gap risk typically is associated with events such as economic data reports, central bank rate decisions, and other major news events. In that sense, most gap risk is identifiable in advance by looking at data and event calendars. Unexpected news or official comments can also trigger price gaps. Breaks of key technical levels are another source of price gaps.

Gaps vary in size depending on the nature of the news, but price gaps of 20 to 80 pips or more are not uncommon in currencies after major news and data events. Gaps occur because the interbank market reduces its bids and offers in the minutes or so immediately before and after major announcements, leaving online currency trading platforms with no prices to show individual traders.

After the news is out, interbank traders adjust their prices to reflect the news, resulting in a price gap higher or lower. It may be up to 30 seconds (or more depending on the news or event) before normal pricing returns.

If you're holding open positions at the time of major data releases or events, you're subject to gap risk. The same goes for stop-loss orders left with online brokers — stop-loss executions are subject to gap risk. Depending on market circumstances, stop-loss order executions will see *slippage* (meaning, your stop-loss order may not be filled at the rate you specified). In the case of price gaps, brokers are obligated only to fill your order on a "best efforts" basis.

Don't expect to be able to leave a stop-loss order nearby on either side of the market before a major news or data event and have it filled at your order rate. Occasionally, the market will take out both sides of the stop-loss orders before the release ever hits the market, locking in your loss. If that doesn't happen, and the market gaps through one side of your order, you're subject to slippage, and you'll be filled where the market resumes trading, which could be substantially different from where you left your order.

If you're thinking that this is some trick that online brokers cooked up to sock it to individual traders, keep this in mind: The big players in the interbank market are subject to the same gap risk as individuals trading online. Even if you were a prop trader (see Chapter 3) at some big bank, with one of your own bank's traders watching your order, you're going to get filled where your trader is able to execute the order in the market. The same applies to online brokerages. ***Bottom line:*** No market-maker will survive very long if he fills his customers at rates even he can't access.

The other type of gap risk stems from events that occur over weekends, potentially resulting in a substantial gap between Friday's closing level and the Sunday/Monday opening price. Weekend gap risk is typically also identifiable in advance because it most often occurs around scheduled events like a G20 meeting or a Chinese data release.

That said, there's still plenty of potential for unexpected events (earthquakes, terrorism, and currency revaluations or devaluations, to name just a few) to happen over weekends. To judge the risks of a weekend gap, you need to have a good sense of what's going on in the major currency nations and a healthy sense of expecting the unexpected. The safest approach is simply not to hold positions over a weekend.

We have a winner here! Protecting your profits

It's one thing to speculate in the market and get the direction wrong. That's good old-fashioned risk-taking, and it's just part of the business of trading. But it's another result entirely to get the direction right and still lose money, or not make as much as you could have, or not keep as much as you'd already made.

Most traders can readily accept the idea of getting the direction wrong. They shrug it off and get back to work in short order. But take a trader with a winning position in the morning that goes south in the afternoon, and you're suddenly looking at a case study of negative trader emotions. With a wrong-way trade, it's a simple case of not missing what you never had. With a good trade gone bad, it's hard not to feel regret or think the market is out to get you.

Experienced traders know that keeping what you've made is often as hard as making it in the first place, so they guard their profits aggressively. The best way to do that is by adjusting your stop loss in the direction of the trade once it's in the money. You can do this by using either a *trailing stop loss* or manually changing your original stop loss based on specific price levels being surpassed.

A trailing stop loss is a stop-loss order that automatically trails the market at a user-defined distance (say, 40 pips). For example, if you're short at 55, and you have a 40-pip trailing stop loss, the stop starts out at 95. As the market moves lower, the trailing stop will adjust so that it is always 40 pips from the low. If the market trades down to 10, your trailing stop is now at 50, guaranteeing you at least a 5-pip profit. Trailing stops are great for catching longer-term movements, because they rely on a market reversal of *x* pips before being triggered.

If you're more inclined to trade according to technical levels, you may want to consider manually adjusting your stop loss after specific levels are broken.

For example, if you're long, you may raise your stop loss from its original level after technical resistance has been broken.

Above all, if the market reverses and your profit starts to decline, don't worry about getting back what you've just lost — worry about keeping what you've still got.

Placing your orders effectively

Currency traders rely on orders to take advantage of price movements when they're not able to personally monitor the market and also to protect themselves from adverse price movements. If you're going to be trading currencies, odds are that you'll be relying on orders as part of your overall trade strategy. I cover the various types of orders in greater detail in Chapter 4.

The two main types of orders are *limit orders,* used to buy or sell at rates more favorable than current market prices, and *stop-loss orders,* which are used to buy or sell at worse rates than prevailing levels. The key difference between the two types is that you generally want your limit orders to get filled, but you don't want your stop-loss orders to be triggered. That's because limit orders are used to take profit and enter positions (which you want), and stop-loss orders are used mainly to exit losing positions (which nobody likes). (The exception is stop-loss entry orders, in which you use a stop-loss order to enter a position — on a breakout, for example [see Chapter 14].)

The risk with using orders is that you miss having your take-profit limit or entry orders filled or that your stop-loss orders are triggered at extreme price points. The catch here is that markets have a penchant for going after stop-loss orders and shying away from limit orders in the routine noise of daily fluctuations.

That makes where you place your orders a critical factor in your overall trading strategy. Deciding where to place orders is definitely more art than science, and even the most experienced currency traders continually grapple with the question of where to place their orders.

Factoring in the dealing spread with orders

Online currency traders face two other complicating factors: the dealing spread of the currency pairs and the order execution policies of online currency trading platforms.

Most online platforms execute on the basis that a limit order to sell is filled when the bid price reaches the order rate and a limit order to buy is filled when the offer price reaches the order rate. In the case of stop losses, a stop-loss order to sell is triggered if the bid price reaches the order rate, and a stop order to buy is executed if the offer price reaches the order rate. In both cases, the dealing spread works against the order, and traders need to take that into account.

For example, you may be long USD/CHF at 1.0250 with a limit, take-profit order, to sell at 1.0330 and a stop-loss order to sell at 1.0200. For your take profit to be executed, the dealing price must print 1.0330/33. If the highest price quoted is 1.2329/32, no cigar. Your stop loss would be triggered if the dealing price ever trades at 1.0200/03; if the lowest quoted price is 1.0201/04, your order is still alive. As you can see, it's frequently a game of inches played out in milliseconds.

Factoring in technical levels when placing orders

Many traders focus on technical levels to decide where to place their orders. Continuing the order example from the last section, if there is resistance from a trend line or hourly highs at the 1.0330 level, many other sell orders could be grouped there. If the selling interest is strong enough, the market may never get that high because sellers step in front of the resistance level, start selling, and stop prices from rising.

In the case of the stop-loss level, it may be placed on Fibonacci retracement support or recent daily lows, which may also attract other technically minded traders to place their stops at the same level. If the market starts to move lower, sellers will frequently try to test key technical-support levels to see if they hold, in the process triggering stop-loss orders left at those levels. The stops may be triggered and the level exceeded briefly, only to see prices rebound and the support ultimately hold.

Getting stopped out at a market top or bottom is a very frustrating experience, but it's happened to everyone at one point or another. *Remember:* Someone has to sell at the low and buy at the high.

Margins of error and market extremes

One way to prevent getting stopped out by market extremes is to factor in a margin of error when placing your orders. Using a margin of error is a fairly sophisticated practice, but the idea is to err on the side of getting your limit order filled — leaving a sell order a few points below key resistance levels or a buy order a few points above support levels. At a minimum, the margin of error should account for the dealing spread of the currency pair you're trading.

For stop losses, the concept is to err on the side of not allowing your stop to be triggered — leaving a stop-loss sell order several points below key support levels and a stop-loss buy order above technical resistance levels.

In both cases, the margin of error will depend on the relative volatility of the currency pair you're trading as well as overall market volatility at the time. Generally speaking, the greater the volatility, the greater the margin of error, and vice versa. (I look at individual currency pair volatility and trading behavior in greater detail in Chapters 8 and 9.). My own preference for limit orders is for a small margin of error of around 5 to10 pips. For stop losses, I like to use a wider margin of error of around 20 to 40 pips, allowing for a greater cushion in case others' stops get triggered and the technical level is briefly broken.

Using a margin of error in placing orders will also require you to rethink the overall trade strategy, especially in terms of position size. If you're going to place stops with a margin of error, and the stop ends up getting triggered anyway, your losses will be greater. So you may need to reduce the position size to mitigate the impact on your margin.

Placing stop-loss orders based on technical or financial levels

There are generally two schools of thought when it comes to the basis for deciding where to place stop-loss orders:

- ✔ **Technical stops:** Placing a stop-loss order according to price levels identified through technical analysis. Whatever technical approach you choose to follow, you'll be looking to identify key technical points that, if exceeded, will invalidate the trade setup and signal that it's time to get out of the trade.

- ✔ **Financial stops:** Based on the amount of money you're prepared to risk on a given trade. You may base the trade on a fundamental view of future developments, but you're willing or able to risk only a certain amount of money on the trade.

Financial stops may be appealing to highly conservative traders who don't want to risk more than a fixed amount on any single trade. If that's your way of maintaining trading discipline, by all means go with it. But I think it's important to note that financial stops are essentially arbitrary and have no relation to the market. They're much more a function of position size and entry price — elements you control — than any objective market measure.

Technical stops, on the other hand, are based on past price action, which is about the only concrete way traders have of gauging future price movements. If GBP/USD has repeatedly failed to trade above 1.6215 in recent weeks, to pick a random price as an example, a move above that level suggests that something has changed. And the market, in its infinite wisdom, has decided that GBP/USD should move higher. We have no way of knowing for sure whether the break will be sustained; we can only go with our best analysis.

My own preference is to base orders on technical levels rather than financial considerations, but the ultimate limiting factor is the amount of money at risk. That may sound like I'm trying to have it both ways — I explain this idea further in the next section.

Applying Risk Management to the Trade

When it comes to trading, risk management is frequently an afterthought — that is, until you take a loss that you weren't expecting. Suddenly, the wisdom of the ages is upon you, and you vow never to let it happen again.

By the way, who in her right mind would ever put on a trade expecting to take a loss, anyway? Sounds crazy, right? But all the experienced traders I know calculate the risk they're facing in every trade before they ever enter it. It's part of their decision-making DNA and goes a long way to determining which trade opportunities they pursue and which ones they skip.

I strongly recommend that traders approach the forex market with risk management as the first thought. It's how you'll be able to get some trades wrong and still survive to get other trades right.

Analyzing the trade setup to determine position size

The starting point for any successful trade is developing a well-conceived trading plan. And the most important element of a trading plan is the size of the position that will be traded. Position size will determine how much money is ultimately at risk, as well as the overall viability of the trade.

But position size is only one half of the equation that determines how much money is at risk. The second half of the equation is the pip distance between the entry price and the stop-loss level. Wait a minute, you may be thinking. Why didn't I mention the upside potential or the pip distance between the entry price and the take profit? Why aren't I looking at how much money I can make on the trade?

Save the rose-colored glasses for buying lottery tickets. When you're plunking down a dollar or two, it's okay to focus only on the upside and dream about winning millions. But when you're trading in any financial market, you have to remember the market is not there to give you money.

I know you're not drawn to currency trading for the chance to lose money. You're interested in making money, and you're prepared to take some risks to do that. The question is how much risk are you prepared to accept. Because you're dealing with finite resources in your trading — the amount of risk capital you've devoted to your trading — you have a definite limiting factor to your trading. If you eat through your trading capital, you're done. So the starting point of a risk-aware trading plan has to focus on the downside risks.

That brings us to the trade setup, which I cover in greater detail in Chapter 12. A *trade setup* is a trade opportunity that you've identified through either fundamental or technical analysis, or a combination of both.

In every trade setup, you need to identify the price point where the setup is invalidated — where the trade is wrong. For example, if you're looking to sell a currency pair based on trend-line resistance above, price gains beyond the trend line would invalidate your rationale for wanting to be short. So the price level of the trend line is the line in the sand for the overall strategy.

Now comes the entry point for the trade. Let's say that current market prices are 50 pips below the trend-line resistance you've identified. That means the market could move higher by 50 pips and your trade setup would still be valid, but you'd be out of the money by 50 pips. You now have a clear delineation of how much risk your trade setup would require you to assume. If you get in now, you're risking at least 50 pips.

Alternatively, you could reduce that risk by waiting and using an order to try selling at better levels — say, 25 pips higher. If the market cooperates and your limit-entry order is filled, you're now risking only 25 pips before your trade setup is negated.

So how large a position should you commit to the trade? From a risk standpoint, it all depends where you're able to enter the trade relative to your stop-out level (see the following section).

Doing the math to put the risk in cash terms

After you've identified where your stop-loss point is — where the trade setup is negated — and where you're able to enter, you're able to calculate the amount of risk posed by the trade. Let's say you're inclined to enter the position at current market levels, and your stop is 50 pips away. For example, if you're trading a standard-size account (100,000 lot size), and the trade is in NZD/USD (where profit and loss accrues in USD), each lot would translate into risking $500 (100,000 × 0.0050 NZD/USD pips = $500).

If your margin balance is $10,000, you're risking 5 percent of your trading capital per lot in this trade, which is frequently cited as the maximum risk in any one trade.

There are no hard and fast rules as to how much you should risk in any single trade, but I recommend limiting your risk to no more than 10 percent of your account balance.

If you're able to enter the position at a better level (say, using the order to sell 25 pips higher), you're now risking only 25 pips on the trade. You could double the position size and still be risking the same amount of trading capital. Or you could stick with the single lot and cut your risk in half.

Devising the trading plan in terms of risk

Risk in the trading plan is not confined simply to losing money on the trade. There are also opportunity risks from trade setups that you're not able to enter. Another old market saying is that some of the best trades are the hardest to get into. You may be eyeing a trade setup that involves buying a dip toward rumored buying orders or significant technical support. But what happens if the dip never comes?

Identifying the trade entry points

Winning or losing on a trade is difficult if you never get into the position in the first place, which makes identifying where to get into the trade one of the most important steps in any trading plan.

I like to use technical analysis as the primary means of identifying entry levels. When looking to identify entry points, I focus on the following technical levels:

- Trend lines in various time frames (daily, four-hour, and hourly)
- Hourly highs and lows for short-term intraday position entries
- Daily highs and lows for medium- to longer-term positions
- Congestion zones
- Fibonacci retracements of prior price movements (38.2 percent, 50 percent, 61.8 percent, and 76.4 percent)
- Spike highs and lows

After you've identified a price point to enter into the trade, double-check the level. Is the entry level realistic? If you're looking to enter a short-term trade, is your entry point likely to be reached in the short-term time frame (minutes to hours)? You can use momentum readings to help gauge the likelihood of an order level being reached. For example, if hourly momentum readings are moving lower, a buy entry to the downside probably stands a better chance of being reached than a sell entry above.

What happens if your entry level is never reached? Do you have a backup plan? If you were planning on selling on further rallies, for example, but the market moves directly lower, is there a price level below that you would consider selling at on a stop-entry basis? What does that backup plan mean for your overall trade stop level? Should you reduce the position size to compensate for the worse entry rate?

Establishing stop losses with foresight

The stop-loss level is the starting point in any trade plan from an overall risk perspective. It's the point where the trade setup is negated and the strategy fails.

When considering where to place the stop level, be aware that the currency market, like most financial markets, has a tendency to try to take out levels where stop losses are likely to be located. Nothing is worse than having the right strategy but being taken out by a short-term, stop-loss-driven price move that eventually reverses and goes in the direction of your outlook.

To guard against the risk of being unnecessarily whipsawed out of a position, you need to approach selecting your stop-loss level from a defensive point of view. Anticipate that the market *will* test the level where the trade setup is invalidated, such as trend-line support or hourly lows. Then consider if the market tests that level, how far must it go through before it's really considered a break?

No set formula exists for this calculation, but allowing for a margin of error can sometimes prevent a stop loss from being triggered unnecessarily. The margin of error you apply will depend on the general volatility of the currency pair you're trading, as well as on the overall market volatility at the time of the trade.

Above all, you need to balance the risk of being taken out on a false move with the larger risk that your overall strategy is wrong. You can be flexible up to a point, but you still need to set your ultimate stop loss and then stick to it.

Setting take-profit objectives dynamically

When it comes to establishing the take-profit objective, a lot of trading books recommend using some sort of risk/reward ratio, like 2:1 (meaning, if you're prepared to risk 50 points on a trade, you should be aiming to make 100 points). That approach is all well and good in theory, but it fails to account for the realities of the market. Just because you've identified a trade opportunity that risks x amount, why would the market necessarily "reward" you with twice that amount in profit?

Instead, I suggest using a much more dynamic market-based approach, one that considers where the market is likely to go based on where it's been (technical analysis) and overall market conditions. The idea is to be *realistic* about how much you can take out of the market, not *idealistic* about how much the market will reward you.

I focus on technical support and resistance levels as the primary guideposts in the progress of market movements. If you're looking to buy based on a Fibonacci retracement level as support, for example, you're going to be looking at technical resistance levels above for your take-profit targets. Chart formations, such as channels and flags, also suggest relatively predictable and attainable price targets.

I look to momentum indicators like Moving Average Convergence/Divergence (MACD) and stochastics as gauges of the underlying speed of the price movement. If short-term momentum is accelerating in the direction of the trade, stay with it, and consider revising your take-profit objectives to capture a larger move. But if short-term momentum in the direction of the trade is slowing or stalling, consider scaling back your profit targets and adopting a more defensive, profit-protecting stance, like raising your stop loss or taking partial profit.

Time is another important consideration in dynamically managing your profit objectives. You need to be aware of and anticipate upcoming events and market conditions. If you've been long for a rally during the North American morning, what's likely to happen when European markets begin to close up for the day? If you're positioned in USD/JPY in the New York afternoon, and Japanese industrial production is slated to be released in a few hours, what can you expect in the interim? Stay flexible and dynamic, just like the market.

Choosing Your Trading Broker

With the explosion in online currency trading over the past several years, dozens of forex brokerage firms now operate all over the world. Competition among various brokerages is fierce, and there's no shortage of advertising seeking to win you as a client. In this section I look at some of the differences between forex brokerages from a risk perspective, because where you trade can sometimes influence your trading outcomes.

In case you skipped the introduction to this book, I think it's important in the interest of full disclosure to note that I am affiliated with FOREX.com. Before you choose a broker, I recommend you take a look at the Cheat Sheet, where I provide a list of questions to ask.

Different business models of brokers

Most online forex brokers function as the market-maker for your trading, meaning that the broker is on the other side of every trade — when you buy, you're buying from the broker; when you sell, you're selling to the broker. Brokerage firms that are market-makers typically provide both consistent liquidity and execution, which allows you to trade your desired amount at all times.

Market-makers typically offer either fixed spreads or variable spreads:

- **Fixed spreads** remain constant all the time, regardless of what's happening in the market. Because the broker must assume the additional market risk of quoting a fixed spread all day long (including in thinly traded or volatile markets, when interbank spreads tend to widen), fixed spreads tend to be slightly wider than variable spreads.

✔ **Variable spreads** fluctuate depending on market interest. In highly liquid periods — such as the overlap between the London and New York sessions — variable spreads will be the tightest (as low as 1 or 2 pips in EUR/USD and the other heavily traded currency pairs). In slower periods (such as 6 p.m. eastern time [ET], when New York is closed and Asia is not yet fully online), spreads will tend to be wider.

Whether you should choose fixed spreads or variable spreads largely depends on your trading style. If you're a short-term trader looking to make just a few pips on each trade, you're probably better off with variable spreads, which are tightest in liquid markets. If you trade around news, fixed spreads will allow you to avoid the inevitable widening of spreads (sometimes by a significant amount) that typically happens around fundamental announcements.

Another model being promoted by a few brokers is the *nondealing desk* model. The term is meant to differentiate these brokers from market-making brokers — who have trading, or *dealing,* desks — that manage the firm's market exposure. Nondealing desk brokers will tell you that the price you're trading on is coming directly from the interbank market and that they route all your trades directly to the banks. But if that's the case, why is the non-dealing desk broker even needed? Online forex brokers have emerged precisely because the large institutional players did not have the capacity to process tens of thousands of individual trades.

More important, if the nondealing desk is commission free and routing every trade to a bank, how does it make any money? A legitimate nondealing desk firm will offer very tight bid/offer spreads and charge commissions for each trade.

Commission-free forex brokers are compensated by the spread between the bid and the offer. If you buy from a broker at 15, for example, and another trader at the same time sells to the broker at 14, 13, or 12, the broker realizes a profit from the spread.

The reality with the nondealing-desk approach is that such trading platforms may display wider prices and sharper price gaps during periods of volatility, all the while claiming no control over the prices being shown. Be careful about promises of dealing in the interbank market —if it sounds too good to be true, it usually is.

Financial risks of brokers

The main financial risk posed by forex brokerages involves the brokerage firm's failing due to mismanagement or fraud, as happened in the case of Refco in early 2006. If a brokerage collapses, your trading account could be frozen and your funds tied up in bankruptcy proceedings for months or lost forever.

To reduce that prospect, you need to make sure your broker is registered with the appropriate financial authorities in the jurisdiction where it operates. In the United States, forex brokers are required to be registered as a Futures Commission Merchant/Retail Foreign Exchange Dealer (FCM/RFED) with the Commodity Futures Trading Commission (CFTC) and are ultimately subject to CFTC rules and regulations. The National Futures Association (NFA) is the self-regulating body for forex brokers, similar to FINRA (formerly known as NASD, or the National Association of Securities Dealers), which oversees stock brokers regulated by the Securities and Exchange Commission (SEC).

You can visit the NFA's website at `www.nfa.futures.org` to check on the regulatory status of a prospective broker. You should also review the brokerage firm's regulatory history and its overall financial condition. Go with firms that have solid histories and strong financials.

Technology Issues and Contingency Planning

Online currency trading presents its own host of potential technological problems that you need to be prepared for. We cover the primary technology risks originating from the broker's side in the previous section, but plenty of things can go wrong on *your* side of the connection.

Unfortunately, it's the Catch-22 of today's technology: Without it, you couldn't access the forex market in the first place — but when there's a problem, it's just another example of modern technology making your life more difficult. The trick is to anticipate what can happen and be prepared for when it does.

Contingency planning is the name of that game, and redundancy is the solution. By *redundancy,* we mean having a backup plan for your backup plan, with a backup plan in case the other backup plan fails. Now try saying that three times fast.

In particular, have backup plans in place for the following contingencies:

- **If your Internet connection is disrupted:** Make sure you're able to call your brokerage's trading desk; memorize its phone number and any account numbers or passwords you need to verify your identity, in case you need to trade or place orders over the phone.

- **If the power goes out:** You may not be able to log on via computer, and your landline phone may be disabled, so make sure your cellphone is reliably charged. (*Note:* Cordless phones are the only landline phones that require electricity to run. That's all the more reason to have access to at least one corded phone.)

> ✔ **If your cellphone fails:** Know where you can access a landline phone, and make sure you have your brokerage's phone number memorized. Saving the number in your cellphone is no good if the phone's battery is dead or the phone isn't working.

Above all, make sure to do the following:

> ✔ **Always have a stop-loss order in place for any open positions.** This is your first and ultimate backup plan for any and all contingencies. Also, make sure your stop-loss order is good until canceled, so it'll never expire while the position is open.

> ✔ **Write down your open positions and orders.** Keep a hard copy of all your trades and orders in a notebook or trading journal so you can refer to it in the event of an emergency. If you can't access your brokerage's trading platform, you won't be able to see your exposure.

Part IV
Executing a Plan

In this part . . .

This is what it all comes down to. You've done the research, you've looked at the charts, you've developed your strategic trade plan, and now it's time to put it to work. If you thought economic data mining and chart analysis were the hard part, wait until your adrenaline starts pumping after you've entered the trade. Here, I take you through the concrete steps of opening a position, monitoring the trade while it's active, closing it out, and doing a post-trade analysis to refine your trading going forward.

Chapter 14

Pulling the Trigger

"You gotta be in it to win it" is a favorite saying that currency traders like to throw around. The "in it" part refers to being "in" the market, having the right directional view expressed with an open position (long/short) in a currency pair.

But there's always a trade-off between having the right position and getting into that position at the most advantageous price. For example, being short AUD/USD may be the correct position to have, but if you enter at the wrong price, you may have to endure some pain before the trade moves your way.

In this chapter, I walk you through some of the different ways of entering trades and establishing the position to fit your overall strategy.

Getting into the Position

You can make trades in the forex market one of two ways: You can trade *at the market,* or the current price, using the click-and-deal feature of your broker's platform; or you can employ orders, such as limit orders and if/then contingent orders. (I discuss order types in Chapter 4.) But there's a lot more to it than that. Certain trade setups suggest a combination of both methods for entering a position, while others rely strictly on orders to capture rapid or unexpected price movements. Then there's the fine art of timing the market to get in at the best price at the moment.

Buying and selling at the current market

Many traders like the idea of opening a position by trading at the market as opposed to leaving an order that may or may not be executed. They prefer the certainty of knowing that they're in the market. Actively buying and selling is also what makes trading as fun and exhilarating as it is hard work.

Deciding whether to enter now (at the market) or wait for better price levels (using orders) depends greatly on the nature of your strategy. If you're aiming to trade short term (minutes/hours) on news or economic data reports, for instance, you're going to be trading mostly at the market. If you're looking to position for a larger price adjustment over the next day(s), you're better off using orders to execute your market entry.

For short-term trade entry at the market, you want a good handle on the recent price action, which means knowing where prices have been over the past several hours. Just because you've settled on a strategy to buy USD/CAD doesn't mean you have to close your chart window, open your trading platform, and pay the offer.

Take a step back and look at shorter-term charts, such as 5 or 15 minutes, to get an idea of where prices have been trading recently. Chances are you'll observe a relatively narrow range of price action, typically between 20 and 30 pips. Unless the situation is urgent, a little patience can go a long way toward improving your entry level. Why buy at 1.0550 when you have a viable chance to buy at 1.0535?

Let the routine price fluctuations work to your advantage by trying to buy on down-ticks and sell on up-ticks in line with your overall strategy. Selecting your trade size in advance helps — so when the price gets to your desired level, you need to click only once to execute the trade. You can also use limit orders to buy or sell just a few pips from the current market, letting the broker's platform execute automatically in case the price moves are too quick to click and deal manually.

As you watch the price action, keep a disciplined entry price in mind, both in your favor and in case prices start to move away from your desired entry level. If the market cooperates and moves to your desired trade entry price, stay with your plan and make the trade. If prices move away from you, have a worst-case entry level in mind and be prepared to pull the trigger so you can still execute your overall strategy. You may not be able to enter at better prices every time, but I think you'll be surprised how often you can.

Averaging into a position

Medium- and longer-term trade strategies typically benefit from averaging into a position. *Averaging into a position* refers to the practice of buying/selling at successively lower/higher prices to improve the average rate of the desired long/short position. The idea here is to allow larger market swings to unfold and use them to establish a larger position at better prices than current levels in anticipation that the market will eventually reverse course in line with your strategy.

Take a look at a detailed example of averaging into a position to see how it works. Imagine that the USD/JPY is moving lower from 82.20 on a weak U.S. economic release, but you think USD/JPY is unlikely to decline below 81.00, where the 200-day moving average is located.

One possible strategy would be to buy USD/JPY on the current weakness, spacing your buys so that you can buy as low as possible, but above 81.00 where you don't expect it to trade. (The stop-loss exit in this example would be somewhere below 81.00.) Imagine that you buy one lot of USD/JPY at the market, now at 82.00, just so you have some piece of the position in case the market rebounds abruptly. You decide that 81.20 is another good level to buy at because it's a margin of error above the key 81.00 level. If your order to buy at 81.20 is filled, you'll be long two lots at an average price of 81.60 ([82.00 + 81.20] ÷ 2 = 81.60).

Take a look at what just happened there. To begin with, you were long one lot from 82.00. To add to the position at 81.20 means the market was trading lower, which also means you were looking at an unrealized loss of –80 pips on your initial position from 82.00. After you buy the second lot, your unrealized loss has not changed substantially (assuming that the market is still at 81.20 and excluding the spread, you're still out –80 pips, now –40 pips on 2 lots), but your position size has just doubled, which means your risk has also just doubled.

If the market rebounds from 81.20, your unrealized loss will be reduced. But if the market continues to decline, your losses are going to be twice what they were had you not added on to your position. If your strategy plays out and the market reverses higher, you now have a larger position from a better entry price than if you had entered the two lot position earlier at higher levels.

I've seen the practice referred to as *pyramiding* in other trading books, and the advice is usually to avoid doing it (as in "Don't pyramid into a losing position"). Sometimes "adding on" to winning positions is acceptable, such as after a technical level breaks in the direction of your trade. The result of adding on to winning positions, however, is a worse average rate for the overall position — a higher average long price or a lower average short price. If the market reverses after you add on, any gains in the overall trade can be quickly erased.

So what's the deal? Should you average into positions or not? As with most questions on trading tactics, the answer is a straightforward "It depends." Before deciding whether to average into positions, consider the following:

> ✔ **Time frame of the trade:** Short-term trades seek to exploit the immediate direction of the market. If you're wrong on the direction in the first place, adding to the position at better rates will likely only compound your losses. For medium- and longer-term trades, averaging into a position can make sense if the trade setup anticipates a market reversal.

(I talk about this a bit more in the "When averaging into a position makes sense" section, later in this chapter.)

- ✔ **Account size:** Depending on your account size, you may not have the ability to add to positions. You also need to keep in mind that adding to a position will further reduce your available margin, which reduces your cushion against adverse price movements, bringing you closer to liquidation due to insufficient margin. If that means trading smaller position sizes, such as 10,000 mini-lots, go with that.

- ✔ **Volatility:** If the overall market or the currency pair you're trading is experiencing heightened volatility, averaging into trades is probably not a good idea. Increased volatility is usually symptomatic of uncertainty or fresh news hitting the market, both of which are prone to see more extreme directional price moves, in which case averaging is a losing proposition. In contrast, lower volatility conditions tend to favor range-trading environments, where averaging can be successful.

Signs that averaging into a trade is not a good idea

Many trading books recommend avoiding averaging into, or adding on to, a losing position — and with good reason. The tactic can lead to dramatically higher losses on smaller incremental price movements. Also, if you're adding on to a losing position, you're missing out on the current directional move. In other words, not only are you losing money, but you're also not making money, which is the opportunity cost of averaging.

But that still doesn't stop people from averaging into losing trades, even professional traders. Here are some indications that averaging is probably not a good idea:

- ✔ **The market just blew through your stop-loss level.** But you didn't have a stop-loss order in place, so you're still holding onto the losing position. First tactical error: Trading without an active stop-loss order. Second tactical error: Instead of exiting the position in line with your trade plan, you're reluctant to take the larger loss than you initially reckoned with, so you decide to hold on to the position, hoping it will recover. This is usually the first wipeout on the slippery slope of relinquishing trading discipline. Save yourself some money and don't commit a third tactical error by averaging into an even larger position (which you had already planned to be out of by that point anyway).

- ✔ **The range just broke.** You may have had great success in recent trades playing a range-bound market, and you're in a position again based on that range. But ranges do break, and prices do move to new levels. Remember the basis for your trade — the range is going to hold — and don't hang on, much less add on, to positions beyond your predetermined stop-loss exit level based on the range.

✔ **News is out, but the currency pair is not responding the way it should.** The news or data may be USD-positive, for example, but the dollar is coming under selling pressure anyway. Keep in mind that multiple cross-currents are at work at any given moment in the forex market. Sometimes they're position related (a large hedge fund may be turning around a multibillion-dollar position); other times they're based on news or information that is not widely known in the market, like a mergers-and-acquisitions (M&A) deal or a rumor. *Remember:* The market reaction to a news/data report is more important than the report itself. If you've taken a position based on the news, don't second-guess the market reaction by adding on to the position if the market doesn't respond the way you think the data indicates. Instead, accept that something else is going on and that the news you based your trade on is not it.

When averaging into a position makes sense

Depending on the trade setup, you may be entirely justified in averaging into a position. In fact, with some trade opportunities, you'll be hoping to have the chance to average into the position at better rates, because if the trade setup is correct, you'll want to have on as large a position as possible.

Even though I'm suggesting that certain trade opportunities warrant averaging into a position, I want to stress that you still need to identify the ultimate stop-loss exit point in every trade setup. In other words, you can average into a position as much as you want up to a certain point, but after that the trade setup is invalidated, and you need to exit the position.

The trade setups I'm referring to are those where a *reversal* is anticipated. Prices frequently move into a *counter-trend consolidation ranges,* where prices move in the opposite direction of the primary trend for a time before the trend resumes. You may see signs of an impending reversal from daily candlestick patterns, such as a shooting star/hammer or a tweezers top/bottom. You may begin to suspect a reversal after a significant intraday spike reversal/rejection from key technical levels. The market may also be nearing important long-term trend-line support or resistance that suggests a medium-term bottom or top is close by.

What all these setups have in common is a price difference between current market levels and the ideal entry point based on the setup. For example, major daily trend-line resistance dating back six months may lie above in EUR/USD at 1.2960/70. Current market levels are well below at 1.2890, and there has been a spike rejection from an intraday test to 1.2930/35. Adding up these observations, we may justifiably conclude that the current market price is just below an area of major resistance, suggesting a short position as the overall way to proceed.

But we have no accurate way of predicting how much higher the market might trade, or even if it will, before the anticipated reversal lower takes place. The market could start moving directly lower from current levels. It could retest the spike highs seen earlier in the day, or it could make it all the way to test the key trend-line resistance before stalling. So where might we look to get short?

The answer is in that zone of resistance we just identified between current market levels and the daily trend-line resistance. This is where it makes sense to average into a trade to exploit the trade setup.

As an example of my own approach, I may not know how much higher the market will go, so I may be prepared to short a portion of the overall position at current market levels, in case the top has already been seen and prices move directly lower. I may also be prepared to sell remaining portion(s) of the position at successively higher levels, if the market allows it. I'll save my last portion of the position for the trend-line resistance level in case it's reached.

When considering where to leave your limit-entry orders to average into a trade, be aware of what your final average rate will be if all your orders are filled. The difference between that average rate and your stop-loss level multiplied by the total position size will give you the total amount you're risking on the trade. (In Chapter 16, I look at the profit/loss implications of closing out a multiple lot position that was averaged into.)

Although there are no 100 percent accurate gauges to tell us how much higher the market is likely to trade, we can use short-term momentum studies — such as stochastic models, the Relative Strength Index (RSI), or Moving Average Convergence/Divergence (MACD) — to make an educated guess as to how much more upside potential there may be.

If hourly momentum studies have already topped out and crossed over to the downside, for example, the upside potential is likely more limited. This may argue for being more aggressive in establishing a short position, such as making the initial sale at current market levels and placing any additional limit orders to sell above at closer levels. But if hourly momentum studies are still moving higher, we can reasonably wait and look to sell at relatively higher levels using limit sell orders.

Averaging into a reversal setup requires that you're able to buy/sell multiple lots over relatively large price zones, sometimes as much as 100 pips or more. Make sure that you have sufficient margin resources available *before* you start averaging into your overall position. Depending on the size of the buy/sell zone and your available margin balance, you may have to space your limit-entry orders farther apart or trade fewer lots overall.

It's always a trade-off between being in the right position to catch the move and getting in at the best price possible. It's quite frustrating to identify a potentially significant market reversal, leave a single limit-entry order, but then see the reversal take place without your order being filled. Averaging into the position starting at current prices is one way to make sure you're on board for at least some of the move.

If the setup works out, you'll have taken advantage of any favorable price moves the market has made, resulting in a better average rate on your position. If the setup fails, averaging into the position at successively better rates will cost less in the end than entering the whole position at the current market level.

Trading breakouts

A *breakout* or *break* refers to a price movement that moves beyond, or breaks out of, recent established trading ranges or price patterns captured with trend lines. Breakouts can occur in all time frames, from weeks and days on down to hours and minutes. The longer the time frame, the more significant the breakout in terms of the overall expected price movement that follows.

In the very short term, prices on a 15-minute chart may establish a trading range of 20 to 30 pips over several hours, for example. A breakout on such a short time scale might result in a 30- to 50-pip movement in a matter of minutes/hours. Daily trading ranges of 300 to 400 pips may see a breakout result in an initial 50- to 150-pip movement in subsequent hours, with more to come in following sessions.

There's no real fixed ratio or scale for range breakouts; I've just given those examples above to give you an idea of the relative scales involved. To be sure, a breakout of a 15-minute range can lead to the break of an hourly range, which can lead to a breakout of a daily range.

 Breakouts are important because they represent a shift in market thinking. Most trading theories start with the premise that the current price reflects all the known information on that market at the moment. But rather than settling on one price and stopping, markets tend to consolidate into a zone of prices, or a range, where relatively minor price fluctuations are simply noise in terms of the grand theories of market price behavior.

For a range to break, then, by definition something must have changed in the market's thinking. And there's only one thing that will change the market's thinking: new information. New information can be anything from news and data to rumors or comments, down to the prices themselves. Many traders rely on price information as their primary source of decision-making information. If prices in USD/CHF have been capped by 1.0500 for the past four weeks, a price move above that level is new information and requires adjustments in the market.

The beauty of breakouts from an individual trader's perspective is that you don't necessarily need to know the reason for the breakout — just that prices have broken out. Of course, being aware of what's going on and what news is driving the market always helps give you a leg up in anticipating and preparing for potential breakouts.

In terms of entering a position, breakouts frequently represent important signals to get in or out of positions. In that sense, they take a lot of the guesswork out of deciding where to enter or exit a position.

Identifying potential breakout levels

The first step in trading on a breakout is to identify where breakouts are likely to occur. Pinpointing likely breakout levels is most easily done by drawing trend lines that capture recent high/low price ranges. In many cases, these ranges will form a sideways or horizontal range of prices, where sellers have repeatedly emerged at the same level on the upside and buyers have regularly stepped in at the lower level. Horizontal ranges are mostly neutral in predicting which direction the break will occur.

Other ranges are going to form price patterns with sloping trend lines on the top and bottom, such as flags, pennants, wedges, and triangles. These patterns have more predictive capacity for the direction of the eventual breakout and even the distance of the breakout. (I review the most common patterns and what they imply in greater detail in Chapter 11.)

The time frame that you're looking at will determine the overall significance of the breakout and go a long way toward determining whether you should make a trade based on it. Very short time frames (less than an hour) are going to have much less significance than a break of a four-hour range or a daily price pattern. The length of time that a price range or pattern has endured also gives you an idea of its significance. A break of a range that has formed over the past 48 hours is going to have less significance for price movements than the break of a range that has persisted for the past three weeks.

Trading breaks with stop-loss entry orders

After you've identified a likely breakout point, you can use a resting stop-loss entry order placed just beyond the breakout level to get into a position if a break occurs. To get long for a break to the upside, you would leave a stop-loss entry order to buy at a price just above the upper level of the range or pattern. To get short for a break lower, you would leave a stop-loss entry order to sell at a price just below the lower level of the range or pattern. Figure 14-1 is a chart showing EUR/USD and where stop-loss entry orders could be placed to trade breakouts.

The appeal of using stop-loss entry orders is that you're able to trade the breakout without any further action on your part. Breakouts can occur in the blink of an eye. Just when you thought the upper range level was going to hold and prices started to drift off, for example, they'll come roaring back and blow right through the breakout level.

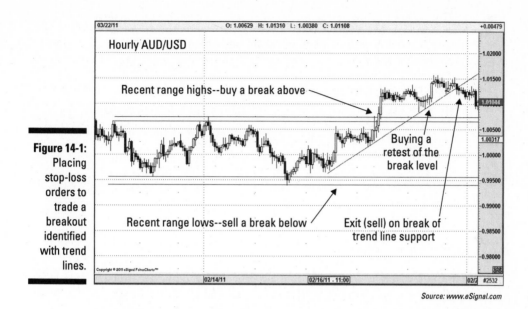

Figure 14-1:
Placing
stop-loss
orders to
trade a
breakout
identified
with trend
lines.

Price moves like that can leave the most experienced traders caught like deer in the headlights. By the time they react, the break has already seen prices jump well beyond their desired entry level. Worse, by trying to trade at the market in a fast-moving breakout, you may miss your price and have to reenter the trade, by which time prices may have moved even farther in the direction of the break.

When placing a stop-loss entry order to trade a breakout level, be aware of any major data or news events that are coming up. If your stop-loss entry order is triggered as a result of a news event, the execution rate on the order could be subject to slippage, which may reduce much of the gains from getting in on the breakout. (We discuss slippage in Chapter 13.)

Trading the retest of a breakout level

The other way to trade a breakout is after the break has occurred. You may not have noticed the significance of a particular technical level, or you may not have left orders in overnight to exploit a break. You turn on your computer the next morning to discover that prices have jumped higher overnight and feel like you've missed the boat. But you *may* still get a chance to trade the breakout if prices return to re-test the breakout level.

A *retest* refers to prices reversing direction after a break and returning to the breakout level to see if it will hold. In the case of a break to the upside, for example, after the initial wave of buying has run its course, prices may stall and trigger very short-term profit-taking selling. The tendency is for prices to return to the breakout level, which should now act as support and attract buying interest.

You can use these retests to establish a position in the direction of the break-out, in this case getting long on the pullback. Figure 14-1 shows where you could have bought on the retest of the break higher in AUD/USD. Note that prices did not make it exactly back to the breakout level. When trying to get in on a retest, you may consider allowing for a margin of error in case the exact level is not retested. You could also consider using a strategy of averaging into a position, discussed earlier in this chapter, to establish a position on any pullbacks following a breakout. Here the averaging range would be between current prices and the break level.

Earlier I wrote that you *may* get the chance to buy/sell a retest of a breakout level. The reason is that not every breakout sees prices return to retest the break level. Some retests may retrace only a portion of the breakout move, stopping short of retesting the exact break level, which is typically a good sign that the break is for real and will continue. Other breakouts never look back and just keep going.

But to the extent that it's a common-enough phenomenon, you still need to be aware of and anticipate that prices may return to the breakout level. From a technical perspective, if prices do retest the breakout level, and the level holds, it's a strong sign that the breakout is valid, because market interest is entering there in the direction of the break.

Guarding against false breaks

Breakouts are relatively common events in currency trading, especially in the very short-term. But not every breakout is sustained. When prices break through key support or resistance levels, but then stop and reverse course and ultimately move back through the break level, it's called a *false break*.

There's no way to tell whether any given breakout is going to turn out to be a false break except in hindsight. To protect against false breaks (as well as maintaining trading discipline and sound risk management), you also need to follow up your stop-loss entry with a contingent stop-loss exit order to close out the position if the market reverses course.

Although there's no surefire way to tell whether a breakout is a false break or a valid one that you should trade, a few points to keep in mind are:

- ✔ **Time frame of the breakout level:** The shorter the time frame you're looking at, the greater the potential for a false break. The break of a price range on an hourly chart may trigger stop losses only from short-term intraday traders. But the break of a daily price range dating back several weeks is likely to spark greater interest from the market, especially systematic models.

- ✔ **Significance of the price level:** The more important the price level that's broken, the more likely it is to provoke a market response and to be sustained. A break of a three-month daily trend line is more likely to trigger a market response than the break of recent hourly highs/lows.

✔ **Duration of the break:** The longer the breakout level is held, the more likely the breakout is to be valid. Many false breaks are reversed in a matter of minutes. An hourly closing price beyond the break level increases confidence that it's a valid breakout, and a daily close beyond confirms it.

✔ **Currency pair volatility:** Relatively volatile currency pairs, such as GBP/USD and USD/CHF, are more prone to false breaks than others, especially in short-term time frames. Look for confirmation in bigger pairs, like EUR/USD and USD/JPY. If they're pressing against similar price levels, the less-liquid pairs could be leading the way.

✔ **Fundamental events and news:** What's the fundamental reason for the breakout? Did someone say something? Have major market expectations on monetary policy, for example, been disappointed or surprised? Sustained breakouts tend to have a fundamental catalyst behind them — a significant piece of news that has altered the market's outlook. If the news is relatively minor or not entirely "new" news, it increases the chances it's a false break.

Trading breakouts is a relatively aggressive trading strategy and is certainly not without risks. Until you've gained some experience in the forex market you're probably better off focusing only on breaks of levels identified by trend-line analysis in longer time frames, such as daily charts, or breaks of longer-term price levels, like daily or weekly highs/lows. They may not occur as frequently, but they'll tend to be more reliable.

Making the Trade Correctly

When using an online trading platform, entering a position is as easy as making a few simple mouse clicks. At the same time, the simplicity and speed of online trading platforms make those simple mouse clicks a done deal that puts your trading capital at risk.

That's why it's important to understand from the get-go that any action you take on a trading platform is your responsibility. You may have meant to click Buy instead of Sell, but no one knows for sure except you.

If you do make a mistake, correct it as soon as you discover and confirm it. Don't try to trade your way out of it. Don't try to manage it. Don't start rationalizing that it may work out anyway. No trader is error-proof, and you're bound to make a mistake someday. Just cover the error and get your position back to what you want it to be. Covering errors immediately is one of the few hard-and-fast rules I subscribe to in trading any market.

Buying and selling online

I take you through the basic steps of making a trade online in Chapter 4, but here I aim to clue you in to some of the human and technical aspects common to online trading.

Most every online trading brokerage now provides for click-and-deal trade execution. *Click and deal* refers to trading on the current market price by clicking either the Buy button or the Sell button in the trading platform. Before you can click and deal, you have to:

1. **Select the right currency pair.**

   This may sound silly, but make sure you've selected the currency pair that you actually want to make a trade in. When the market gets hectic, and you're switching between your charts and the trading platform, you could easily mistake EUR/USD for EUR/CHF if you're not careful. This can also happen when different currency pairs are trading around similar price levels. If EUR/USD is trading at 30/33 and USD/JPY is trading at 31/34, it's easy to home in on the price and overlook the big figures, which would tell you you're in the wrong pair.

2. **Select the correct trade amount.**

   Make sure you've specified the correct amount you want to trade. Different platforms have different ways of inputting the trade amount. Some use radio buttons, others use scroll-down menus, and others allow you to type the amount manually. When the trading is fast and furious, make sure your selection has been properly registered on the platform. Some trading platforms allow you to customize your default trade sizes in advance, so you're able to simply click and deal on the currency pair of your choice.

3. **Double-check your selections.**

   Remember: This is your money; be certain now or be sorry later. In case you think input errors can't happen to you, think about the equity trader at a New York investment bank who meant to sell 10 million shares of a stock but ended up entering 10 *billion.* By the time the trade was stopped, the system had sold several hundred million shares. Ouch!

4. **Click Buy or Sell.**

   Be sure you know which side of the price you want to deal on. If you want to buy, you'll need to click the higher price — the trading platform's offer. If you want to sell, you'll have to click the lower price — the platform's bid. Most platforms have labeled the sides of the prices from the user's perspective, so the bid side will be labeled Sell, and the offer side will be labeled Buy.

After you've clicked Buy or Sell, the trading platform will confirm whether your trade went through successfully, usually within a second or less. If your trade request went through, you'll receive a confirmation from the platform. Double-check your position, and make sure it's what you want it to be.

If the trading price changed before your request was received, you'll receive a response indicating "trade failed," "rates changed," "price not available," or something along those lines. You then need to repeat the steps to make another trade attempt.

Attempts to trade at the market can sometimes fail in very fast-moving markets when price are adjusting quickly, like after a data release or break of a key technical level or price point. Part of this stems from the *latency effect* of trading over the Internet, which refers to time lags between the platform price reaching your computer and your trade request reaching the platform's server.

If you're continually getting failed trade responses, it may be due to the speed of your Internet connection, which is preventing your trade requests from getting to the brokerage trading platform in a timely way or delaying the incoming prices you're seeing so that they're always behind the real market.

Whatever the outcome of your trade request, you need to be sure you've received a response from the trading platform. If you have not gotten a response back after more than a few seconds, you need to call your broker immediately and confirm the status of the trade request. The deal may have gone through, but confirmations may be delayed due to processor slowness. Or the trade may have never been received by the trading platform because your computer lost its Internet connection.

Placing your orders

Orders are critical trading tools in the forex market. Think of them as trades waiting to happen because that's exactly what they are. If you enter an order, and subsequent price action triggers its execution, you're in the market. So you need to be as careful as you are thorough, if not more so, when placing your orders in the market.

We go over the different types of orders and how they're used in Chapter 4, and we look at the finer points of placing orders in Chapter 13. Here are some additional important tips to keep in mind when placing and managing your orders:

✔ **Input your orders correctly.** Make sure you've correctly specified the currency pair, order type, amount, and price. Most trading platforms are designed to reject an order that is obviously wrong, such as a stop-loss order to buy at a price below the current market, and will prompt you to correct it. But other errors, such as a wrong big figure on the order price, can be accepted and end up being your problem. Double-check your order after it has been accepted by the trading platform. If it's wrong, edit it or cancel it and start again.

✔ **Note the expiration of your orders.** Order expirations are typically good-'til-cancelled (GTC), where the order remains active until *you* cancel it, or good until the end of the day (EOD), which means that the order automatically expires at the end of the trading day (5 p.m. eastern time [ET]). If you had an intraday position with a stop-loss good until EOD, and you later decide to hold the position overnight, you'd need to revise the expiration. GTC orders will expire on some trading platforms after an extended period of time, such as 90 days, so be clear on your broker's policy.

✔ **Cancel unwanted orders.** Some trading platforms allow orders to be *associated with a position,* meaning that the order will remain valid as long as the position is open. Such *position orders* will also usually adjust the order amount if you increase or reduce the associated position. Other orders are *independent of positions,* so even if you close out your position, the independent orders will remain active. Make sure you understand the difference between the two types, and remember to cancel any independent orders if you close the position they were based on, such as take profits, stop losses, or OCO.

Chapter 15

Managing the Trade

· ·

In This Chapter

▶ Staying on top of prices and news

▶ Listening to what other markets are saying

▶ Updating the trade plan over time

▶ Protecting profits and extending gains

· ·

So you've pulled the trigger and opened up the position, and now you're in the market. Time to sit back and let the market do its thing, right? Not so fast, amigo. The forex market isn't a roulette wheel where you place your bets, watch the wheel spin, and simply take the results. It's a dynamic, fluid environment where new information and price developments create new opportunities and alter previous expectations. Actively managing a trade when you're in it is just as important as the decision-making that went into establishing the position in the first place.

I hope you'll take to heart my recommendations about always trading with a plan — identifying in advance where to enter and where to exit every trade, on both a stop-loss and take-profit basis. (I go into more detail about developing trading plans in Chapters 10, 12, and 13.) Bottom line: You improve your overall chances of trading success (and minimize the risks involved) by thoroughly planning each trade before getting caught up in the emotions and noise of the market.

Depending on the style of trading you're pursuing (short-term versus medium- to long-term) and overall market conditions (range-bound versus trending), you'll have either more or less to do when managing an open position. If you're following a medium- to longer-term strategy, with generally wider stop-loss and take-profit parameters, you may prefer to go with the "set it and forget it" trade plan you've developed. But a lot can happen between the time you open a trade and prices hitting one of your order levels, so staying on top of the market is still a good idea, even for longer-term trades.

Shorter-term trading styles looking to capture intraday and even smaller price movements will necessarily have more frequent adjustments to overall trade strategies. I say *necessarily* because short-term price movements can be extremely rapid as well as short lived. If your trade strategy is designed to capture only smaller price shifts, say, on the order of 30 to 50 pips, you'll need to be more proactive in guarding against short-term reversals of 15 to 25 pips, which constitute nearly half of your expected upside.

On top of that, short-term price movements are the market noise that makes up larger price movements. There will be a lot more 30- to 50-point moves than 100- to 200-pip moves. If you're going after the more frequent fluctuations, you'll have to be more nimble when it comes to adjusting to incoming news and price developments.

Monitoring the Market while Your Trade Is Active

No matter which trading style you follow, it'll pay to keep up with market news and price developments while your trade is active. Unexpected news that impacts your position may come into the market at any time. News is news; by definition, you couldn't have accounted for it in your trading plan, so fresh news may require making changes to your trading plan.

The starting point for any trading plan is determining how much you're prepared to risk, which is ultimately the result of the size of the position and the pip distance to the stop-loss point. When I talk about making changes to the trading plan, I'm referring only to reducing the overall risk of the trade, by taking profit (full or partial) or moving the stop loss in the direction of the trade. The idea is to be fluid and dynamic in one direction only: taking profit and reducing risk. Keep your ultimate stop-out point where you decided it should go before you entered the trade, when your emotions weren't in play.

Following the market with rate alerts

One way to follow the market from a distance is to set rate alerts from either your charting system or your trading platform. A *rate alert* is an electronic message that alerts you when a price you've specified is touched by the market in a currency pair you specify. Rate alerts are a great way to keep tabs on the market's progress.

Rate alerts on charting systems usually have the capability of alerting you to price developments only while you're logged on to your computer and the charting service. With charting systems, you're able to work on other tasks on your computer and keep the charting system minimized or in the background, which means you can use these at your job. If your requested price level is hit by the market, the chart system will typically start beeping or flashing and send a pop-up message.

Some forex brokers, including FOREX.com, can send rate alerts to clients via e-mail and SMS (short message service) text message to devices such as a cellphone, PDA, or pager. Many brokers are also expanding communication services to sites like Twitter and Facebook.

Still another way to keep tabs on the market while you're on the go is through wireless trading applications from your broker. FOREX.com offers a cellphone trading platform and iPhone and Droid apps that allow you to get market rates, place orders, execute live trades, and view charts and research.

When you're deciding which charting service and forex broker to use, make sure to find out if rate alerts and wireless access are available, what systems are required, and which devices are served.

Rate alerts are a convenient way to follow the market remotely, but they don't take the place of live orders and should never be substituted for stop-loss orders. By the time you respond to a rate alert and log on to the trading platform or call your broker's trading desk, prices may have moved well beyond your desired stop-out level, leaving you with a larger loss than you anticipated. Rate alerts are a nice little extra service, but only orders represent obligations on the part of your broker to take an action in the market for your account.

Staying alert for news and data developments

Every trade strategy needs to take into account upcoming news and data events before the position is opened. Ideally, you should be aware of all data reports and events scheduled to occur during the anticipated time horizon of your trade strategy. You should also have a good understanding of what the market is expecting in terms of event outcomes and anticipate how the market is likely to react.

For instance, if the Fed chair is scheduled to deliver remarks on the economy or the monetary policy outlook, find out what his recent comments have been. Is he currently leaning hawkish or dovish? If it's an economic data release, make sure you understand what the report covers and what it means for the market's current expectations. At the minimum, be sure you know what the consensus expectations are for the report and what the data series has been indicating recently.

It's often said that the market's reaction to news and data is more important than the news or data itself. But you can't properly interpret the market's reaction if you don't have a grasp on what the news means in the first place. (See Chapter 7 for a detailed look at economic reports and Chapters 5 and 6 for major fundamental drivers and how the market interprets them.)

The other reason to stay alert for news while your trade is active is that many trade strategies are based on fundamental data and trends. If your trade rationale is reliant on certain data or event expectations, you need to be especially alert for upcoming reports on those themes.

Part of your calculus to go short EUR/USD, for instance, may be based on the view that Eurozone inflation pressures are receding, suggesting lower Eurozone interest rates ahead. If the next day's Eurozone consumer price index (CPI) report confirms your view, the fundamental basis for maintaining the strategy is reinforced. You may then consider whether to increase your take-profit objective depending on the market's reaction. By the same token, if the CPI report comes out unexpectedly high, the fundamental basis for your trade is seriously undermined and serves as a clue to exit the trade earlier than you originally planned. There's no sense hanging on until the bitter end if your trade rationale has already been knocked down. You may even consider reversing your position in light of the new data.

Speculating based on expected event or data outcomes is perfectly okay. It becomes a problem only if you maintain the trade even after the data/event outcome has come out against your expectations and strategy. Always relate incoming news and data back to the original reason for your trade, and be prepared to adapt your trade strategy accordingly.

Keeping an eye on other financial markets

Forex markets function alongside other major financial markets, such as stocks, bonds, and commodities. Although these financial markets have seen higher long-term correlations with FX in recent years, short-term correlations are far less reliable.

But there are still important fundamental and psychological relationships between other markets and currencies, especially the U.S. dollar. In that sense, I look to developments in other financial markets to see whether they confirm or contradict price moves in the dollar pairs. So even though there may not be a statistically reliable basis on which to trade currencies based on movements in other financial markets, you'll be a step ahead if you keep an eye on the following other markets.

U.S. Treasury yields

U.S. government bond yields are a good indicator of the overall direction of U.S. interest rates and expectations. I focus on the benchmark ten-year Treasury-note yield as the main interest rate to monitor. I also keep an eye on shorter term rates, like three-month T-bills and two-year notes. Rising yields tend to be dollar positive, and falling yields tend to be negative for the dollar. If yields are rising, but the dollar isn't, it suggests that other factors are at work keeping the dollar down and that dollar bulls should be cautious. If yields are falling and the dollar is falling, too, you're getting confirmation from the bond market of a negative U.S. dollar environment — lower interest rates.

Make sure you understand the reason for the bond yield's movements, because it can suggest different interpretations. If it's based on interest rate expectations — due to data or Fed comments, for instance — it's more likely to reflect overall dollar direction. If it's due to market uncertainty and a flight to quality — due to European debt concerns, for example — the impact on the U.S. dollar may be more positive. The larger the change in yields, the more important is the message that's coming from the bond market. Yield changes of more than 5 basis points (1/100 of a percent) should get your attention.

Gold and silver prices

Precious metals like gold and silver are typically viewed as hedges against inflation and safe-haven investments in times of financial market uncertainty. In recent years, gold and silver have seen heightened demand as alternatives to the major currencies, most especially the U.S. dollar, but also the euro, as the European debt crisis has threatened the single currency. As such, gold and silver prices tend to move in the opposite direction of the U.S. dollar overall (inverse correlation), but the short-term correlations are trickier. Gold and silver are relatively illiquid markets and mostly take their cues from the larger forex market, but the metals are no stranger to their own market-specific gyrations, typically based on breaks of technical levels.

Look for confirmation of the U.S. dollar direction in gold and silver prices. If the dollar is rallying and the metals are falling, for instance, it's a good sign that the dollar's gains are for real. If the dollar is rallying but gold is holding steady or even rising, the dollar's strength looks more suspect.

Oil

Oil is similar to the precious metals and other commodities in that it has a long-term inverse correlation to the U.S. dollar (dollar down/oil up and vice versa). But the same caveat also holds true — shorter-term correlations are less reliable, and oil is especially vulnerable to oil specific supply/demand shocks. I would also note an *asymmetric bias* to the relationship between oil and the U.S. dollar. What that means is that oil is likely to experience greater strength on a falling dollar than weakness on a rising dollar, if all else is equal.

I also like to look to oil price developments for what they suggest about interest rate expectations and relative economic growth. Higher oil prices tend to increase inflation pressures, which may lead to higher interest rates. At the same time, higher oil prices tend to reduce economic growth by undermining personal consumption. Between the two, oil's impact on the growth outlook is more important due to the speed with which consumers react to changes in oil prices. Interest rate changes take longer. The recent surge in emerging market nations' growth has also heightened global demand for oil, so oil increasingly functions as a barometer for overall global growth.

Stocks

Long-term, such as over the last decade, there is very little correlation between stock markets and currencies. However, since the Great Financial Crisis of 2008–2009, there has been a stronger relationship between stocks and FX, especially the U.S. dollar. The relationship is best described as risk on/risk off (see Chapter 5 for more on risk sentiment), where stocks are considered risk-seeking assets and the dollar is viewed as the safe haven asset, as investors buy USD to buy U.S. Treasury debt, the ultimate safe harbor. In recent years, the risk on/risk off scenario has typically played out as follows: When the overall market environment is positive, investors embrace risk and buy stocks, reducing the demand for dollars, usually leading to dollar weakness. When the news turns bad, however, investors have dumped stocks and fled to the safety of U.S. Treasuries and the greenback. As long as recent financial travails plague the global economy, this relationship seems set hold. But when economic and financial conditions begin to improve to something resembling normalcy, I would expect the stocks/FX relationship to return to lower historical correlations.

Updating Your Trade Plan as Time Marches On

If you're like most traders, after you enter a position you're going to be keenly aware of every single pip change in prices, at least as long as you're watching the market. Every little price change, and the attendant change in your unrealized profit and loss (P&L), will evoke emotions ranging from joy to despair and everything in between. And that's to be expected. After all, at the end of the day, it's the P&L that matters, and pips are how that's measured.

But one element that tends to receive remarkably little attention from traders, at least on a conscious level, is the passage of time. Prices may seem to stand still for extended periods — when a currency pair may be stuck in a range (that is, it keeps trading back and forth over the same ground) — but time is constantly moving forward.

Staying aware of time and its passing is an important skill for traders to develop. You know where the market price is now, so the question is really: Where will the market price be in the future? As soon as you think of the future, it becomes a question of time: *When* will it be there? If you consider these questions as you formulate each trade strategy, you'll go a long way toward incorporating time into your overall trade planning. More important, you'll gain an intuitive appreciation of the importance of time in trading, and you'll find yourself asking *when* as often as *why* or *where*.

On the most concrete level, as time progresses, it brings with it routine daily events, such as option expirations and the daily fixings, to name just two. These are specific time periods where traders can reasonably expect a flurry of activity, though it doesn't always materialize. (I run through the series of regular trading day time events in Chapter 2.)

Time's passing also brings you nearer to scheduled news or data events. The *pricing in* of market expectations for major events occurs in the hours and days ahead of the event or data release. As the release time draws closer, anticipative speculation generally declines, and price movements can become more erratic as traders take to the sidelines ahead of the release. Prices may chop around more, but ultimately not go anywhere. All these market reactions are as much the result of time as they are of the event itself.

On a more objective level, as time progresses, it can add significance to, or detract significance from, price movements that have already occurred, frequently providing trading signals as a result. For instance, the failure of prices to make an hourly close below a break of trend-line support suggests that it may be a false break and that prices are likely to rebound higher. But if the break occurred at 10:12 ET, for instance, you won't know until the next hourly close in 48 minutes. Potentially more significant trading signals are generated from longer time periods, such as a daily close above long-term trend-line resistance or a prior daily high.

Trend lines move over time

If you're basing your trading strategies on trend-line analysis, you need to be aware that price levels derived from trend lines will change depending on the slope of the trend line. The *slope* of a trend line refers to the angle of a trend line relative to a horizontal line. The steeper the slope of the trend line, the more the relevant price level will change over time; the shallower the slope, the more gradually the price levels will change with time.

Figure 15-1 gives you a good idea of how short-term price levels based on a 15-minute trend line will shift over the course of just a few hours. Note how steeply the trend line is sloping upward. For prices to continue to move higher in line with this trend line, they must stay above the trend line as it rises over time, suggesting price gains of 10 to 15 pips per hour are needed.

03/22/11		O: 1.42190 H: 1.42500 L: 1.41780 C: 1.42071		-0.00119

```
OP 1.42050
HI  1.42080
LO  1.42020
CL  1.42071
```

5-minute EUR/USD

...but rises to
1.4215 by 4 pm

Trend line is at
1.4200 at 2 pm

Date and time indicator

`01:00 02:00 03:00 04:00 05:00 06:00 07:00 08:00 09:00 10:00 11:00 12:00 13:00 14:00  03/22/11 - 16:00` #10019

Copyright © 2011 eSignal ForexCharts™

Figure 15-1: Trend-line levels can change over time, depending on their slope.

Source: www.eSignal.com

Using your charting system, you can pinpoint relatively accurately where prices must be in the future for the trend line to remain active as a support/ resistance level. To do this, slide the cursor along the trend line, and note the time that appears on the horizontal axis at the bottom of the chart.

The same applies with longer-term charts, but the price shifts are typically less pronounced, meaning an hourly trend line may see levels adjust by 10 to 15 pips every 6 to 12 hours, and daily charts may see levels shift by 10 to 30 pips over a few days. But there are no concrete rules on this; it all depends on the slope of the trend line.

No matter what time frame you're trading, be sure to factor in the shifting levels of trend lines, if they're part of your trade strategy. You may need to adjust your order levels accordingly. In particular, consider the following:

✔ **Short-term and overnight positions:** Consider where trend-line support or resistance will be over the next 6 to 12 hours, when your position is still active but you may not be able to actively follow the market. You may want to use a trailing stop as a proxy for changes in trend-line-based support/resistance levels.

✔ **Limit-entry orders:** If your limit buying/selling order is based on a sloping trend line, periodically adjust your order so that it's still in play according to changes in the trend line. You may miss a trade entry if the trend line is eventually touched, but, in the meantime, its level has shifted away from where you first placed the order.

> ✓ **Breakouts:** A significant trend line that looks to be a mile away one week may suddenly be within striking distance in the following week or two weeks, substantially altering the market's outlook. Alternatively, the market may be focused on a price high/low as a breakout trigger, when a sloping trend line touching that high/low may actually be the catalyst for a breakout.

Impending events may require trade plan adjustments

As you develop your trading plan, I strongly recommend that you look ahead to see what data and events are scheduled during the expected life of the trade. If you follow that simple advice, you strongly reduce the chances of having your trade strategy upset by largely predictable events. More important, you'll be able to anticipate likely catalysts for price shifts, which will give you greater insight into subsequent price movements. Forewarned is forearmed.

If you've entered into a trade strategy based on an upcoming event — an expected weak U.S. data report, for instance — and the market has cooperated and priced in a lower U.S. dollar before the report is released, you may be looking at a profitable position before the data is even released. As the release time draws near, you may consider taking some profit off the table and holding on to the remaining partial position.

Consider the possible outcomes. If the data comes in negative for the U.S. dollar, and the market reacts by selling the U.S. dollar, you're still in the partial position to gain from further dollar weakness. But what if the data comes in stronger than expected? Or what if the data comes in weak as expected, but the market takes profit on short-dollar positions made in advance, in a "sell-the-rumor/buy-the-fact" reaction? You've protected your profit and taken some money out of the market before the event ever transpired. Now, that's called playing the market!

In the preceding scenario, I intentionally depict a short trade to remind you that being short is as common as being long in currency trading. You may be more familiar with "Buy the rumor, sell the fact." I just want to make sure you know that it works both ways.

Before major data and events, the market also frequently goes into a sideways holding pattern. The event speculators have all put on their positions, and the rest of the market is waiting for the data to decide how to react. These holding patterns can develop hours or days in advance, depending on what event is coming. Especially if you're trading from a short-term perspective, be prepared for these doldrums and consider whether riding through them is worthwhile.

Updating Order Levels as Prices Progress

Just because you've got a well-developed and considered trade plan doesn't mean it has to be carved in stone. Well, at least the ultimate stop-loss exit should be carved in stone. But when you're in a position, and the market is moving in your favor, it's important to be flexible in adjusting take-profit targets and amending stop-loss orders to protect your profits.

The key to being flexible in this regard is also being prudent — don't adjust your take-profit targets without also adjusting your stop-loss order in the same direction. If you're long, and you raise your take profit, raise your stop loss too. If you're short, and you lower your take profit, lower your stop-loss order as well.

Increasing take-profit targets

You've put together a well-developed trade strategy ahead of your trade, as I've recommended, so now that you're in the trade, why would you change your take-profit objective? That's a very good question, and you'd better make sure you have a very good answer, because I've also touted the virtues of not tampering with a trade plan after the position is opened.

So what constitutes a very good reason to extend your take-profit objective? Keep an eye out for the following events to consider extending your take-profit targets:

- **Major new information:** More likely than not, the new information will have to come out of left field. If it was a scheduled event, like a data report or speech, the market speculation surrounding it would have sopped up all the interest and muted its impact. *Major* means it has to come from the very top echelons of decision-making, like the Fed chairman, the European Central Bank (ECB) president, or other central bank chiefs; the U.S. Treasury secretary; or, increasingly, China. Surprise interest rate changes or policy shifts are always candidates. The more at odds the information is with current market expectations, the better the chances that it will generate an extensive price move.

- **Thinner-than-usual liquidity:** Reduced liquidity conditions can provoke more extensive price movements than would otherwise occur, because fewer market participants are involved to absorb the price shocks. Reduced liquidity is most evident during national holidays, seasonal periods (late summer, Christmas/New Year's), end of month, end of quarter, and certain Fridays.

- ✔ **Breaks of major technical levels:** Trend lines dating back several months or years, Fibonacci retracement levels of major recent directional moves, and recent extreme highs and lows are likely to trigger larger-than-normal price movements.

- ✔ **The currency pair:** The more illiquid and volatile the currency pair you're trading, the greater the chances for an extreme move. GBP, CHF, and JPY are the most common culprits among the majors, and the commodity currencies (AUD, CAD, NZD, and ZAR) are also candidates.

As you can see, the list is pretty short, and there may be only a dozen or so events in the course of a year that warrant altering your trade plan. Be careful about getting caught up in the day-to-day noise and routinely extending your profit targets — it undermines trading discipline and the basis for your trade strategy.

Tightening stop-loss orders to protect profits

I'm generally reluctant to extend our take-profit objectives unless there are significant grounds to do so (see the preceding section) or I'm using a trailing stop loss. But when it comes to protecting profits, I'm much more comfortable about adjusting stop losses to lock in gains. When you've got a profit in the market, taking steps to protect it is always a smart move.

When formulating your overall trade plan, always consider what price levels need to be surpassed to justify moving your stop loss. If it happens in the market, you'll be ready and know exactly what to do.

I like to focus on hourly and daily trend-line levels, highs/lows, and breaks of Fibonacci retracement levels. When these technical support/resistance points are exceeded, it's an indication that the market has seen fit to move prices into a new level in the overall direction of the trade. When that happens, consider moving your stop-loss order to levels just inside the broken technical level. If the market has second thoughts about sustaining the break, your adjusted stop will then take you out of the trade.

For example, say you're long GBP/USD at 1.5250, your original stop loss is at 1.5180 below, and your take-profit objective is above at 1.5380. Also above is resistance from yesterday's high at 1.5335. If that level is surpassed, consider raising your stop loss to break even (where you entered, at 1.5250) at the minimum. To more aggressively protect profits, you may raise the stop further to 1.5315 or 1.5325, locking in 65 to 75 pips minimum, on the basis that 1.5335 should now act as support.

The risk with adjusting stops too aggressively is that the market may come back to test the break level (1.5335, in this example), triggering your adjusted stop loss if it's too close, and then go on to make fresh gains. But the trade-off in that situation is between something and more of something, or potentially nothing and more of nothing. I prefer to have something to show for my efforts.

Another way to lock in profits in a more dynamic fashion is by using a trailing stop-loss order (see Chapter 4). After a technical level in the direction of your trade is overcome, similar to the preceding example, you may consider instituting a trailing stop to replace your fixed stop-loss order. Set the trailing distance to account for the distance between the current market and the other side of the technical break level, possibly allowing for a margin of error in case the break level is retested.

Chapter 16

Closing the Position and Evaluating Your Results

- -

In This Chapter

▶ Closing out trades to maximize results

▶ Taking profits and stopping losses

▶ Exiting trades at the right time and price

▶ Looking at your trading results to improve performance

- -

Deciding how and when to exit, or close out, an open currency position is obviously one of the last steps in any currency strategy, but it's also one of the most important. In my trading experience, no other part of a trading strategy has the potential to stir up greater feelings of self-recrimination by traders.

The classic trader's lament is "coulda, woulda, shoulda." And at no time is that sentiment more palpable than after a trade is closed out because that's when the profit or loss has been registered and you're looking at real money made or lost.

Coulda, woulda, shoulda refers to actions you may have taken in the market, but for some reason didn't. In the context of exiting a position, it captures after-the-fact thoughts like "I could've taken profit when it was testing x level," "I would've cut my losses sooner if I'd known it was going to keep going," or "I should've stayed in longer for the big move." The key is to understand beforehand that you're never going to know with 100 percent certainty how the actions you take now will pan out in the future. In currency trading, you're going to be making more decisions in an hour or a day than most people make in a month, and that's half the excitement.

In terms of maintaining a positive trading attitude, you have to accept that you're not going to be right all the time, so why should you kick yourself when a trade doesn't work out? The answer is, you shouldn't — unless you failed to actively plan and monitor your trades. If you didn't do that, you have every reason to blame yourself.

If you ever find yourself thinking coulda, woulda, shoulda — and everyone does — you need to look back not at what you failed to do, but at *why* you failed to do it. This chapter covers some of the main considerations you face when it's time to close out a position.

Closing Out the Trade

If you've embraced the idea of always trading with a plan — and I hope you have — you're way ahead of most of the market. Developing a thorough trading plan (trade size; entry levels; and exit levels, both stop-loss and take-profit) while you have a clear head (no open market risk and its attendant emotional distractions) is the first step to actively trading in the currency market.

Taking profit and stopping out

On the most basic level, every trade ends with either a profit or a loss. Sure, some trades finish *flat,* which is when you exit the trade at the same price you entered, producing no gain or loss. Most of the time, though, you'll be dealing with the agony of being stopped out or the ecstasy of taking profit.

Taking profit too soon or not at all

Taking profit is usually a positive experience for most traders. But if the market continues to move in the direction of your trade after you've squared up and taken profit, you may begin to feel as though you're missing out or even losing money. This is where traders may begin to fear they've taken profit too soon. The emotional element can become very strong, and past trading experience can begin to color your current thinking. The alternative is usually not taking profit at all, which ultimately leaves you exposed to continued market risk.

The important factor to remember is that you took profit based on your trade plan, whether it was based on a technical level being reached or an event playing out. You identified a trade opportunity and went with it, so enjoy the fact that you've got something to show for it. And don't get greedy. No trader ever captures 100 percent of any price movement, so keep your gains in perspective and remember: The market is not there to *give* you money. That's why it's called *taking* profit.

Above all, avoid making rash trading decisions after you've taken profit. The market may continue to move in the direction of your earlier position, and you may be tempted to reenter the same position. In some cases, reentering the same position may be the right thing to do, but until you reevaluate the market objectively and without the emotional baggage of previously being right (but not as right as you could've been), you run the risk of overstaying your welcome.

Also, avoid the urge to suddenly take a position in the opposite direction. If you were short and prices moved lower, for example, and your analysis and strategy have led you to buy back that short, you may be tempted to venture into a long position. After all, if you were right that prices would move lower, and you're now buying back your position, it stands to reason that the market may begin to move up — otherwise, why would you be buying now? But this trade is another trade entirely and not the one you identified earlier.

Treat each trade independently, and recognize that the outcome of one trade has no bearing on the next trade. Instead, take a step back and reassess the market after you've regained the objectivity that comes from being square.

Taking partial profits

One way in which traders are able to stay in the market with a profitable position and hang on for a potentially larger move is to take partial profits on the overall position. Of course, taking partial profits requires the ability to trade in multiple lots — at least two. The idea is that as prices move in favor of your trading position, you take profit on just a portion of your total position.

For example, you may have bought 15 mini-lots for a total position size of 150,000. If prices begin to move higher, you may sell out pieces of the overall position, realizing profit on a part of your position, but hold on to the rest if prices continue to move in your favor. If prices reverse course, you've reduced your market exposure and may still have a profit to show for the overall trade. If prices continue to rise, you can continue to take profit until your position is completely closed out.

Whenever you're taking partial profits, you need to modify the size of your stop-loss and other take-profit orders to account for the reduction in your total position size. Some online brokers offer a position-based order-entry system, where your order size automatically adjusts based on any changes to the overall position.

Depending on the jurisdiction in which you're trading, closing partial positions may be treated differently. In the United States, forex providers are required to account for your trades on a first-in, first-out, (FIFO) basis. For example, if you buy one lot at 30, one at 20, and one at 10, you're long 3 lots at an average of 20. When you close out your first lot, you're going to be selling the one you first bought at 30. In most other jurisdictions, you're able to choose which individual lot you want to close.

There's no practical difference on your margin balance between the two, but some traders like the idea of closing out the lots with the most profit. The key here is that you've averaged into a position, and the market needs to reverse beyond your average for you to realize a profit under either system. If you take profit only on those lots that are in the money, you're still exposed to a loss from the ones that remain out of the money. If the market never fully reverses, it means it's still moving against you, and you'll need an exit strategy.

Stopping out before things get worse

As part of any trade strategy and to preserve your trading capital for future trading, you always need to identify where to exit a trade if the market doesn't move in the direction you expect. Devote as much time and energy to pinpointing that level as you need, always keeping in mind that a lot of short-term price action can be stop-loss driven.

Anticipate that key technical and price levels will be tested to see if stop-loss or market orders are there. Testing levels is what trading markets spend a lot of time doing. For this reason, I like to factor in a margin of error in placing my stops, based on the individual currency pair and the current market environment. (I discuss the pros and cons of applying a margin of error for stop-loss orders in more detail in Chapter 13.)

In my experience, no one is ever happy when a stop-loss order gets triggered. The fact of the matter is that stop losses are a necessary evil for every trader, big and small. I never know beforehand where a price movement will stop, but I can control where I exit the market if prices don't move as I expect. Most important, stop losses are an important tool for preventing manageable trading losses from turning into disastrous ones.

No trader is right all the time, so getting stopped out is simply a part of trading reality. Traders who apply intelligent and disciplined stop-loss orders occasionally may suffer setbacks, but they'll avoid getting wiped out, and they'll still be around to trade the next day. Traders who fail to use stops, or who move them to avoid having them triggered, run the risk of getting wiped out if the move is large enough.

Trailing stop losses for larger price movements

The one type of stop loss that traders may actually enjoy seeing triggered is trailing stop-loss orders, which are often used to protect profits and enable traders to capture larger price movements. (I explain how trailing stop-loss orders work in Chapter 4.)

Trailing stops are no surefire guarantee that you'll be able to stay on board for a larger directional price move, but they do provide an element of flexibility that you should consider in adjusting your trade plan. For example, if your position is in the money and holding beyond a significant technical break level, you may want to consider adjusting your stop loss to a trailing stop that has its starting point on the other side of the technical level. If the break leads to a more sustained move, you'll be able to capture more than you otherwise might. If the break is reversed, the trailing stop will limit the damage.

Setting it and forgetting it: Letting the market trigger your order

When you've identified a trade opportunity and developed a risk-aware trading plan, you're going to have active orders out in the market to cover your position one way or the other (stop-loss or take-profit). Depending on your trading style and the trade setup, you can reasonably follow a set-it-and-forget-it trade strategy where your orders will watch the market and your position for you.

Medium- to longer-term traders are more likely to rely on set, or *resting*, market orders to cover open positions due to the longer time frame of such trade strategies and the burdens of monitoring the market overnight or for longer stretches of time.

Remember to use rate alerts to update you on specific price movements (see Chapter 15). The archetypical picture of the currency trader sleeping with a phone under the pillow is not really that far off. Depending on how your trade is developing, you can make order adjustments typically in a matter of seconds or minutes and get back to sleep (or whatever it was you were doing).

Shorter-term traders are more likely to follow a more dynamic approach, again based on the shorter time frame of such trades. Short-term traders are more apt to be in front of their trading monitors while their trade is still open, but they should always still have an ultimate limiting set of orders to cover the trade strategy.

You may want to be flexible with where you leave your take-profit order, but always have a stop-loss order in place to protect you in case of unexpected news or price movements. If you're trading the market from the long side (meaning, you think prices in a currency pair are likely to move higher), you need to pinpoint the ultimate price level on the downside, which negates this short-term view.

Squaring up after events have happened

Depending on the basis of the trade opportunity you've identified, there will be very real hallmarks indicating what, if any, adjustments you should make.

Trades based on fundamental events (like a data report or an expected monetary policy statement) have a very real basis in both time and content. If you've taken a position based on a data release, for example, when the report is issued, you and the rest of the market now have that information.

If you've anticipated various outcomes to the report, you'll have a leg up on the market in interpreting the subsequent price action. If the market is not reacting the way you expected, it's a strong sign that other forces are at work. The market reaction to the data or news is usually more important than the event itself.

Most important, though, is that the basis for your trade strategy — the event — has taken place. If the market doesn't react as you thought it would, you have very little reason to continue to hold onto the position. Always relate your original rationale for holding your position back to the reality on the ground. When events turn out differently from what you expected, start looking for the exit sooner rather than later.

Exiting at the right time

In trading, it's frequently said that timing is everything. Truer words were never spoken. But that line applies to trying to time your entry and exit to capture tops and bottoms in the market — market timing, in other words.

But I'm talking about the time on the clock on the wall. The time of day and the day of the week can frequently influence how prices behave and how your ultimate trade strategy plays out. If you're trading ahead of major data releases, for example, you need to be aware that price action is going to be affected in the run-up to the scheduled release, not to mention in its aftermath. There's no set way that prices will behave before data releases, but you still need to be alert to upcoming events that may dictate changes to your trade plan.

Similarly, if you've been positioned correctly for a directional price move in the New York morning, for example, you need to be aware that there may be a price reaction as European traders begin to wind up their trading day. Some London closes may see the price move continue in the direction it was going; other times, the price move may reverse. The question for you as a trader, though, is: Do you really want to find out which way it plays out?

At the minimum, you may want to make adjustments to your trade strategy to limit any negative impact from session closes, such as reducing your position size, tightening stop losses, or squaring up altogether.

Depending on the day of the week, you may be looking at different liquidity conditions (such as a holiday, a month end, or a quarter end, which frequently see lower liquidity and the chance for outsize volatility). If it's a Friday, the market will be closing for the weekend in a matter of hours. If you hold on to your position, you run the risk of being exposed to weekend gap risk. Do you want to wait 'til the last minute and expose yourself to the uncertain price action?

Staying on top of the time of day is as important a trading consideration as having the right position. When it comes to adjusting your trading plan or closing out your position, it frequently pays to be a clock watcher.

Getting out when the price is right

When it comes to market information, the most reliable information is always the prices themselves. Sharp price reactions are usually strong indicators of significant market interest — interest that is either pushing prices faster in the same direction or repelling them in the opposite direction.

As you're monitoring your position in the market, you need to be closely attuned to significant price reactions, such as spike reversals or price gaps, with a good benchmark being typically more than 20 points over a few minutes. The sharp move in prices may be due to news or rumors, or it may just be a pocket of illiquidity. Either way, the sharp price move carries its own significance that is information to you. There's no set way such moves always play out, but if you're alert for them, you've got one more piece of information to help you decide when and how to exit your position.

If the rapid price movement was in your favor, you can look at it as a new high-water mark, or as a new support or resistance level. If the move is reversed, the tide is reversing, and you should consider exiting sooner rather than later. If the tide doesn't reverse, you've got a solid short-term price level on which to base your decisions going forward. If the price move was against you, you may want to consider that the market is not cooperating and adopt a more defensive strategy, such as tightening stop losses, reducing your position, or exiting altogether.

Assessing Your Trading Strategy

Active currency trading is as much a learning process as it is a speculative endeavor. Good traders learn from their mistakes and try to avoid repeating them in the future. Bad traders keep making the same mistakes over and over again until they give up in frustration or are forced to for financial reasons.

Successful trades also represent excellent learning opportunities, both about how different trading strategies work best and about your own personal response to them. Successful traders remember what they did right and try to emulate it in the future, knowing full well that no two trades are ever the same. Bad traders only remember that they won, but they fail to take the lessons of why they won to heart.

The best way to learn from each trading experience — both good and bad — is to make post-trade analysis part of your regular trading routine.

Identifying what you did right and wrong

Regardless of the outcome of any trade, you want to look back over the whole process to understand what you did right and wrong. In particular, ask yourself the following questions:

✔ **How did you identify the trade opportunity?** Was it based on technical analysis, a fundamental view, or some combination of the two? Looking at your trade this way will help identify your strengths and weaknesses as either a fundamental or technical trader. If more of your winning trades are being generated by technical analysis, you'll probably want to devote more energy to that approach. If more of your winning trades are coming from the fundamental approach, you're probably better off concentrating on a fundamental style.

✔ **How well did your trade plan work out?** Was the position size sufficient to match the risk and reward scenarios, or was it too large or too small? Could you have entered at a better level? What tools might you have used to improve your entry timing? Were you patient enough, or did you rush in thinking you'd never have the chance again? Was your take profit realistic or pie in the sky? Did the market pay any respect to your choice of take-profit levels, such as stopping short of it, or did prices blow right through it? Ask yourself the same questions about your stop-loss level. Use the answers to refine your position size, entry level, and order placement going forward.

✔ **How well did you manage the trade after it was open?** Were you able to effectively monitor the market while your trade was active? If so, how? If not, why not? The answers to those questions will reveal a lot about how much time and dedication you're able to devote to your trading. Did you modify your trade plan along the way? Did you adjust stop-loss orders to protect profits? Did you take partial profit at all? Did you close out the trade based on your trading plan, or did the market surprise you somehow? Based on your answers, you'll learn what role your emotions may have played and how disciplined a trader you are.

There are no right and wrong answers in this review process; just be as honest with yourself as you can. No one else will ever know your answers, so you have nothing to lose by being candid. On the contrary, you have everything to gain by identifying what you're good at, what you're not so good at, and getting to understand how you as a currency trader should best approach the market.

Updating your trading record

Recollections of individual trades can be hazy sometimes. Some traders may tend to favor remembering winning trades, whereas others may remember only the losing trades. The only way to get to the heart of the matter is to look at the numbers — the results of your trades over a specific time period, such as a month.

A trading record doesn't lie, but you still have to interpret it properly to glean any useful lessons from it. I find that depending on your trading style, it's best to approach analyzing your trading record from two different angles, each with a common denominator — average wins and average losses.

- ✔ **Long-term and medium-term traders:** Tend to have fewer overall trades because they're more likely to be looking at the market from a more strategic perspective, picking trade opportunities more selectively. If that's you, you'll want to tally your results on a per-trade basis, totaling up separately the number of winning trades and the number of losing trades, along with the total amount of profits and the total amount of losses. Divide the number of profits by the number of winning trades to find your average winning trade amount. Do the same with your losing trades.

- ✔ **Short-term traders:** Tend to have a larger number of trades due to their short-term trading style. If that's you, you're going to want to measure your results on a per-day basis. Tally up your daily profit and loss (P/L) and note the number of winning/losing days in a month, along with the average win/loss per day.

Your results can be very helpful in allowing you to further identify your strengths and weaknesses as a trader. The main focus is to evaluate how good you are at spotting trades and how your financial successes compare to your financial losses.

If you have more winning trades or trading days per month than losing ones, you're on the right track and are likely adept at spotting trading opportunities or actively trading in and out in the market. If your losing days or trades outnumber your winners, you probably need to take a good hard look at how you're identifying your trades or making your short-term decisions.

You next want to look at the size of your average win and average loss. Again, if your average win is larger than your average loss, you're doing something right, and that bodes well. When you're right, you're right for a larger amount than when you're wrong — and that's just the way you want it to be.

Focus on what you're doing right, but also figure out what you're doing wrong. Refine your analysis of your trading results by breaking them down to smaller categories, such as day of the week and currency pair or even trade size. Are your losing days or trades concentrated on certain days of the week, such as Fridays or Mondays? For example, in my own experience, trading on the last day of a month was a losing proposition. Are your losing trades concentrated in certain currency pairs? Does the position size of each trade have any relationship to wins and losses? Are you winning more on large trades, for example, or are you giving up larger losses on smaller trade sizes?

Look at your results as dispassionately as possible. They're the real reflection of your currency trading. Learn from them, and use them to:

- ✔ **Keep yourself honest.** You may remember only the winning trades and not realize you're developing bad risk-management habits.

- ✔ **Spot dangerous habits or lapses.** Over time, you'll develop and refine your trading style. If you're successful, you'll want to stay that way, and monitoring your trading results on a regular basis is the way to do that. If you lose more than you normally do on a losing trade, you may want to consider scaling back. If you're winning on more days or trades than normal, you'll also want to do a reality check and make sure you aren't overextending it.

- ✔ **Be your own best teacher.** Identify your strengths and weaknesses, as well as trading styles and market conditions that fit your temperament and discipline best. Focus on those where you experience the greatest success, and avoid those with bad results.

- ✔ **Identify market sessions and currency pairs that suit you best.** Interpret your trading results to help pinpoint currency pairs where you've had the most success and avoid those where you don't. You may need to adapt your trading schedule and concentrate on only a portion of a particular trading session.

Currency trading is all about getting out of it what you put into it. Evaluating your trading results on a regular basis is an essential step in improving your trading skills, refining your trading styles, maximizing your trading strengths, and minimizing your trading weaknesses.

Part V
The Part of Tens

The 5th Wave   By Rich Tennant

"Eat your cereal. Your father's heavily invested in grain."

In this part . . .

I assembled several great lists to help you identify important habits shared by successful currency traders as well as common errors that beginners frequently make. I also provide a concrete set of rules to manage your risks effectively. Finally, I include a list of additional resources for you to take your currency education and trading to the next level.

Chapter 17

Ten Habits of Successful Currency Traders

In This Chapter

▶ Getting in the groove of positive trading habits

▶ Staying on top of market events and price levels

▶ Narrowing your trading focus

▶ Trading with a plan and sticking to it

*H*ere are ten rules I think define the best currency traders I've ever seen. Many of these rules apply to traders in any market, but some of them are unique to the currency market. The important idea to keep in mind: No one is born with all these habits. The only way to acquire them is the way other successful currency traders have — through patience, discipline, and experience.

Trading with a Plan

No successful trader will last very long without a well-conceived game plan for each trade. Sure, you may have some short-run success winging it, but the day of reckoning will surely come. Successful currency traders have a specific plan of attack for each position, including position size, entry point, stop-loss exit, and take-profit exit.

They stay flexible with their take profits, sometimes settling for less if they judge that that's all they can take out of the market at the moment, other times extending their profit targets if market developments are shifting in their favor. But they never move their stop-loss orders from the original setting unless it's in favor of the position to lock in profits.

Anticipating Event Outcomes

Trading is very similar to chess, in which the best players are thinking several moves ahead of their opponents. Successful forex traders look ahead to future events and consider how much the market has (or has not) priced in an expected outcome. They also consider the likely reactions if the event matches, or fails to match, those expectations. Then they construct trading strategies based on those alternative outcomes. While the rest of the market is trying to figure out what to make of the event, checking charts and redrawing trend lines, the forward-looking trader has a game plan already in place and is ready to trade.

Staying Flexible

Successful currency traders resist getting emotionally attached to positions. They recognize that it's not about being right or wrong — it's about making money. They adapt to incoming news and information, and quickly abandon an open position if events run counter to it instead of waiting for price action to take them out of their trade. At the same time, they're alert to fresh opportunities that may develop in the market and are prepared to react. To be prepared, they must keep sufficient margin available for additional positions. Also, they need an ongoing mental model of other major pairs so they can factor in fresh news and events. They may not be actively trading AUD/USD, but they still know the lay of the land for Aussie.

Being Prepared for Trading

Successful currency traders are always prepared, at least as much as possible in a market that's open 24 hours a day and subject to random events from half a world away. To stay on top of their game, successful currency traders are prepared for:

- **Upcoming economic data releases in the next week to two weeks:** Know what the prior report indicated and what's expected in the upcoming report.

- **Scheduled speakers:** Find out who's speaking (central bankers or finance officials), what they've said in the past, and what they're likely to say this time.

- **Central bank interest rate setting meetings and announcement times:** Know when they're scheduled and what decision the market is expecting.

✔ **Important gatherings of financial leaders, such as G7/G20 meetings or monthly get-togethers of Eurozone finance ministers:** Get a sense of whether currencies are on the agenda and what actions are expected.

✔ **Liquidity conditions:** Stay aware of time periods — such as end of month, market closings or holidays, and time of day (for example, European close, option expirations, or daily fixings — when market liquidity may be affected.

✔ **Unexpected events:** Use rate alerts to stay on top of price movements outside expected ranges. Follow up on alerts to check for significant news and to assess potential trading opportunities.

Keeping Technically Alert

Even if they're not pursuing a technical-based trading strategy themselves, successful currency traders are still aware of important technical levels in the currency pairs they're trading. For instance, they know the key Fibonacci retracement levels, where various moving averages are, important short- and long-term trend lines, and major recent highs and lows (see Chapter 11).

You may be trading based on price behavior or momentum analysis, but be sure to stay abreast of key technical levels as part of your overall strategy.

Going with the Flow/Trading the Range

Successful currency traders are able to assess whether the market is trending or likely to remain confined to ranges. If they think the market is trending, they aim to go with the flow more often than against it. When the short-term trend is higher, they're looking for levels to get long at, and vice versa when the direction is down. At the same time, they're aware that trends pause and frequently correct, so they're also actively taking profit at key technical points as the larger trend unfolds.

If the environment favors range trading, successful currency traders are able to switch gears and become contrarians, selling near the top of the range when everyone else is buying, or buying near the bottom of the range when everyone else is selling. Just as important, when they're in range-trading mode, they've defined an ultimate point when the range is broken. If that point is hit, they throw in the towel without any remorse, possibly even reversing direction and jumping on the breakout.

Focusing on a Few Pairs

Many successful forex traders focus on only one or two currency pairs for most of their trading. Doing so enables them to get a better feel for those markets in terms of price levels and price behavior. It also narrows the amount of information and data they need to monitor. Above all, they recognize that different currency pairs have different trading characteristics, and they're able to adjust their tactics from one pair to the next.

Focus on gaining experience and success in just one or two major pairs before trying to broaden out and take on the whole market. Look at other pairs only when they're trending or trading at key levels.

Protecting Profits

There are numerous market aphorisms on the benefits of taking profits, such as "You can't go broke taking profit." One of my favorites is "Bulls and bears each get a seat at the table, but pigs get slaughtered."

Successful traders take profit regularly, whether it's a partial take profit (reducing the size of a winning position) or squaring up completely and stepping back after a profitable market movement. Above all, when a trade is in the money, successful traders focus on keeping what they've made and not giving it up for the chance to make a little more.

If you don't take some money off the table from time to time, the market will do it for you.

Trading with Stop Losses

All successful traders lose money from time to time. What makes them successful in the long run is that their losses are relatively small compared to their average winning trades. The absolute key is to have a stop loss in place at all times to prevent an everyday losing trade from becoming an account killer.

No one likes to lose money, but the best traders are able to accept it as part of the cost of doing business. And the only way they can regularly accept losses is by keeping them small in the first place. Master this habit, and you're halfway there.

Watching Other Markets

Currencies don't trade in a vacuum, and smart traders keep an eye on other major financial markets as a matter of routine. The primary markets they focus on are benchmark bond yields of the major currencies (U.S., German, UK, and Japanese ten-year government notes); oil; gold; and, major global stock indexes.

On an intraday basis, they look to these other markets for confirmation of short-term U.S. dollar directional bias. For example, if the dollar is moving higher, U.S. ten-year yields are rising, and gold is falling, it's confirmation from other markets in favor of the dollar's move higher. If yields are flat or down, and gold is higher, the dollar's move up may be only short lived. On a longer-term basis, currency traders analyze those other markets for significant technical levels and overall directional trends, just as they do the currencies.

Spend the extra money for charting services that include live rate feeds for those other markets.

Chapter 18

Ten Beginner Trading Mistakes

I call these "beginner" trading mistakes, but they're made by everyone — from total newcomers to grizzled market veterans. No matter how long you've been trading, you're bound to experience lapses in trading discipline, whether they're brought on by unusual market developments or emotional extremes.

The key is to develop an intuitive understanding of the major pitfalls of trading, so that you can recognize early on if you're letting your discipline slip. If you start to see any of the following errors in your own trading, it's probably a good idea to square up, step back from the market, and refocus your concentration and energies on the basic trading rules.

Running Losers, Cutting Winners

By far the most common trading mistake is holding on to losing positions for too long and taking profit on winning trades too soon. By cutting winners too early, you may not make as much — but then again, you literally can't go broke taking profit. That said, you *will* deplete your trading capital if you let losses run too long.

The key to limiting losses is to follow a risk-aware trading plan that always has a stop-loss order and to stick to it. No one is right all the time, so the sooner you're able to accept small losses as part of everyday trading, the sooner you'll be able to refocus on spotting and trading winning strategies.

Trading without a Plan

Opening up a trade without a concrete plan is like asking the market to take your money. If the market moves against you, when will you cut your losses? If the market moves in your favor, when will you take profit? If you haven't determined these levels in advance, why would you suddenly come up with them when you're caught up in the emotions of a live position?

Resist the urge to trade spontaneously based on your instincts alone without a clearly defined risk-management plan. If you have a strong view, go with it, but do the legwork in advance so you have a workable trading plan that specifies where to enter and where to exit — both stop-loss and take-profit.

Be aware of the increased risk of trading around important news and data releases. Study economic and event calendars to identify future event risks, and factor them in to your trading plan. That may mean stepping out of the market in advance of such events.

Trading without a Stop Loss

I can't stress this enough: Trading without a stop loss is a recipe for disaster. It's how small, manageable losses become devastating wipeouts. Trading without a stop loss is the same as saying, "I know I'm going to be right — it's just a matter of time." That may be so — but it may take a lot longer than your margin collateral can support.

Using stop-loss orders is part of a well-conceived trading plan that has specific expectations based on your research and analysis. The stop loss is where your trade strategy is invalidated.

Moving Stop-Loss Orders

Moving your stop-loss order to avoid being stopped out is almost the same as trading without a stop loss in the first place. Worse, it reveals a lack of trading discipline and opens a slippery slope to major losses. If you don't want to take a relatively small loss based on your original stop loss, why would you want to take an even larger loss after you've moved your stop? If you're like most people, you won't — and you'll keep moving your stop to avoid taking an ever-larger loss until your margin runs out.

Move your stop loss only in the direction of a winning trade to lock in profits, and never move your stop in the direction of a losing position.

Overtrading

Overtrading comes in two main forms:

- ✔ **Trading too often in the market:** Trading too often in the market suggests that there is *always* something going on and that you *always* know what it is. If you always have a position open, you're constantly exposed to market risk. But the essence of disciplined trading is minimizing your exposure to unnecessary market risk. Instead, focus on trade opportunities where you think you've got an edge, and apply a disciplined trade strategy to them.

- ✔ **Trading too many positions at once:** Trading too many positions at once also suggests that you're able to spot multiple trade opportunities and exploit them simultaneously. More likely, you're throwing darts at the board, hoping something sticks. Trading too many positions also eats up your available margin collateral, reducing your cushion against adverse market movements.

Be careful about trade duplication and overlapping positions — a long USD/CHF position can be the same as a short EUR/USD or GBP/USD (all long USD versus Europe), while a short EUR/USD and a long EUR/JPY position nets out to be the same as being long USD/JPY.

Overleveraging

Overleveraging is trading too large a position size relative to your available margin. Even a small market move against you can be enough to cause an overleveraged position to be liquidated for insufficient margin.

This common no-no is made more tempting by the generous leverage ratios available with some online forex brokers. Just because they offer you 100:1 or 200:1 leverage does not mean you have to use it all. Don't base your position size on your maximum available position. Instead, base your position size on trade-specific factors such as proximity to technical levels or your confidence in the trade setup/signal.

Failing to Adapt to Changing Market Conditions

Market conditions are always changing, which means your trading approach needs to be flexible, too. Trends give way to consolidation ranges, and breakouts from ranges may lead to new trends. Stay flexible with your trading approach by first evaluating overall market conditions in terms of trends or ranges. If a trending move is under way, using a range-trading style won't work, just as a trend-following approach will fail in a range-bound market. Use technical analysis to highlight whether range or trending conditions prevail.

Being Unaware of News and Data Events

Even if you're a dyed-in-the-wool technical trader, you need to be aware of what's going on and what's coming up in the fundamental world. You may see a great trade setup in AUD/USD, for instance, but the Australian trade balance report in a few hours could blow it out of the water.

Make data/event calendar reading a part of your daily and weekly trading routine. The market throws enough curve balls with unscheduled developments, so make sure you at least have a handle on what's coming up. A forward-looking mindset also allows you to anticipate potential data outcomes and market reactions and to factor them into your trading plan.

Trading Defensively

No trader wins all the time, and we've all experienced losing streaks. After a series of losses, you may find yourself trading too defensively, focusing more on avoiding losses than spotting winning trades. At those times, it's best to step back from the market, look at what went wrong with your earlier trades, and refocus your energies until you feel confident enough to start spotting opportunities again.

Keeping Realistic Expectations

Face it: You're not going to retire based on any single trade. The key is to hit singles and stay in the game. Be realistic when setting the parameters of your trading plans by looking at recent market reactions and average trading ranges. Avoid holding out for perfection — if the market has achieved 80 percent of your expected scenario, you can't go wrong locking in some profits, at the minimum.

Chapter 19

Ten Rules of Risk Management

*W*hen people think about risk management in the context of currency trading, the natural tendency is to zero in on the risk of losing money. No two ways about it, that's the ultimate risk. But traders can head down many different streets before they get to their final realized profit or loss address.

Throughout this book, I stress that risk management is a multifaceted process that ends only with the final trading tally. In case you skipped it, check out Chapter 13 for more detailed ideas on the various forms of risk. Sometimes, what you don't know *can* hurt you.

How you navigate the avenues of risk has as much to with trading outcomes as it does with whether you ever reach the final destination. In this chapter, I group ten practical rules of risk management to guide you in your forex trading.

Trade with Stop-Loss Orders

Stop-loss orders are the ultimate risk-limiting tools. (The exception is data/ events where stop-loss order executions may be subject to substantial slip-page. Avoid that risk by not carrying positions into news releases.) If you trade without stop-loss orders, you're exposed to virtually unlimited risk. Always have a stop-loss order in place for every open position, and don't move the stop-loss order except to protect profits. Do your analysis and risk calculations before you enter the trade, and then stick to your trading plan.

Leverage to a Minimum

Position size will ultimately determine how much financial risk you're exposed to — the larger the position, the greater the risk. Don't be seduced by high leverage ratios and take too large a position. Trading too large a position relative to your available margin reduces your cushion against routine, adverse price movements. Keep your use of leverage to the minimum needed to trade your strategy.

You can request a lower leverage ratio from most forex brokerages to systemically limit your leverage utilization. Just because they offer 50:1 or 100:1 leverage doesn't mean you have to use it all.

Trade with a Plan

The best way to limit the inevitable emotional reactions that come with trading is to develop a complete trading plan from entry to exit (stop loss and take profit) before you ever open a position. (I devote most of Part III to the merits of trading with a plan.) Committing yourself to having a trade plan for every strategy will also keep you from speculating on a whim or *overtrading* (always having an open position). Of course, no trading plan will work if you don't follow it, which brings me back to the human risks in trading. You stand a much better chance of sticking to a trading plan if you've drawn one up in the first place.

Stay on Top of the Market

Make sure you have a firm grasp of what's happening in the market and the currency pair you're trading. Know what data and events are scheduled in the days and weeks ahead. Consider liquidity conditions during your trade plan's time horizon. What has the market priced in and priced out? Anticipating market events and conditions won't guarantee a winning trade, but it will alert you to potentially disruptive circumstances that you can factor into your trading plan to limit overall risk.

Trade with an Edge

The currency market trades around the clock, but that doesn't mean you have to be in it all the time. Pick your spots, and choose your timing; don't get pulled in by the noise. Keep your ammunition dry, and look for trade setups with a clearly defined risk/reward scenario. Be opportunistic, and spend your time and efforts looking for trading opportunities still to come instead of getting caught up in the market move of the moment. Other opportunities will surely develop, and you'll be ready for them.

Step Back from the Market

When you're not involved in the market, a funny thing happens: Your perspective is clearer; your objectivity is at its peak; you're not emotionally invested in a market position. Make it a point to square up and step back from the market on a regular basis. Use the downtime to catch up on your charting and fundamental analysis. Take time off completely, and just forget about the markets for a while. When you return, you'll be refreshed and thinking more clearly, ready for new trading opportunities.

Take Profit Regularly

Taking profit regularly is the surest way to limit risk. By definition, if you take profit, even partial profit, you're reducing your exposure to market risk. Your trade plan may have a more aggressive profit target, but if market events play out in your favor, it pays to protect what you've gained by taking partial profit or adjusting your stop-loss orders to lock in some of the gains. It may be a fluke that the market jumped 40 pips in your favor on a data release, or it may be a fluke that the market dropped back by 50 pips 10 minutes later. The only way to be sure is to take some profit. You can't go broke taking profit.

Understand Currency Pair Selection

Market risk varies significantly from one currency pair to the next, based on volatility, liquidity, data sensitivity, and many other factors. Each currency pair brings its own idiosyncrasies to the table, requiring different analytical tools or strategic approaches. Different currency pairs also carry higher or lower margin utilizations and pip values. Make sure that you understand what currency pair you're trading and that your trading plan reflects that pair's characteristics. (Chapters 8 and 9 look at the trading behavior and drivers of the most heavily traded currency pairs and crosses. Not all currency pairs are the same.)

Double-Check for Accuracy

Currency trading is a fast-paced environment made even faster by electronic trading. The risk of human error in inputting trades and orders is ever present and requires diligence on your part to avoid costly errors. A stop-loss order won't help if it's entered for the wrong currency pair or the wrong amount. Make it part of your routine to double-check every trade and order entry you make, ideally before you submit it but at least immediately after you make it. Mistakes happen to everyone, but only careless traders let minor errors slip through and become big disasters.

Take Money out of Your Trading Account

Here's one you won't see in many trading books: If you've made some money in the market, make periodic withdrawals from your trading account. I call it *taking money off the table.* If your profit stays in your margin account, it's subject to future trading decisions, which represents an unknown risk. Keep your margin balance at a level that allows you to trade in sizes you're comfortable with. Also, remember why you're trading — it's not just about the money, but what you can do with it. Withdraw your profits, and spend or invest them the way you always said you would.

Chapter 20

Ten Great Resources

This book gives you a solid foundation for understanding the ins and outs of currency trading, but it can't cover all the subdisciplines of trading, such as technical analysis, market psychology, and strategy development. Those subjects are deep enough and rich enough to warrant further study on their own as you develop your own trading style and favorite techniques. Indeed, those topics are important enough that entire books have been written on them. I think you'll find the following suggested additional resources very helpful in gaining a deeper understanding of the technical tools, economic data reports, and practical applications of strategy and psychology.

Technical Analysis of the Financial Markets, by John Murphy

Technical Analysis of the Financial Markets: A Comprehensive Guide to Trading Methods and Applications, by John Murphy, is *the* encyclopedia of technical analysis, written by perhaps the most prominent technical practitioner in the market. Murphy covers all the tools and all the rules in depth, from both a theoretical and a practical standpoint. Murphy also lays out one of the most comprehensive reviews of chart patterns you'll find anywhere. If you're going to have only one book on technical analysis in your library, make it this one.

Japanese Candlestick Charting Techniques, by Steve Nison

I'm a huge proponent of candlestick charting, and for my money, *Japanese Candlestick Charting Techniques: A Contemporary Guide to the Ancient Investment Techniques of the Far East,* 2nd Edition, by Steve Nison, is the best book on candlesticks out there. Nison takes you inside the linguistic and cultural meanings behind the myriad candle patterns, which leaves you with a more intuitive understanding of the patterns. With that greater understanding, you're more likely to spot viable candlestick patterns and understand what they're telling you. I keep this book handy and refer to it frequently in my own candlestick observations. (I look at several key candlestick patterns in Chapter 11.)

Elliott Wave Principle, by A. J. Frost and Robert R. Prechter, Jr.

Elliott Wave Principle: Key to Market Behavior, by A. J. Frost and Robert R. Prechter, Jr. (Wiley), is the go-to guide if you're interested in learning more about the Elliott wave principle. Elliott wave patterns are an important part of currency price movements, especially if you're intending to trade from a medium- to longer-term perspective. This book explains the philosophy behind Ralph Nelson Elliott's theories of price patterns and provides practical examples of how to apply those theories to all financial markets.

Technical Analysis Explained, by Martin J. Pring

Technical Analysis Explained: The Successful Investor's Guide to Spotting Investment Trends and Turning Points, 4th Edition, by Martin J. Pring, is an excellent alternative to Murphy's more encyclopedic volume (see earlier in this chapter). Pring covers all the components of trend behavior, and focuses heavily on momentum analysis and other keys to successful market timing. He also has a good chapter on automated trading, if that's your objective.

Technical Analysis For Dummies, by Barbara Rockefeller

Technical Analysis For Dummies, by Barbara Rockefeller (Wiley), is an excellent introduction to the many and varied tools and methods of technical analysis, all delivered in the easy-to-read *For Dummies* style. Rockefeller takes you through all the important tools and approaches, and provides plenty of real-life dos and don'ts that you can apply to your own trading.

The Book of Five Rings, by Miyamoto Musashi

The Book of Five Rings, by Miyamoto Musashi, is known as *Go Rin No Sho* in Japanese. This relatively short book (about 150 pages) is a fascinating exposition on the philosophy of strategy and rules of tactical warfare. Musashi was the greatest samurai to ever live, and this book is his end-of-life distillation of all the rules of strategy and swordsmanship gained in his lifetime.

Musashi's exhortations on timing and staying calm in the midst of chaos are as applicable to successful trading today as they were to martial artists in the mid-17th century, when the book first appeared. This book is not for a single reading only. Pull it out and reread it often. Not only does it contain advice on strategy and mental discipline, but it also offers lessons on personal fulfillment and finding a spiritual, focused, and balanced existence.

Reminiscences of a Stock Operator, by Edwin Lefèvre

Reminiscences of a Stock Operator, by Edwin Lefèvre (Wiley), is as relevant today as when it was first published in 1923. Although the book deals with stock markets, Lefèvre's observations on price behavior and market psychology make it universally applicable to all financial-markets trading. Lefèvre, who made and lost several fortunes in his trading career, relates his good and bad experiences and those of his peers from the individual trader's point of view, making it resonate with other aspiring traders. This is another book you can pick up and reread often, and still find something new each time.

Market Wizards: Interviews with Top Traders, by Jack D. Schwager

In *Market Wizards: Interviews with Top Traders,* Jack D. Schwager, a veteran trader himself, interviews the legends of the trading world for their insights and philosophies of trading. *Wizards* is not confined strictly to the forex market; it offers a wider-ranging discussion of stocks, futures, and currency trading. In it, you learn how the likes of Richard Dennis, Bruce Kovener, and Paul Tudor Jones, to name just a few, approach trading. These traders are living legends today, but they all started out relatively modestly and succeeded through discipline, strategy, and diligence while managing intense psychological pressures. If you're in search of a trading style, these guys have plenty to offer.

The Secrets of Economic Indicators, by Bernard Baumohl

The Secrets of Economic Indicators: Hidden Clues to Future Economic Trends and Investment Opportunities, 2nd Edition by Bernard Baumohl is an excellent guide for any trader pursuing a fundamental trading approach. This book actually makes economic statistics into an exciting story. Baumohl covers all the key U.S. economic reports, how to read and interpret the data, and what they imply for the U.S. outlook. He also looks at some of the most prominent international data reports, like the German IFO survey and Japanese industrial production. Baumohl also provides the best websites to find United States and international economic data, so you can follow the data trail to the source. Read in advance about each U.S. economic release; over the course of a month, you'll have learned about every major monthly indicator.

Come into My Trading Room, by Alexander Elder, MD

Come into My Trading Room: A Complete Guide to Trading, by Alexander Elder, MD (Wiley), was written by a practicing psychiatrist and trader. Elder's observations on the personal psychology and emotions of trading are especially insightful if you're new to the markets. His book is a well-rounded overview of all aspects of individual trading, from understanding emotions to managing money and risk to following the habits of an organized trader.

Index